TRACING TECHNOLOGIES

Tracing Technologies

Prisoners' Views in the Era of CSI

HELENA MACHADO
University of Minho, Portugal

BARBARA PRAINSACK
Brunel University, UK

Routledge
Taylor & Francis Group
LONDON AND NEW YORK

First published 2012 by Ashgate Publishing

Published 2016 by Routledge
2 Park Square, Milton Park, Abingdon, Oxon OX14 4RN
711 Third Avenue, New York, NY 10017, USA

First issued in paperback 2017

Routledge is an imprint of the Taylor & Francis Group, an informa business

British Library Cataloguing in Publication Data
Machado, Helena.
Tracing technologies : prisoners' views in the era of CSI.
1. Forensic sciences. 2. Forensic sciences on television.
3. Mass media and crime. 4. Crime prevention. 5. DNA
fingerprinting. 6. DNA data banks. 7. Criminals--Austria--
Attitudes. 8. Criminals--Portugal--Attitudes.
I. Title II. Prainsack, Barbara.
363.2'5-dc23

Library of Congress Cataloging-in-Publication Data
Machado, Helena.
Tracing technologies : prisoners' views in the era of CSI / by Helena
Machado and Barbara Prainsack.
p. cm.
Includes bibliographical references and index.
ISBN 978-1-4094-3074-2 (hbk)
1. Forensic sciences. 2. DNA fingerprinting. 3. Prisoners--Attitudes. 4. Evidence, Criminal--Psychological aspects. 5. Criminal justice, Administration of.
I. Prainsack, Barbara. II. Title.
HV8073.M2192 2011
363.25--dc23

2011047490

ISBN 13: 978-1-138-10750-2 (pbk)
ISBN 13: 978-1-4094-3074-2 (hbk)

Contents

List of Figures and Tables

Figures

Tables

Foreword: *CSI* in Fiction, Fantasy and Fact

Troy Duster

Introduction

Crime Scene Investigation stories have captured and held the public's imagination as have few other genres – reaching an apex with Conan Doyle's super-sleuth Sherlock Holmes. Indeed, a full century of murder mysteries and detective novels, from Agatha Christie to Erle Stanley Gardner to Dashiell Hammet have fuelled the fantasies of audiences and filled the coffers of book publishers, radio programs, and most recently producers of ongoing television series. The most popular of these programs is aptly and simply called *CSI*, but their spin-offs and penetration into far-flung areas across the globe represent an astonishing success. This outcome is not merely to be understood in terms of economic rewards, but is also a socio-political development that has perceptibly penetrated real-life criminal justice systems in ways worthy of serious study and focused intellectual effort. This book is Exhibit A.

Several years ago, I was invited to give a lecture at a university in Singapore on the social and political context of new and developing technologies in human molecular genetics. When I reached the point in my presentation where I turned to forensics, I decided to ask my audience of about 350 students and faculty 'how many had seen or heard of a *CSI* television program?'. Nearly everyone raised their hands. Intrigued by this response, a few months later when I was speaking before an audience mainly of social scientists in London, I decided to ask the same question. The results were similar. While this seemed anecdotal at first, as the authors point out at the beginning of the first chapter, we now know that *CSI* has become the most popular crime series across the globe (Brewer and Ley 2010: 111).

In part because sensational public cases go to jury, in part because crime novelists and fictional portrayals in both movies and television, the popular imagination casts 'the jury' foremost as the main agent in determining guilt or innocence for those who are accused and brought before authorities in the criminal justice system. We all have seen a movie or a television program in which the jury is swayed by the work of a key legal aide who rushes in at the eleventh hour with critical new information that dramatically turns the case – and justice is done. So it comes as a surprise to most when they learn that less than 10 per cent of all convictions in any nation-state are the result of a jury's deliberations. Indeed, the public is completely shut out of the most important deliberations that will send a citizen to prison, or set him or her free (because charges are either dropped or never formally brought).

A bit of background is needed in order to explain why this is so, and most significantly, why this matter is central to understanding the importance of this book.

It has been known for more than three decades that approximately 90 per cent (or more in some jurisdictions) of those defendants who end up incarcerated pled guilty to a crime rather than take their case to a jury (Alschuler 1979, Heumann 1978). This saves the state the problem of convening a jury and going through a lengthy trial. Indeed, if even a third of those in prison requested or demanded jury trials, the system would be clogged up for decades. So, the plea bargain is a Faustian bargain of sorts – and everyone in the criminal justice system knows it. The segment of the society that is surprised by the ubiquitous nature of the plea bargain is – everybody else, i.e., the general public. Mesmerised by decades of radio and then television portrayals of criminal court jury proceedings, from *Perry Mason* to *Law and Order*, from *Closer* and *Cold Case* to the *Crime Scene Investigation* series, the public is more likely to think that juries play a decisive role in the determination of guilt or innocence. Indeed, the so-called *CSI* effect – the idea that the prosecution needs to come up with DNA evidence has made some penetration into jury selection and jury membership (Willing 2004).

Jury trials are very expensive and time-consuming, and each one takes an ordinate amount of energy and effort on the part of both prosecutors and those in the role of legal defenders of the rights of the accused. In the United States (US), for example, in order to seat a jury of 12 members, the state typically will send out at least 200 'calls to citizens'. In the process of getting 14 (two alternates), each person called to possible duties is asked a number of questions to determine their capacity for impartiality, for example.

Jurors are paid a pittance – and many complain that they can not afford to be away from gainful employment for an extended period.

For these and many other reasons, prosecutors and defence attorneys prefer 'out of court settlements' to the huge costs of a jury trial. Which brings us to that often opaque negotiation, far from public scrutiny, called 'the plea bargain'. When a prosecutor confronts the accused with evidence of his or her guilt, the preferred outcome is that the accused confess to the crime. Let us take the example of armed robbery, where the prison sentence is set at 20 years. The prosecutor may 'bargain' with the accused, and suggest that if he/she pleads guilty to robbery, the prison sentence will be just seven years. The bargain is struck, the deal is made – no jury trial!

In the US, almost all convictions are determined by this negotiation called the plea bargain, all out of the sight of the public (Oppel 2011: 1). We have no idea about what goes on in the bargaining process, at least from the point of those most at risk – the accused. Now, for the first time, in this volume, we are provided with a substantial amount of data from the point of view of those who were incarcerated after being convicted of a crime. This begins to fill a huge lacuna in our understanding of the process of the plea bargain. We start to get a picture of the *CSI* effect – not on juries, which as noted above, are a small fraction of all cases where there is a conviction. Rather, the authors provide a megaphone for those otherwise silent partners in the bargaining process. What do prisoners think about the role of DNA evidence in claims of forensic information being brought before the court? Is it one more grenade in the prosecutor's arsenal at the plea bargaining table? Does the *CSI* effect penetrate the consciousness of those who are on the receiving end of claims that 'the DNA evidence is in – and it is definitive' so don't bother to bargain down beyond what is being offered? 'Equally important, how do those captured by the criminal justice system think about strategies for avoiding being caught in a DNA net at their next crime scene? Do they give as much credence to claims of the definitive nature of DNA evidence as the prosecution, or even more? This manuscript addresses each of these questions, and many more.

In the DNA databanks used by criminal justice authorities, biological samples are collected from crime scenes – in this case just as popularised by the television series *CSI*. These are called 'forensic samples', or 'crime scene samples'. A second kind of data collection is from persons who are known-to-the-police, mainly because they have been convicted of a crime, or more recently, merely arrested. These are called variably 'known samples', 'offender samples', or 'subject samples'. The US National DNA Index contains over 10,061,069 offender profiles and 388,979 forensic profiles as of August 2011.[1] When someone who has been arrested has his or her DNA profile uploaded into the CODIS database, it can be compared to the scores of thousands of crime-scene samples in the CODIS forensic database.

The 'One in a Million' Claims

Under what conditions does the criminal justice system conclude that a DNA sample sufficiently matches that in their forensic database to accuse someone of a crime? A forensic sample is a digitalised description of 26 specific points of the DNA molecule.[2] These 26 points were chosen because they are thought to be sufficiently distinctive from other segments of the DNA. This actually translates to mean 13 loci, but since the DNA is a double-helix, there are thus 26 points.

> If enough of the loci from the suspect's DNA line up with those from the DNA found at the crime scene (and if none are found to be different), a match is declared. Once that happens, a statistic is generated that shows how rare (or common) the matched genetic profile is in the general population. Statisticians call this 'random match probability' and it is often a very small number, which can be very helpful to a prosecutor trying to win a conviction. (Humes 2009: 2)

1 http://www.fbi.gov/about-us/lab/codis/ndis-statistics [accessed: 30 September 2011].

2 There are 3 billion base pairs in the human genome, and even though we are 99.9 per cent alike, that still leaves *several million* points-of-difference between any two people.

In cold-hit cases, the task is to try to obtain a match at a set of as many as possible of the 13 loci. However, when starting with a database of hundreds of thousands of DNA profiles *instead of that of a specific suspect*, statisticians are in general agreement that Random Match Probability is the wrong statistic. The appropriate question to be answered is the likelihood that the technology will mistakenly identify an innocent person.

In the fall of 2006, the US Congress passed legislation authorising a thorough study of forensic science – to be conducted by the National Research Council. The report, *Strengthening Forensic Science in the United States: A Path Forward*, was released in early 2009 and raised serious questions about how the science was being neglected, even blocked out, in claims-making by prosecution experts:[3] 'There is no uniformity in the certification of forensic practitioners, or in the accreditation of crime laboratories' (National Research Council 2009: 6).

Indeed, here is what 25 leading statisticians signed on to in a letter to the California Supreme Court in *People v. Johnson* [139 Cal. App. 4th 1135 (2006)]:

> The fact that a suspect is first identified by searching a database unquestionably changes the likelihood of the matching being coincidental. … We all agree that the fact that the suspect was first identified in a DNA database search must be taken into account (i.e., when asserting probabilities about chances for a coincidental match).

This has important bearing on all cold hit cases, but especially ones in which this is the solitary evidence. John Davis is a California state prisoner who had been linked by a 'cold-hit' to a 1985 rape-murder in San Francisco. Davis had been arrested for robbery, and thus his DNA had been collected and was entered into the state's database:

> 'The only evidence against him was the DNA (match), plus the fact that he'd lived in the area at the time.' … The … match occurred after DNA was eventually extracted from semen found on the body of the murder victim. … The cold-hit match held good across 13 different sections, or loci … [and] a 13-locus match seemed unassailable … (Jefferson 2008)

However, Davis' defense attorney, Bicka Barlow, is not only a lawyer, she also holds an advanced degree in genetics. Barlow had read about an interesting case in Arizona, where two people matched at nine loci. Conventional and prevailing statistical wisdom says that the odds of a random match at nine loci would be one in a billion. She filed a subpoena seeking more data on this case, and learned in November, 2005, that Arizona's offender database contained genetic profiles of 65,493 offenders, and 'within that pool, 122 pairs of people had DNA that

3 Available free to the public from the National Academy Press website, http://www.nap.edu/catalog/12589.html [accessed: 1 September 2009].

matched at nine loci – and 20 pairs had profiles that matched at 10 loci' (Jefferson 2008: 32).

Now the story turns into an interesting melodrama about the search for truth versus the organisational imperatives of the FBI and prosecuting attorneys' interest in protecting the image of DNA cold-hit technology as definitive. Barlow posted her results on a website in order to alert other public defenders of her findings. Then she subpoenaed California's Department of Justice to compel the state's crime lab to analyze how common such unexpected pair matches were in the California offender database.

> The FBI sent out a nationwide alert [to state crime labs] saying, 'notify us if you get any requests like this,' she says, and '… the Arizona Attorney General faxed me a letter from CODIS that said basically, "if you don't take this [Barlow's web posting] down, we'll bar your state from participation in the national database."' (Jefferson 2008: 33)

A San Francisco judge refused to permit her to probe California's database.

Forensic Science vs. Science

Barlow is not alone in her scepticism about DNA cold-hit technology. Erin Murphy (2007) has raised similar issues of the limits of asserting just how definitive DNA matches can be in 'cold hit' cases. Yet, this is a world in which the *CSI* effect has captured the public imagination, and where DNA evidence has come to be seen as nearly infallible (Willing 2004).

We now have some data suggesting that defendants confronted with the 'information' that there is DNA evidence against them are far more likely to see this as 'definitive evidence' – and thus more likely to accept a less advantageous plea bargain (Prainsack and Kitzberger 2009). Murphy (2007) and others have noted the successful 'creep' of the *CSI* effect on the general public. But Prainsack and Kitzberger's earlier work suggests that there are predictable circumstances in which defendants are perhaps even more susceptible to the *CSI* effect, i.e., the tendency to believe that DNA evidence is sufficient to secure a conviction. Their work with prosecutors and interviews with defendants in Austria documents just how much the technology of the *DNA Mystique* (Nelkin and Lindee 1995) has become a part of the taken-for-granted features of the *zeitgeist*. Since prosecutors have become increasingly aware of this, they can and do tell those arrested and accused of a crime that 'they have the DNA fit' – whether or not they do!! This is legally permitted. Second, more and more cases will be brought before prosecutors using 'cold hits' (that match 'known offenders' – which will increasingly include those merely arrested).

Which brings us to a crucial distinction between science and forensic science. One of the most essential elements of science is replication of findings by an independent investigator. If a researcher claims to have discovered some empirically derived finding (think of cold fusion), s/he must make available the method of investigation, and open up for scrutiny the procedures so that other scientists can determine whether the finding was spurious, unique, doctored, a fluke, etc. Not so with empirical evidence on DNA matches in a court of law. The crime labs are routinely held proprietarily, where the government agency *refuses* to permit independent laboratory work by 'outsiders' who could use the same 'scientific methods' to either corroborate or refute a finding of a DNA match (Murphy 2007). This barrier to comparative laboratory analysis is not science – but it is the current state of forensic science. The stakes are not just scientific reputation of some principal investigator – the stakes can involve the death sentence to an innocent person – the life imprisonment of a citizen falsely accused of rape and homicide.

From the current monograph by Machado and Prainsack, we learn that views about a universal database (that is, one in which all residents or citizens have their DNA deposited) differ dramatically in Portugal and Austria. In 2005, Portugal announced a plan to create a universal database (see Chapter 3 for an elaboration of this development). Funding for such a project was never provided, so eventually the plan did not materialise. Nonetheless, this signals just how non-controversial such a move would be, at least politically. In sharp contrast, we learn that Austrians are overwhelmingly opposed to such a national database.

These findings are reminiscent of the substantial divide in the US, where whites are more likely than blacks to support 'neutral' collection of DNA data across a wide swath of the citizenry (Duster 2006a). Indelible memories of recent twentieth century social history for both Austrians and African Americans in the US play a vital role in their respective scepticisms about the neutrality of universal databases. In the US, part of that history resonates still because of the patterns of drug arrests are so sharply different by race.

We know African Americans are being arrested at a rate of at least five times greater than whites for minor violations such as marijuana possession, even though the best available evidence suggests that whites are more likely than blacks to use (and thus possess) marijuana at every age level (Levine and Small 2008). The DNA of arrestees is being collected more and more routinely (in the US, 12 states now collect DNA from those merely arrested), and thus we are witnessing a new kind of convergence with portents for even greater racial disparities in convictions and rates of incarceration. As noted, the overwhelming majority of persons convicted of crimes plead guilty, without their case ever going to trial.

Part of this story examines prosecutorial claims trumpeting DNA fingerprinting as unassailable, definitive evidence. A recent book by Lynch et al. (2008), and new research by Kahn (2009) and Murphy (2007, 2008) each provide historical accounts of how these claims developed. But another part of the story has to do with the age-old balancing act between security and freedom – the 'special needs' of government to protect its citizens *versus* the individual's right to privacy. For example, there are constitutional limits that prevent the government from entering your home and searching your belongings without demonstration of good reason (warrant). Yet the government can and does search your DNA – as we shall see – without any 'cause' save arbitrary social and political forces happened to turn you up in a DNA database. Over the last three decades, the prison population of the US dramatically increased, more than doubling to now hold over two million of its citizens (Austin et al. 2007). Many end up incarcerated because they happen to live in communities where police systematically practice 'buy and bust' drug operations. It will come as a surprise to many that these operations are rare in white neighborhoods, where drug use is *relatively higher* than in African American and Latino communities (Levine and Small 2008). As more and more arrestees are locked into national DNA forensic databases, we will see an increasingly volatile intersection of race and ethnicity and the 'certainty' of DNA forensics. This brings us to the necessity to address a common misconception about the use of DNA evidence to exonerate *versus* convict. Erin Murphy has a graphic analogy that explains why the two strategies involve very different levels of certitude:

> … the use of DNA typing to inculpate a person – by which I mean to say that a suspect is the likely source of a sample – fundamentally differs from its use to exculpate. The simplest analogy is to blood typing. Imagine a murder scene at which police find a blood sample certain to belong to a killer. Crime scene technicians test the blood sample and show that it is type O. Later, the police find and draw blood from two suspects. One suspect is type AB; the other is type O. We can, with unreserved confidence, say that the first person is not the killer, but regarding the second suspect, we can only say that she is included within a class of people that includes the killer. The probability that she is the actual killer turns on how many other people have that blood type, along with any other evidence that we might be able to adduce. (Murphy 2008: 493)

Some of the differences between Austria and Portugal can be explained by the respective and distinctive social histories of the two countries. In the chapter that focuses on Austria, we learn that the reluctance to place faith in a system that collects DNA on the total population relates in some considerable measure to the lack of transparency of the way 'networks of power' operate. Thus, it is not so much that the citizenry is inclined to challenge the scientific legitimacy of DNA forensics, more that there is free-floating anxiety about secret and powerful interests, intermingled with fears of the corruptibility of those in opaque networks of power. This is not to dismiss the larger socio-political context of Austrians' antipathy to genetic technologies – as reflected in the strong rejection of genetically modified foods. Rather, more emphasis can be placed upon sensational media accounts of crime scene laboratory-based mix-ups, as reflected in the 'phantom of Heilbronn' (see chapter 2). For more than a decade, the police were looking for a female who purportedly left her DNA at a wide variety of crime scenes, but only later turned out to be a female worker who was packaging the content of the swabs taken from those crime scenes.

In sharp contrast with the unease and general scepticism about un-checked police power that the Austrians have exhibited, the Portuguese have had a long and uninterrupted history of passively accepting the state's collection of personal identification data. Indeed, we learn that Portugal has a history going back a full century before the DNA technologies of classifying and registering its citizens, and issuing identification cards based upon such personal information. In the late 1920s, new regulations required fingerprints on applicants to any secondary school or university. By 1944, the Department of Identification Services set up a system that would include requirements for both ordinary citizens and convicted criminals to supply fingerprints in order to obtain and identity card. So Portugal had a long history of citizen compliance with state requirements to collect personal data that set the stage for announcing that the government was willing to prepare pioneering legislation of the new DNA period, to become the first nation to require that all citizens and residents submit DNA for a national databank in 2005. For a host of reasons having little to do with public outcry (there was none), this plan was never implemented.

While this social history provides the useful and important backdrop and context, the chapter on Portugal contributes yet further analytic insights about how the media's sensational treatment of a crime would reinforce and solidify public readiness to accept the call for universal DNA data collection. Yet there are also important 'breaks' from that history – most particularly the new development where the Portuguese will include ethnic classification along with other identification data. As I have argued elsewhere (Duster 2006a), this has some troubling if not ominous features. Once DNA can be grouped by ethnic and racial categories, there is a strong push to correlate the two – and any association can easily be transmogrified into what would seem to be a legitimate scientific basis for concluding a genetic basis to complex human behavior. This is a new development in Portugal, since criminal statistics have been collected only by nationality up until this point.

Given the considerable differences in the social histories and the state policies regarding DNA collection, it was counter-intuitive to learn that the cases of full one-third of the Austrian prisoners interviewed had involved DNA evidence, while less than two per cent of the Portuguese prisoners had been implicated by DNA. The far greater acceptance by the Portuguese to the deployment of these technologies would lead one to suspect that these figures would be reversed.

Perhaps the most interesting finding is that prisoners accept that 'the evidence does not lie' when it comes to DNA, and that instead they attribute inaccuracy or inconclusiveness of DNA evidence to either human error or human purposeful manipulation. That is, prisoners make the same mistake as the general lay population, in confusing the definitive nature of a DNA mismatch with the definitiveness of a DNA match. As noted earlier, a 'definitive match' is dependent upon the assumption that no other matches are possible, or that the probabilities are so astronomically low as to be conclusive. That in turn, is dependent upon the deployment of appropriate and *socially relevant* population parameters – and a host of other decisions made by the analysts that are never context-free. Here, of course, there is always the possibility of inadvertent human error – but more disturbing is the fact that a number of laboratories have made consistent errors in their reports of matches that could have been detected had their been minimally cross-checking by an independent analyst.

In late 1999, and for nine months of ensuing testimony, it was revealed how police in the Rampart division of the Los Angeles Police Department were planting drugs and guns on defendants – mainly African Americans and Latinos – then testifying in court, under oath, that they had found these items, in order to secure convictions.[4] These machinations came to light only because a police officer working in a special unit of Rampart (Community Resources Against Street Hoodlums, or CRASH) began testifying against his fellow officers while he was awaiting re-trial on charges of stealing impounded cocaine. The officer, Rafael Perez, testified that he and other police officers had planted guns on suspects, fabricated drug evidence, and lied in arrest reports. As a result, more than 120 criminal defendants had their convictions vacated and dismissed, and more than $42 million dollars has been paid in civil settlements (Glover and Lait 2003).

In the last ten to fifteen years, major police corruption scandals have come to light in Dallas, New Orleans, Philadelphia and Chicago. In Dallas, police framed 39 Latinos and had them deported, by planting what they testified to be cocaine on them. This turned out to be powdered wallboard gypsum, not cocaine (Harrison 2002). Also of interest is the infamous Tulia, Texas drug bust, where a corrupt police officer jailed and then helped convict nearly three dozen people by planting drugs and testifying against them. These convictions were later over-turned when the governor pardoned 35 persons, and the police officer was indicted for perjury (Gold 2003). This came to national attention only after Bob Herbert kept up a steady stream of revelations in his column in *The New York Times*.

A few more examples should suffice to begin to fill in the contours of a suggestive national pattern in the US, a mosaic of dotted lines that can be connected to provide at least a plausible account of suspicion. In the early 1990s, in Philadelphia's 39th police district, five officers pled guilty to setting up suspects, bribing witnesses, and planting evidence – resulting in the vacating of more than 50 convictions and an investigation of another several thousand arrests. Lynn Washington, legal scholar and editor of the *Philadelphia New Observer*, recognised deeper issues involved in this case, stating 'what's most disturbing about the Philly corruption, is that the DA knew what the cops were up to, but tolerated their use of planted evidence because it boosted conviction rates' (Parenti 1996). New York City police were rocked by a similar scandal, when 16 officers of the Bronx 48th precinct were arrested and indicted 'on charges ranging from falsifying evidence to stealing weapons and money from illegally-raided apartments'.

---

4 The next three pages are adapted from my article that appeared in the *Journal of Law, Medicine and Ethics* (Duster 2006a).

It is possible to provide more reason for this scepticism by describing the basis for the different perspectives on just how 'definitive' DNA testing has come to be perceived. On the one hand, there is the possibility of exoneration of someone convicted when analysis of the crime scene DNA does not match that of the person convicted. On the other hand, there is the arrest and conviction of a person not previously a suspect, when there is a match between that person's DNA and the DNA found at a crime scene (known as a 'cold hit'). If DNA is the only evidence against the accused in the larger context of the framing scandals just described, we can see how some will fear the considerable abuse potential by rogue police officers doggedly committed to obtaining convictions. That is, if police can plant cocaine and guns on those that they later testify against, and obtain a conviction, they can *surely* plant DNA. The legitimacy of the criminal justice system rests primarily on fair application of laws. Who (or what part of society) would believe that police would actually plant DNA evidence, and even if they did, can DNA evidence ever stand alone without other circumstantial evidence?

Conclusion

The answer to this last question is vital to our understanding of how and when the gears of the criminal justice system no longer mesh – and where there ensues a 'crisis of legitimacy' for the key participants. Machado and Prainsack have allowed us to peer into the 'black box' of the plea bargaining process, and in so doing – provide the beginnings of a process to fill in our understanding of *how justice is done*. The old *cliché* about how we really don't want to know how beer and sausages are made is an apt metaphor for justice, but may impede our collective capacities to reduce injustice. In the Afterword to this book, Robin Williams provides an excellent summary distillation of the field of forensic DNA research, in which he points out that this is the first monograph to systematically address how prisoners experience this new technology. This is an important beginning, and a useful foot-in-the-door. It is bound to inspire more much-needed research on this topic, most especially in the country with the highest rate of incarceration in the world, the US. In the last 30 years, the nation has experienced a 500 per cent increase in citizens placed behind bars and prisons and jails, and now totals 2.3 million. And by what process did they get there?

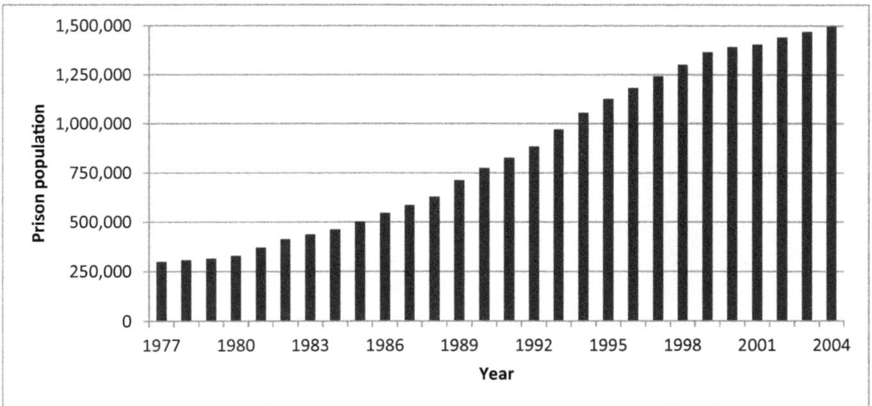

Figure F.1 Prisoners under state or federal jurisdiction 1977–2004

In late September, 2011, the *New York Times* published a front-page story with the astonishing news that plea bargaining is even more extensive than has been uncovered in previous investigations. Now, in most jurisdictions, the plea bargain accounts for 97 per cent of all convictions (Oppel 2011: 1). The pages that follow provide a useful model for how to contextualise such findings – using the social and political history of the nation-state to situate and explain the public's level of acceptance of expanding DNA forensic technologies.

Acknowledgments

We would like to thank all those who have contributed to this book. First and foremost we are grateful to our interviewees in Austria and Portugal, without whom this book could not have been written. We also thank the authorities that facilitated and funded out research: in Austria, the Federal Ministry of Science and Research (and their Genomeresearch in Austria programme, www.gen-au.at), the Federal Ministry of the Interior, and the Federal Ministry of Justice. In Portugal, the Foundation for Science and Technology (Portuguese Ministry of Education and Science, http://alfa.fct.mctes.pt/) through a post-doctoral fellowship (SFRH/BPD/34143/2006) and the project 'Forensic DNA databasing in Portugal: contemporary issues in ethics, practices and policy' (FCOMP-01-0124-FEDER-009231). We are grateful to many colleagues and friends who were extremely generous with their time and expertise: António Amorim, Troy Duster, Martin Kitzberger, Reinhard Kreissl, and Robin Williams. We are indebted to Christian Gesek, Andrea Lehner, Diana Miranda, Helena Moniz, Filipe Santos, Reinhard Schmid and Alípio Ribeiro for supporting us with access to materials and sources, as well as helpful conversations on many of the topics covered in this book; and to the following individuals for valuable comments on our manuscript at various stages: Manuela Cunha, Catarina Frois, Jean Lo, Stefan Gschiegl, Daniel Meßner, Victor Toom, and Susana Silva. We are also grateful to Filipe Santos for editorial assistance in preparing the manuscript. A big thank you goes to Claire Jarvis at Ashgate for having been such a wonderful editor.

All translations of interviews, policy documents and laws from German and Portuguese into English were done by the authors.

Chapter 1
Introduction

> If there is a drop of blood at the crime scene, that is irrefutable evidence, it's almost a confession…
>
> Feliciano

> We always leave some trace behind. It's not as if you can seal yourself inside a bubble.
>
> Micael

> The DNA trace does not only prove that I am guilty, and I think that's a good thing, because it can also prove my innocence.
>
> Hubert

Tracing Technologies

The human body leaves physical and biological traces that can suggest that a person has been in a particular place or in contact with other person or object. The capability of scientific and technological knowledge to detect the presence of the human body at a crime scene has provided invaluable support to the criminal justice system to identify perpetrators of crime in the last decades. The term 'bioinformation', in the context of criminal investigation, pertains to data derived from the analysis of a range of physical or biological characteristics of a person (Nuffield Council on Bioethics 2007: 5), which may include DNA and fingerprints (trace evidence), iris scans, photographs, or images on CCTV cameras. These, as we call them in this book, 'tracing technologies' have obtained a special role not only in criminal investigations and in criminal trials but also in public imaginaries, due to the television series such as *Crime Scene Investigation – CSI*, the most popular crime series in the world (Brewer and Ley 2010: 111). Scholars and practitioners speak of a *CSI* effect which captures, broadly speaking, the notion that the wide popularity of technocentric television drama has coloured our perception of what forensic technologies can and should do (see Chapters 4–5).

This book is about the views on forensic technologies held by a group that has so far received relatively little attention in the discussion of the benefits and risks inherent in the use of forensic technologies, namely prisoners. Our study was carried out in two different national contexts – Austria and Portugal. The fact that our data come from two different countries has allowed us to do two things: first, to highlight the similarities in the views held by prisoners in both countries; here, our data indicate that there could indeed be some shared public imaginaries facilitated by the global success of American technocentric crime drama. Second, the comparative dimension also allowed us to identify areas where prisoners in Austria and Portugal held different views, such as with regard to the question whether a universal DNA database comprising profiles of all residents would be desirable – a scenario that was supported by many Portuguese but none of our Austrian interviewees. These differences and similarities held by convicted offenders raise intriguing questions about the effects of different legal, political, discursive, and historical configurations on perceptions of crime scene technologies, and their use within the criminal justice system.

In this book we explore how prisoners described and interpreted the rules and practices followed by the police and other actors in the justice system to utilise bodily traces to establish a link between a specific criminal act to a specific body and person. How did the prisoners' views of 'tracing technologies' relate to popular assumptions about forensic technologies that are mobilised in TV shows and other media? A way to answer this research question was to explore the nexus between crime, technology and the media in the accounts of prisoners. This book thus foregrounds forensic identification technologies from the point of view of prison inmates. Their representations of the value of science and technology in fighting crime in particular is deeply interconnected with the cultural images disseminated by the media about DNA technologies and other methods in criminal investigation.

Forensic Technologies in the Era of *CSI*

As argued by Cole (2001), the twentieth century was the 'age of dactyloscopy' in the history of criminal identification. Fingerprints are physical characteristics that develop before birth and remain unchanged throughout a person's life. Dactyloscopy, the method of fingerprint identification, comprises the comparison between two (or more) instances of friction ridge skin impressions from human fingers, the palm of hand or even toes, to determine whether these impressions could have come from the same individual. No two people have been found with the same fingerprints, not even identical twins. Although the late twentieth century is often seen as marking the shift from the era of dactyloscopy to the era of DNA, which has been hailed as the new 'gold standard' of identification techniques, fingerprints have remained the most commonly used method of identification in forensic crime scene investigation (Bradbury and Feist 2005, McCartney 2006a, Nuffield Council on Bioethics 2007: 15). This raises the question why DNA evidence has received so much attention both within scholarly and public discourse, when other forensic methods are at least equally important in terms of how many cases they help to solve: is it just because DNA technologies are newer and thus more exciting?

The forensic analysis of DNA usually involves comparisons between profiles obtained from bodily samples to determine the likelihood that they came from the same person. Each person's DNA is unique, with the exception of identical twins or multiples. Biological substances like blood, hair, semen, urine, skin, saliva, sweat and tears, which are collected at crime scenes, all contain DNA. A DNA sample can also be obtained from an identified individual through the buccal swab method – which involves lightly scraping the inside of a person's cheek with a swab to collect saliva and cells – or by taking hair samples (including the roots, since these contain the cells required for analysis), or blood samples (by a finger prick), or by rubbing off a small sample of a person's skin (this method is used in Austria, for example, when people who are legally obliged to provide a DNA sample refuse to cooperate).[1]

In this book we also discuss how the genetic age in criminal investigation has been captured by the media's cultural messages, thereby feeding into a phenomenon we call the era of *CSI* in a reference to the aforementioned TV series. Although there is no consensus on whether or not a *CSI* effect exists and what exactly it consists of (see Ley et al. 2010), the claim that people's views and practices pertaining to DNA evidence in particular have been influenced by media representations (e.g., judges and jurors putting more weight on forensic evidence that has been produced with high-tech tools than on other kinds of evidence, see Cole and Dioso-Villa 2007, 2009, Podlas 2006, Robbers 2008, Tyler 2006) have received so much attention in the scholarly literature and public media that some authors have started speaking about a '*CSI* effect effect': the phenomenon that *assumptions* about how people's expectations and behaviours have changed based on public media representations of forensic technologies have started to change people's expectations and behaviour (Cole and Dioso-Villa 2007, 2009, see also Chapter 5).

Regardless of where one stands in the debate on the *CSI* effect – or the *CSI* effect effect – it is apparent that twenty-first-century institutions of criminal justice embody very positive views of the potential presented by bioinformation to identify criminals. The fact that international collaboration in crime control is catalysed by the creation of infrastructures for easier access of law enforcement and criminal justice agencies to bioinformation, illustrates this.[2] Also fictional representations of criminal investigations focus on technologies: the heroes of television crime shows are no longer police detectives but forensic identification technologies (Kruse 2010a), in particular DNA evidence, symbolising an ideology where machines are more reliable and 'safer' than human action and expertise.

In recent years, a considerable body of research has paid attention to how the media portrays the uses of forensic identification technologies in criminal

---

1 In Israel, in contrast, hair roots are the only samples that may be taken by force (if suspects refuse to provide any samples voluntarily (Zamir et al. 2012: 286)). This reflects interesting cultural and national differences in understandings of what is the least physically intrusive method of obtaining DNA from a non-compliant person.

2 Recent examples are the Prüm Decision in the EU (Prainsack and Toom 2010), and bilateral treaties between the US and individual European countries facilitating the exchange of fingerprints (the existing Treaties are devised in such a way that they can be extended to the exchange of DNA profiles by means of signing an additional protocol).

investigation work and to the effects this may have on different audiences. While many scholars have examined the *CSI* effect on publics (Brewer and Ley 2010, Cavender and Deutsch 2007, Schweitzer and Saks 2007) jurors, judges, and police investigators (Cole and Dioso-Villa 2007, 2009, Durnal 2010, Huey 2010, Robbers 2008, Shelton et al. 2006) prisoners' views on forensic technologies have been under-explored in this context, despite the situation that convicted offenders represent an important stakeholder group: they constitute part of the group who commits crimes, and most of them already have their fingerprints, DNA profiles, and other data stored in police databases. Sometimes, false claims pertaining to the availability of incriminating crime scene evidence are used by the police to elicit confessions from innocent people and in such cases DNA technologies can be particularly useful to exculpate the wrongfully suspected, and to exonerate the wrongfully convicted (see Chapter 7).

High-tech crime drama circulates cultural images that reflect dominant and taken-for-granted assumptions about crime and criminals (Jewkes 2004), about the work of investigators and the authoritative power of forensic identification techniques – in particular the interpretation of DNA fingerprinting – as 'infallible evidence'. This imagery is not only constructed and perpetuated by popular television shows but also by journalists, lawyers and legal scholars. Our book is driven by the desire to explore to what extent these cultural images are reproduced by prison inmates.

Literature on the alleged *CSI* effect has mainly discussed the influence of the television series in shaping perceptions of DNA technology, crime scene examination procedures and the identification of offenders on audiences who are removed from the 'real world' of criminal investigation and the work of courts of law. Hence the prevailing focus on the influence of *CSI* and similar series on juries – ordinary citizens summoned by the courts to assess criminal cases that may be complex and may involve DNA evidence. Prisoners' perspectives have not yet been given a lot of attention,[3] and that is precisely what this book sets out to accomplish.

Based on data from 57 qualitative interviews with prison inmates in Austria and Portugal we discuss the ways in which this particular group's representations of forensic genetics reveal forms of exposure to, but also a distancing from, the cultural images circulated by the media which portray DNA evidence as highly reliable and almost infallible. The intention is to contribute towards a more empirically grounded approach and greater sensitivity to the situatedness of the *CSI* effect (Duster 2006a, Huey 2010, Mopas 2007) by emphasising the fundamental role of the personal experiences of prisoners and the fact that they are in a special position to acquire knowledge of forensic identification technologies, due to their place in the real world of crime and criminal investigation.

---

3 For exceptions see Duster (2004, 2006a), Machado et al. (2011), Machado, Santos and Silva (2011), Prainsack 2010b, Prainsack and Kitzberger 2009, and also Bhati (2010).

We will, in many places, speak of 'the' understandings and views of our interviewees, as if they were homogenous. We do this to refer to views and understandings that were held by the majority of our informants. Where there were opposing views, we will mention them and clearly state that these were expressed by a minority. However when we speak of 'the' prisoners and their views, we do this solely for the sake of readability. By no means do we want to make it seem as if there were no nuances and differences also within 'the' mainstream view. To borrow the words of Gresham Sykes (2007 [1958]: 63), one of the pioneers of prison studies:

> It might be argued, of course, that there are certain dangers in speaking of the inmates' perspective of captivity, since it is apt to carry the implication that all prisoners perceive their captivity in precisely the same way. It might be argued that in reality there are as many prisons as there are prisoners – that each man brings to the custodial institution his own needs and his own background and each man takes away from the prison his own interpretation of life within the walls. We do not intend to deny that different men see the conditions of custody somewhat differently and accord these conditions a different emphasis in their personal accounting. Yet when we examine the way the inmates of the New Jersey State Prison perceive the social environment created by the custodians, the dominant fact is the hard core of consensus expressed by the members of the captive population with regard to the nature of their confinement. The inmates are agreed that life in the maximum security prison is depriving or frustrating in the extreme sense.

The Aims of this Book

A good body of literature exists about how the media portray prisoners and incarceration (Altheide and Coyle 2006, Cheliotis 2010, Jewkes 2007, Mason 2006), and on how the media provide reference points for identity construction and power relationships among inmates (Jewkes 2002). This book seeks to provide a contribution to that research field by exploring prisoners' views of criminal technologies in the era of *CSI* as a complex combination of media influence, individuals' biographical trajectories, and 'deviant careers'. More specifically, this book explores how prisoners' views on forensic technologies, the work of police and courts, the body and instances of surveillance, processes of exclusion and social categorisation, are interrelated with media representations of criminality, crime investigation, prisons and prisoners, and also with the inmates' own experiences when dealing with the criminal justice system.

At the same time, forensic uses of DNA technologies have become crucial elements of national criminal justice systems. While the legal and criminological implications of forensic and police uses of DNA analysis and databasing have received ample attention in the last decade (Schroeder and White 2009, Pratt et al. 2006, Williams et al. 2004, Williams and Johnson 2008), this applies less to their social and societal dimensions (yet see Jasanoff 1998, 2004a, 2006, Lynch 2003, Williams 2010a, 2010b, Williams and Johnson 2008, as well as Lynch and McNally 2009, and Heinemann et al. 2012). Empirical social science research on how DNA technologies are used in criminal investigations are relatively scarce (for notable exceptions see the aforementioned work of Williams (Williams et al. 2004; Williams and Johnson 2008), as well as Kruse 2010b, Toom 2010, and Lynch et al. 2008), and there is virtually no comparative social science research on this topic.

This book seeks to contribute to filling these gaps in several ways: first, it explores how prisoners view crime scene traces, how they understand crime scene technologies, and what effect do they attribute to the existence of large, transnationally networked police databases with regard to their own criminal careers and their future lives. Second, the book does not aim at producing an evaluation of the ethicality or the legal provisions pertaining to high-tech crime scene work, but instead provides an in-depth discussion of the meanings and effects of crime scene technologies in the era of *CSI* from a social science perspective. Third, as argued above, the book also develops a comparative perspective on the basis of two case studies which represent two different contexts for the forensic uses of DNA technologies in particular: one country (Austria) holding one of the largest DNA databases in the world, and the other one (Portugal) having only recently established such a database for criminal investigation. Thus, these case studies shed some light on how differences in discursive, political, operational, and also historical contexts, influence the way in which DNA technologies are utilised by law enforcement agencies and related to by our interviewees – and vice versa. At the same time, it should be noted that despite the obvious differences between the two countries, there are also significant similarities, especially when we compare these countries to systems outside of continental Europe: both Austria and Portugal are countries where prisons are state-run, and market forces do not play a large role in service provision (neither in the context of criminal investigation, where the provision of forensic expertise is largely restricted to state-run or state-affiliated institutions, nor within the penal system). Moreover, neither in Portugal nor in Austria does crime dominate public media and public policy agendas to the extent that it is the case in the UK or in the US, for example. Austrians often pride themselves with the country's low crime rate – apart from burglaries and theft, which are being blamed on criminal gangs coming from abroad. Also Portugal has a relatively low rate of serious crimes in the European context. Finally, both Austria and Portugal are countries with aspects of a 'deep state', without a strong tradition of transparency and openness in policy making, and with informal networks playing a large role in the distribution of political and administrative functions. There is a growing public sentiment in both Austria and Portugal that corruption is on the rise, and that anti-corruption measures undertaken by their governments are ineffective (Transparency International 2010).

This book also discusses topics which are of a cross-cultural and transnational relevance, rather than being generated by a configuration of national idiosyncrasies. Examples for such themes with wider relevance are: the prevalence among the prisoners of an exposure to the *CSI* effect by which the TV series acts as an educational vehicle for criminals, helping them to become 'experts' in avoiding leaving traces at crime scenes (Chapter 4); prevalent beliefs in the efficacy and 'truthfulness' of DNA technologies both in identifying criminals (Chapter 5) and in exonerating individuals (Chapter 7); the view that forensic DNA databases are of limited value for crime prevention and deterrence (Chapter 6); and perceptions that DNA databasing adds another dimension to the stigmatization of prisoners and their overall negative perception of the police and the criminal justice system (Chapter 8).

The Study

Our study involved in-depth interviews with a total of 57 prisoners in two prisons in Austria (2006-2007) and in three prisons in Portugal (in 2009). Although the main focus of this book is the prisoners' views of 'tracing technologies', in particular their assessment of the practices of using bioinformation in criminal investigation, our research required us to seek additional information from practitioners in the criminal justice system. We interviewed attorneys, public prosecutors, police officers and criminal investigators who provided technical clarifications about legislation, criminal investigation and trial procedures. These informants have also provided valuable information about the real and practical uses of forensic identification technologies, police archives and databases containing various sorts of data – from DNA profiles and samples, to criminal psychological profiles, photos and biographical details about active criminals. We also collected and analysed documents and media coverage of criminal cases that had a high exposure to the public and which involved a relevant role of DNA technologies.

We obtained permission to conduct interviews with prisoners from the Austrian Federal Ministry of Justice and the Portuguese General Board of Prison Services. Administrators of the prisons in both countries were approached with requests to provide a list of potential interviewees. A theoretical sample was devised, based on representativeness by diversity and exemplariness (Hamel et al. 1993), combined with convenience sampling. The prisoners in our study were diverse in terms of socio-demographic profile (age, civil status, education and profession) and criminal record (type of offence and length of sentence). We interviewed both prisoners in whose cases bioinformation (mostly fingerprints or DNA evidence) had played a significant role in the investigation and/or trial, and others for whom this had not been the case (Table 1.1a and 1.1b). In other words, a prisoner's personal experience with DNA evidence or fingerprints was not a requirement to be included in the study; we sought to speak to a broader range of prisoners

Table 1.1a Characterisation of the sample of prisoners in Austria

Prisoner (name)	Year of birth	Primary crime that led to imprisonment	Sentence (duration)	Fingerprints or DNA traces played a significant role in investigation/trial	Notes
Anton	1965	Aggravated sexual abuse of minors	3 years	No	
Bernhard	1979	Burglary	3 years	Yes	Mentioned that he was detected based on DNA (blood that he had left on the crime scene)
Christoph	1967	Kidnapping, blackmail	10 years	No	Said he did not worry about leaving traces during the kidnapping because the police '*had no DNA of me*' [his profile was not yet on the national database]
Dorian	1947	Murder	15 years	No	
Ernst	1977	Fraud	3 years	No	
Fritz	1975	Drug trafficking, burglary, robbery	8 years	No	
Gert	1977	Rape	3 years and 6 months	Yes	Mentioned that he was detected based on *DNA* found at the crime scene
Hubert	1966	Sexual abuse of minors	7 years and 6 months	No	Said that 'A *DNA examination* was carried out [bed sheets were searched for DNA traces] but no *DNA traces* were found'
Ingo	1964	Robbery, murder	Life	Yes	Mentioned that they cut off the head and the hands of the victim and burned the corpse out of fear that '*DNA* or fingerprints or something like that' could be 'found'
Jürgen	1978	Aggravated battery	5 years	No	
Karl	1957	Murder, attempted murder	17 years	No	
Ludwig	1978	Murder	15 years	No	
Matthias	1974	Murder in two cases	Life	Yes	
Norbert	1957	Attempted murder in three cases	Life	No	

Oliver	1973	Attempted murder, attempted rape	Open (depending on evaluation by psychologist)	Yes	When describing the evidence against him he mentioned a 'blood-stained textile handkerchief'; and that the *DNA* from the handkerchief belonged neither to him nor to the victim
Paul	1970	Aggravated robbery, armed theft	15 years	Yes	Mentioned a *DNA trace* found at one of the banks he had robbed
Quentin	1982	Arson	8 years	No	
Richard	1959	Aggravated sexual abuse of minors, rape	5 years	No	
Sigi	1970	Battery, coercion	18 months	No	
Thomas	1987	Arson	24 months	No	
Uwe	1974	Murder, battery, disturbing the peace of the dead	Open (depending on evaluation by psychologist)	Yes	Mentions that police found a *stain* on the carpet in the trunk of the car that came from the victim – and that the stain convinced him that he should confess
Vincent	1968	Drug trafficking, illegal possession of firearms, aggravated battery, theft	8 years	No	
Walter	1978	Rape and several cases of attempted rape	Open (depending on evaluation by psychologist)	Yes	Mentions a dragnet that was carried out to look for the rapist (*'They took thousand DNA'* [sic])
Xaver	1980	Battery	18 months	No	
Ygor	1985	Attempted rape	18 months	Yes	
Zeno	1978	Drug trafficking, battery, attempted severe burglary	6 years	No	

Table 1.1b Characterisation of the sample of prisoners in Portugal

Prisoner (name)	Year of birth	Primary crime that led to imprisonment	Sentence (duration)	Fingerprints or DNA traces played a significant role in investigation/trial	Notes
Amadeu	1966	Murder, burglary, theft	23 years	Yes	
Amândio	1978	Murder and attempted murder, drug trafficking, theft, aggravated burglary	25 years	No	Was convicted based on co-defendants' confessions
Amaro	1969	Murder and attempted murder	20 years	No	
António	1983	Drug trafficking	5 years	No	Has had pictures taken of his scars and tattoos
Artur	1971	Aggravated burglary, burglary, attempted aggravated theft	12 years	No	Refused submitting to DNA sampling. Claims that the police tried to accuse him of a crime he did not commit saying that his fingerprints were found at the scene. He was exculpated of that crime
Carlos	1957	Procurement, rape, aggravated rape, child and drug trafficking, sexual abuse	7 years and 6 months	No	
Daniel	1973	Murder and attempted murder, arson, grievous bodily harm	24 years	Yes	
David	1967	Attempted murder	3 years and 10 months	No	
Emílio	1977	Murder, sexual coercion, theft	15 years	Yes	
Feliciano	1975	Murder	12 years	No	
Frederico	1955	Criminal association (leader), extortion, drug trafficking, fencing	20 years	No	
Gaspar	1970	Burglary, drug use, theft	5 years and 6 months	No	Claims to have been previously convicted with fabricated fingerprint evidence
Gil	1976	Drug trafficking	6 years	No	

Henrique	1972	Burglary and forgery	3 years	No	Submitted to DNA analysis and fingerprinting. It is not clear whether these were determinant for his conviction, as he claimed to take every precaution
Jaime	1980	Murder	16 years	Yes	
João	1960	Rape, battery	5 years and 4 months	No	
Joaquim	1960	Severe sexual abuse of minors	6 years	No	
Joel	1987	Aggravated rape	5 years and 6 months	No	
Lucílio	1975	Driving without permit	2 years	No	
Luís	1983	Aggravated burglary, theft, trespassing, fencing	9 years	No	
Manuel	1982	Murder and drug trafficking	14 years	No	
Mariano	1980	Murder	17 years	No	
Martim	1982	Rape, attempted coercion, kidnapping	9 years and 3 months	Yes	
Micael	1978	Rape	12 years and 1 month	No	
Miguel	1965	Driving without permit	5 Months	No	Submitted to DNA analysis and fingerprinting in Canada
Nelson	1974	Sexual abuse of a minor, burglary, theft, perjury	9 years	No	Said he had his DNA taken 'many times at the hospital'
Olegário	1978	Theft and perjury	3 years and 6 months	No	
Ovídio	1976	Drug trafficking, possession of an illegal weapon	8 years	No	
Rúben	1978	Fraud and aggravated fraud, forgery, illegal access to a computer system or network, perjury	6 years	No	Was submitted to handwriting analysis and fingerprinting
Tomás	1981	Rape and murder	21 years	Yes	
Valter	1984	Kidnapping, rape, theft, aggravated burglary, possession of an illegal weapon, forgery	18 years	Yes	DNA sampling successfully exculpated him of a crime of rape. Was convicted for burglary based on fingerprints

than those who could be expected to have fairly specific knowledge of forensic technologies in this field due to their first-hand experience.

In the recruitment process, prisoners were asked to participate in a social science research project on forensic identification technologies, crime traces and DNA databasing. All of the 57 prisoners we interviewed were male, which is due to the fact that interviews were carried out in prisons for males only. The effect of this bias is mitigated by the fact that only approximately five per cent of all prisoners in Austria and in Portugal were female at the time when we carried out our interviews (Austrian database search courtesy of the Enforcement of Sentences Office of the Republic of Austria; official statistics provided by the Portuguese General Board of Prison Services – DGSP 2009).[4]

Respondents were between 20 and 60 years old at the time of the interview, with most of them aged between 25 and 35 years (n=31). A large majority was unmarried (n=39), while seven were married, eight divorced, and three widowed. With regard to these parameters, the prisoners we interviewed were 'typical' of the prison population also in other countries (Tonry 2001; for more details, see Chapter 9). Twenty-six of our informants were Austrian, 30 were Portuguese, and one was a Ukrainian citizen in a Portuguese prison. Levels of formal education ranged from four years of schooling (n=4) to a higher education degree (n=2), but most interviewees had no more than 9 years of schooling (n=46). The professional occupation of most interviewees previous to incarceration was in the secondary sector, namely in the civil construction and industry (n=26). In the Austrian group, there was a disconcertingly high number of trained cooks (n=6).

The crimes which led to the incarceration of the prisoners in this study were (this list is not exhaustive; for more details, see Table 1.1a and 1.1b): battery; drug trafficking; coercion; murder (including attempted murder); rape; robbery (both armed and unarmed); and sexual abuse of minors. Prison sentences ranged from five months to life imprisonment. In just under half of all cases, bioinformation (fingerprints or DNA evidence) played a significant role in the investigation and/or trial (see Table 1.1a and 1.1b).[5]

Once respondents had been recruited, individual interviews were conducted with only the interviewer and the inmate present. In Austria, the interviews were conducted by a single interviewer (Barbara Prainsack), whereas in Portugal there were three interviewers (Helena Machado, Filipe Santos, and Diana Miranda),[6]

4 In Austria, on 1 September 2007, 209 (4.2 per cent) of 4,983 individuals serving prison sentences of more than 18 months were female. In Portugal, on 31 December 2009, 613 (5.5 per cent) out of a total of 11,099 individuals serving prison sentences were female.

5 The year of birth was modified slightly in order to minimise the risk of identification of our informants.

6 Filipe Santos and Diana Miranda were junior researchers working on the projects 'Justice, Media and Citizenship' (FCOMP-01-0124-FEDER-007554, 2007-2010) and 'Forensic DNA databasing in Portugal: contemporary issues in ethics, practices and policy' (FCOMP-01-0124-FEDER-009231, 2010-2011), hosted at the Centre for Social Studies,

all duly trained in accordance with the objectives of the research. Each inmate met the interviewer in a room normally used for interrogations and counselling, unattended and unsupervised by prison guards, other representatives of authorities, or surveillance cameras. The interviewer provided a brief oral explanation of the overall purpose of the research project. Interviewees were also told that the risk of breach of confidentiality would be kept to a minimum (through usage of pseudonyms, changing of potentially identifying information such as year of birth and year in which the crime was committed in all published material), and that their participation was to be voluntary, gratuitous and that they could, at any moment, withdraw their participation in the study. These conditions were also confirmed on a written informed consent form.

Interviews lasted between 13 and 120 minutes; most took between 50 and 80 minutes. All interviews were transcribed and the collected data were systematically compared, contrasted, synthesised and coded according to themes and, within these, by categories, closely following the principles of the *Grounded Theory* approach (Glaser and Strauss 1967, in the tradition of Charmaz 1990. See also Charmaz 2000) by which the objective is to raise new concepts from the empirical reality under observation.

The semi-structured interview agendas entailed a list of questions covering the following wide subjects: a) the interviewee's life prior to the crime which lead to his imprisonment; b) the crime that lead to imprisonment with a particular focus on fingerprints and DNA evidence (if it played a role at all); c) sources of knowledge about DNA technologies and fingerprints and criminal investigation databases; d) a more general discussion about crime scene traces and the interviewees' conceptualisation of the nature of these traces, their incriminating potential, their scientific background; e) assessment of the actions of law authorities and opinions about desirable and undesirable future scenarios of criminal investigation and functioning of the criminal justice system; f) value of DNA profiling and databasing in crime prevention and deterrence; g) expectations towards social reintegration and experiences of stigma related to incarceration.

A few publications resulting from this study preceded this book. The first one was a paper summarising findings from the Austrian case study published in *Social Studies of Science* in 2009 (Prainsack and Kitzberger 2009). Findings pertaining to DNA technologies from this case study also informed the chapter on Austria (Prainsack 2010b) in Hindmarsh and Prainsack's (2010) edited volume *Genetic Suspects: Global Governance of Forensic DNA Profiling and Databasing.*

University of Coimbra, Portugal and funded by the Foundation for Science and Technology (Portuguese Ministry of Education and Science, 2010-2013); and '*CSI* behind Bars' (funded by the Research Centre for the Social Sciences, University of Minho, Portugal, 2009). Their work was supervised by Helena Machado, the scientific coordinator for both studies. The Austrian study received generous support from the GEN-AU (Genomeresearch in Austria, www.gen-au.at) ELSA programme of the Austrian Federal Ministry of Science and Research in 2006 and 2007.

With regard to the Portuguese case study, an article with a focus on the prisoners' perspectives on the potential surveillance effects of the DNA database was published in *Forensic Science International* in 2011 (Machado, Santos and Silva 2011).

Our Book in Context

As discussed above, scholarship employing social science perspectives on forensic technologies is currently still relatively limited. With regard to the specific topic of the book – prisoners' views on crime scene technologies – we have pioneered this research and carried out research that provides an empirically informed study of the understandings of crime scene work in this particular stakeholder group.

Also the wider field of social science perspectives on forensic technologies is presently still very limited. We are not aware of any monographs, neither already published or in preparation, that provide an in-depth analysis of understandings of crime scene work in a particular stakeholder group (not only prisoners). Although there are a range of recent books addressing forensic DNA technologies, the emphasis is normally on different aspects from social science analyses of crime scene work (both by investigators and offenders).

Most of the existing literature on forensic technologies from a social sciences or legal studies perspectives focuses on DNA profiling and databasing in the UK and in the US. We should start with Simon Cole's (2001) seminal work on the history of criminal identification techniques and technologies, which focuses on fingerprinting, the 'gold standard' of forensic identification from the early twentieth century onwards. Pertaining to the era of DNA, Robin Williams and Paul Johnson (2008) employ a socio-historical perspective in their analysis of the development of the UK's National DNA Database (NDNAD). These authors focus on the legal and technical aspects of the uses of DNA profiling and databasing for criminal identification purposes. Michael Lynch et al. (2008) examine the controversial development of DNA fingerprinting and the evolution of its uses in civil and criminal cases, albeit mainly in adversarial legal contexts. These particular settings offer unique insights into the challenges and dilemmas at the intersections between science and law which is also discussed in some works of Sheila Jasanoff (2004a, 2006). Jay Aronson (2007) provides an historical account of the early practices and uses of DNA in the USA and its trials to become a contemporary success. The edited volume *Genetic Suspects: Global Governance of Forensic DNA Profiling and Databasing* (Hindmarsh and Prainsack 2010) comprises contributions from academics and practitioners in different disciplines and regions of the world discussing the history, regulation, practical workings of, and public discourse on national DNA databases for forensic and police purposes. Also from a comparative perspective – comprising chapters on the forensic DNA databases in the UK, Japan, Australia, Germany, and Italy – Krimsky and Simoncelli (2011) provide an analysis of the establishment of forensic DNA databases in these countries. However, their focus is predominantly set on rights, ethics and liberties issues and consequences for citizenship. There are other works that revolve mainly around legal aspects of DNA uses, such as Kobilinsky et al. (2004), Semikhodskii (2007). Furthermore, the work of Lee and Tirnady (2004), a forensic pathologist and a lawyer, discusses the wider scientific applications and implications of DNA technology, although focusing more on a 'popular science' view than adopting a critical stance. Charlotte Spencer (2003) also provides an accessible account of the basic concepts underlying DNA technologies for criminal identification by using past criminal cases as practical examples.

Focusing on legal and ethical dimensions, the edited volume convened by David Lazer (2004) comprises contributions from authors with different backgrounds and fields of expertise to discuss the impacts of DNA technology on the criminal justice system, particularly in the USA. Topics covered in the book range from the importance of meaning and context of DNA in a crime scene, to its use in post-conviction examination, as well as the social, legal and ethical issues associated with DNA databases. Finally, Carole McCartney's *Forensic Identification and Criminal Justice: Forensic Science, Justice and Risk* (2006a) uses excerpts from a series of interviews with anonymous persons involved in the British criminal justice system in order to illustrate the practical issues of DNA technologies in several instances, from the legal framework to criminal investigation, the courts, or the establishment of DNA databases. McCartney's book critically assesses the societal dimensions of DNA profiling and databasing, considering the limitation, risks and future impacts for contemporary societies.

A topic which has been widely discussed in the context of forensic DNA profiling and databasing in particular is the risk of discriminating 'ethnic' minorities. Troy Duster's (2004, 2006b) work has made a great contribution to increasing awareness of such issues among scholars and publics. Also relevant in this respect are Krimsky and Simoncelli's (2011) book on DNA databasing and civil rights, and Harriet Washington's (2010) chapter on 'racial aspects of US DNA forensics'. Amade M'Charek (2008, see also M'Charek et al. 2011) has lead the efforts to deconstruct the claim inherent in forensic genetics that 'race' can be objectified and emptied of its political and social meaning. Yet issues pertaining to 'race' and 'ethnic' minorities are one area that we leave unaddressed in our own book. This is not because we do not recognise their importance (the opposite is the case; one of us has also published on this topic, see M'Charek et al. 2011), but because the data collected in our studies would not have provided a firm basis for such work. Neither did our studies in Austria and Portugal include observations of criminal profiling, nor did the groups of prisoners we interviewed represent a diverse sample in terms of cultural and religious backgrounds. Although the Austrian sample contained individuals whose parents had immigrated (mainly from regions in the former Republic of Yugoslavia), and in the Portuguese case we interviewed an immigrant from Ukraine and an individual who had emigrated to Canada but was deported to Portugal for having committed a crime there, language barriers prevented us from including more recent immigrants in the group of our interviewees.

Structure of the Book

Prisoners' views on forensic technologies adhere far less to a cliché of a 'crook's view' than one may assume. This was apparent both within the Austrian and the Portuguese group, despite the fact that these countries represent most-different cases regarding the scope and contexts of use of DNA technologies, with Austria having started very early (1997) and running one of the largest databases in Europe, and Portugal having started relatively late (2008). Chapters 2 and 3 are dedicated to describing the specific features of the Austrian and the Portuguese contexts in order to give insights into the conditioning of DNA technologies and genetic databasing by particular legal culture and different history of technology and governance. Both chapters start out with a discussion of the landmark cases that are commonly seen as having opened the door to the establishment of the forensic DNA database in Austria and in Portugal. Chapter 2 contains also an overview of the ongoing process of harmonising standards and facilitating systems for the exchange of fingerprint and DNA data in Europe, where Austrian authorities are playing a leading role (whereas Portugal started to actively exchange data within the Prüm Treaty, for example, only in July 2011). We then go on to describe the history of the use of forensic technologies for criminal investigation in these countries, starting by outlining the beginnings of the use of fingerprints and police archives and arriving at a discussion of current legal provisions and practices pertaining to the taking of DNA samples and fingerprints from suspects and convicted offenders. Our focus here is on the historical, legal and cultural framework which integrates the use of science and technology in the 'fight against crime' and explains the different levels of public trust in the justice system and its operators. We conclude that in both of the countries where our case studies were set, looking at the role of public media when reporting high-profile criminal cases is crucial for our understanding of the nexus between crime investigation, the justice system, and public assessments of those activities.

But not only public media play an important role in this: high-tech crime television series, such as *CSI*, are valuable sources of information about forensic technologies, as well as of the sorts of biological traces that may lead to identification. Chapter 4 is dedicated to prisoners' reflections on these media representations and the ways in which they have influenced their own practices. We address questions such as: do *CSI* and other technocentric crime series increase the 'forensic awareness' of (potential) offenders (Beauregard and Bouchard 2010)? Chapter 4 thus explores also the possible effect of the interviewees' contact with forensic science fiction TV series, discussed in the literature as another variant of the aforementioned *CSI* effect, according to which the series acts as an educational vehicle for criminals or potential criminals, teaching them how to avoid or remove traces from crimes scenes. We argue that our interviewees' representations of DNA technologies and its uses in criminal investigation cannot simply be explained by the *CSI* effect. Rather, while on the one hand being inspired by what they saw in television crime shows, our interviewees assumed a critical distance from the high tech scenario projected by *CSI* on the other, pointing out what was 'unrealistic' in television representations of crime scene work (both on the side of the criminals and on the side of the crime scene investigators). Thus, they made sense of what they saw on television by merging certain elements of representations of high-tech crime scene work with their own experiences.

The discussion of the cultural imaginary disseminated by *CSI* and similar series provides also provides the point of departure in Chapter 5, where we analyse the meanings and values that biological traces had for prisoners. Most of our respondents saw DNA evidence as 'truth machines' (Lynch et al. 2008 use this term to refer to the popular conception of DNA as infallible) because of the scientific power ascribed to the way in which it is produced. The belief in its 'fool-proof'-nature, and its alleged capacity to produce unambiguous evidence led our informants to perceive DNA technologies as having an almost absolute power in terms of identification, and unique status among the range of forensic technologies; the majority of our interviewees considered it a technology far superior to fingerprints. However, while much of the power ascribed to DNA technologies was attributed to the fact that DNA evidence was seen as being produced by machines and not by humans (see also Mnookin 2008), the infallibility of DNA technologies was not taken to be absolute in connection with the possibility of human errors. Our interviewees expressed strong suspicions regarding police officers or people with malicious intentions deliberately 'planting' biological traces at crime scenes in order to incriminate them, or regarding authorities lying about the availability of DNA evidence to elicit confessions.

Bioinformation has been described as an important tool for crime prevention, detection and deterrence. Chapter 6 starts by discussing how the adoption of scientific and technological devices for corroborating or inferring identities has been part of a developing instrumentality of modern state surveillance. It then analyses prisoners' assessments of the role of the DNA databases in crime prevention and deterrence by taking into account, for example, their evaluations of scenarios of further expanding uses of DNA profiling and more inclusive forensic DNA databases. Our findings show that prison inmates established a hierarchy between 'professional' criminals and 'lower class criminals' when speaking about the DNA databases' potential to prevent and dissuade crime. DNA databases were seen to represent a greater probability of detection, identification and conviction for 'lower class criminals', insofar as these were supposed to lack the experience and 'selective gaze' of 'professional' criminals, or to be too drunk, drugged, or simple-minded to care about leaving traces at crime scenes. On the other hand, 'professional' criminals were said to need to afford greater care and take additional measures in order to avoid detection and identification, as part of their risk management and control associated with the planning of a crime.

Chapter 7 is dedicated to reflections on the capacity of high-tech crime scene traces, and DNA evidence in particular, to exculpate the wrongfully suspected, and to exonerate the wrongfully convicted. High-tech crime scene work was seen by our respondents as a potential 'ally' of both suspects and convicted criminals, because it shifted agency from the hands (and minds) of humans, who were seen as prone to errors and bad intentions, to allegedly objective and infallible machines, who could correct the errors of human beings. This chapter also provides an overview of the role of high-tech evidence in the work of the Innocence Project, an organisation in the US dedicated to exonerating wrongfully convicted individuals that has also been reproduced in other countries, such as UK.

Chapter 8 discusses the ways in which the interviewees talk about their 'criminal' bodies and the underlying potential stigma. The same body that can be used to commit a crime also represents a risk of detection and identification of the criminal. Through externally visible characteristics, such as scars, tattoos, hair colour or peculiar physical features, criminals can be identified and incriminated. Bodily substances such as DNA or fingerprints are also a subject of management and control and a factor involved in risk assessment by criminals, while their storing into forensic databases may also represent a 'deepening' of the stigma of delinquency in their bodies and selves. Hence, this chapter provides insights into social processes by which the prisoners apply their knowledge of crime scene traces, and DNA traces in particular, to their own experiences of dealing with the police and criminal justice system, about whose work many interviewees share rather negative opinions.

The final chapter of this book provides concluding reflections about the prisoners' accounts and understandings of forensic technologies, and their narratives pertaining to the value and utility of DNA profiling and DNA databasing within the criminal justice system. We explore the idea that the serious concerns that the prisoners had about the mis- and abuse of technologies and the dubious effect of DNA databasing for crime prevention and deterrence should inform debates and create implications for policy making in this area. We conclude that there are great similarities between the Austrian and the Portuguese prisoners in their understandings and relations to tracing technologies, despite the relevant differences between criminal justice systems and the conditions of imprisonment in Austria and Portugal. Chapter 9 calls for more empirical and comparative work on social and regulatory aspects of forensic sciences.

Chapter 2
Setting the Scene: Austria

Introduction[1]

In 1974, the 24-year-old Austrian Johann ('Jack') Unterweger – the son of a Viennese prostitute and a member of the US Armed Forces – was sentenced to life in prison for the murder of an 18-year-old woman. The victim, as Unterweger stated later, had reminded him of his mother (Gepp 2007). Unterweger spent his time in prison writing short stories and authoring an autobiography titled *Purgatory – A Journey to Jail* (1983), which had also rendered him the darling of the local celebrity scene. Prominent Austrian artists and writers – such as the later Nobel laureate in Literature (2004), Elfriede Jelinek – signed petitions on his behalf, resulting in his early release from prison after having served only 16 years of his life sentence. Unterweger, initially celebrated as a model case of successful reintegration, soon returned to his old passion of murdering women. Over two years, he strangled at least nine women in Austria, the Czech Republic, and in the US, mostly prostitutes. In 1992, he was arrested in Miami, Florida, and extradited to Austria. On 29 June 1994, he received his second life sentence for nine counts of murder (Leake 2007). In the same night, he hanged himself in his cell with the string of his track bottoms.

The Unterweger case was the first instance in Austrian history in which decisive evidence for the conviction was provided by DNA analysis. Unterweger had hidden the bodies of his Austrian victims in the *Wienerwald*, the woods surrounding most of the city of Vienna, where they were discovered months later. A hair of one of the victims found in Unterweger's car, as well as a fibre of his scarf on one of the corpses, eventually gave him away.

Less than three years later, on 1 October 1997, the Austrian Forensic DNA Database became operational as one of the first worldwide, with Europe's first forensic DNA database having become operational about two years earlier in England and Wales. The custodian of the Austrian forensic DNA database is the Federal Ministry of the Interior (*Bundesministerium für Inneres*, BMI). One year after the establishment of the database, 149 crimes had been solved on the basis of profiles stored in the database; by 2004, that number had grown to over 1,400. In December 2010, a survey carried out by the European Network of Forensic

1 Parts of the introductory section to this chapter, as well as the section on the legal and regulatory background pertaining to DNA profiling, were taken (modified and updated) from Prainsack (2010b). The section on basic principles underlying criminal procedures in Austria was written with the help of Jean Lo.

Science Institutes (ENFSI) reported that the number of matches matches between subject profiles and crime scene stains in the Austrian database had reached 12,990 (ENFSI 2010). Measured by the ratio of the number of subject samples stored in the database to the total population, the Austrian forensic DNA database is among the largest ones in Europe and even worldwide (ENFSI 2010, Prainsack 2008, 2010b).

The history of the use of fingerprints for identification purposes both globally and in Austria is, of course, much older. Let us take a more detailed look into this history in order to understand why fingerprinting has been considered, until very recently, the gold standard of forensic identification (Lynch et al. 2008). As we shall see later, the exchange of dactyloscopic (fingerprint) data still plays a very important role in transnational bioinformation exchange.

As Cole (2001) showed in his book on criminal identification, fingerprinting took the role of a rival system to the so-called Bertillon-system in France at the end of the nineteenth century. The Bertillon-system comprised the detailed description of suspects and convicts on the basis of a large set of standardised measurements of the body, a narrative description (*portrait parlé*), photographs, and, if applicable, the registration of unusual characteristics such as moles or scars. The Bertillon-system, named after its developer, the French criminologist and anthropologist Alphonse Bertillon, rendered possible the first systematic archiving of data obtained for criminal identification. While at the end of the nineteenth century it still looked as if the Bertillon-system would continue to establish itself as the dominant model for criminal identification in Europe and North America, compared to fingerprinting, the Bertillon-system had several disadvantages: the measurements of body-parts of suspects varied when different people carried out the measurements. It seemed that only within France, where virtually all staff had been trained by Alphonse Bertillon himself, the problem of inter-person variation was absent (Cole 2001). In addition, the Bertillon-system was considered unsuitable for use on children and women; in the case of the former, because their bodies still grow, thus measurements of body parts are instable; in the case of the latter, because the close physical contact between the male official and the female suspect or convict which was necessary to carry out the measurements may have been considered inappropriate (Cole 2010, see also Fosdick 1915, Meßner 2010a).

The decisive advantage of fingerprinting over the Bertillon-system, however, had to do with crime scene work. While the personal records containing individual body measurements within the Bertillon-system enabled authorities to ‘recognise’ a person who had already been registered within the system, fingerprinting allowed the establishment of connections between people and crime scenes (Cole 2001). Thus, fingerprinting was – besides the analysis of shoe prints – the first technique with the help of which biological traces at crime scenes that could be linked to concrete suspects, or to individuals in centralised police (or forensic) registries. The result of this advantage was that by 1930, fingerprinting had replaced the Bertillon-system as the dominant method and system of criminal identification practically anywhere, even in France. This technological shift brought about changes in the distribution of power and tasks within criminal justice authorities: within the Bertillon-system, the most difficult part was the taking of the measurements and the collection of other data, while the sorting and archiving of data could be carried out by less well trained staff. In the context of fingerprinting, the opposite was the case: while the collection of fingerprints did not require particular skills or training, the classification, archiving, and interpretation did. This meant that with the emergence of fingerprinting as the 'standard technology' for criminal identification, policing expertise shifted from the front office to the central bureau (see also Cole 2001: 87).

Like many European countries, also Austria had adopted the Bertillon-system, which complemented and extended a photography-based archiving system for records of suspects and convicts since the late 1860s (the so-called 'album of criminals', see Meβner 2010a: 230). However it took over a decade after Bertillon had presented his system internationally for authorities in Vienna to endorse it in 1898. Fingerprinting, on the other hand, was adopted only one year after its establishment in England: as early as 1902, Viennese authorities started to use fingerprinting in parallel to the Bertillon-system. In 1908, criminologist Hans Gross stated that, although the Bertillon-system was very useful, fingerprinting was 'anatomically more certain' (Gross 1908: 458, cited in Meβner 2010a: 240). Less than two decades later, the Bertillon-system had seen the end of its days in Vienna. Many Austrian criminalists and criminologists shared the assessment of their Bavarian colleague Robert Heindl, who saw the Bertillon system as 'useless in daily [criminalistic] practice. It is the result of an almost pathological compulsion to classify' (Heindl 1922: 425, cf. Meβner 2010a: 243, see also Meβner 2010b). Ever since then, fingerprinting has represented a routine step in the process of establishing someone's identity in policing contexts (see below). The reason why Austrian authorities were relatively reluctant to implement the Bertillon-system, while they enthusiastically embraced fingerprinting, is not entirely clear; however historians hold that like in other European countries (Cole and Lynch 2010: 111) it had to do with a rather complicated indexing system for data in the Bertillon-system (Daniel Meßner, personal communication with the authors, January 2011). Possibly it was related also to the preference of a system which would lend itself more easily to standardisation across national borders.

Austria has always been particularly strongly involved in the trans- and internationalisation of data exchange for policing and forensic purposes. Due to there being a strong political commitment to the necessity of transnational collaboration in criminal investigation, Austria played an prominent role in the establishment of Interpol in 1923, contributing with core expertise to the setting up of an Interpol infrastructure for DNA profile exchange in the 1990s, and now provides know-how and hands-on support to countries in the process of establishing national DNA databases in Europe.

In the remainder of the chapter we will first provide an overview of the legal provisions and practices pertaining to the taking of fingerprints and DNA samples and fingerprints from suspects and convicted offenders, and to data storage in the forensic database. Subsequently we will discuss prominent cases which played a role in challenging trust in law enforcement authorities and courts in particular and in governmental authorities in general. Finally, we will address an Austrian characteristic related to the particular political, historical, and cultural heritage of the country, namely a pronounced scepticism towards genetic technologies. The latter is arguably a result of a combination of collective memories of the fateful marriage between science and government in the Nazi period (Barondess 1996), and a certain kind of nature romanticism that dates back to long before World War II (Prainsack and Gmeiner 2008). It shapes attitudes not only of publics but also of stake holder groups – such as convicted offenders, but also law enforcement officers, as we shall see – towards DNA evidence in particular.

Laws and Regulation

Let us start with a few general remarks regarding the procedures for criminal investigations and trials in Austria. Criminal investigations are led by the prosecutor in accordance with the rules of the criminal investigation department. After the investigation is completed and if the prosecutor is convinced that the evidence is sufficient to lead to a conviction, charges will be pressed.

The aim of a criminal trial is the finding of the 'material truth'. This sets criminal trials apart from civil trials, which are characterised by the principle of disposition, namely that the parties constitute 'their own' truth. The notion of material truth guiding criminal trials, in contrast, is not truth as established by the parties, but it is 'what really happened'. This means that all parties are obliged to work towards finding this 'objective' truth, independent of their interest of achieving a particular outcome.

In order to keep this distinction to civil trials, the Austrian procedural system for criminal trials is characterised by the 'principle of prosecution' (*Anklagegrundsatz*). In contrast to the inquisitorial system, where the court investigates, prosecutes and acts as judge, according to the principle of prosecution, only the prosecutor (and in some cases, the plaintiff) is entitled to bring in a charge. Other adversarial elements in the Austrian procedural system for criminal trials are the equal positions of the prosecution and the defence in the search for material truth, and in some cases, juries are installed to answer the question of guilt.

Inquisitorial elements are present with regard to the roles of expert witnesses. Expert witnesses can be called in by the court only (§126 Abs 3 Code of Criminal Procedure, Strafprozessordnung, StPO); they have to be members of state-run registries for expert witnesses (§126 Abs. 2 StPO). The defence cannot call in expert witnesses. They can bring in private experts who help the defence with the interrogation of expert witnesses.

Moving on to forensic identification, the core of fingerprint identification in Austria is the Automated Fingerprint Identification System (AFIS). In the process of establishing someone's identity in the context of an arrest or for the purpose of criminal investigation, fingerprints and palm prints are routinely taken and AFIS is searched to see whether the person's prints match latent prints from crime scenes, or whether the person's prints are already stored under a different name. Since 2003, also fingerprints of asylum seekers, which are sent to the European Eurodac database (see below), are held in AFIS. The legal basis for the taking of prints is provided by the Austrian Security Police Act (*Sicherheitspolizeigesetz*, SPG, BGBl I Nr 56/2006, see in particular § 65).

Also with regard to the taking of DNA samples from suspects, the SPG provides the legal basis. Of particular relevance are §67–75. These sections stipulate that DNA can be obtained in the context of forensic identification only if the person in question is suspected of having committed a dangerous assault,[2] and if, with regard to the deed,[3] or the personality,[4] of the suspect, it can be expected that the person will leave, in the course of committing further dangerous assaults, further traces that enable his or her identification on the basis of the retrieved genetic information (§67.1 SPG).

The law stipulates that the contractor who performs the molecular genetic examination must not receive any information about the identity of the person (§67.2 SPG). Laboratories may examine only parts of the DNA that serve the purpose of identification, which rules out phenotypic profiling – the analysis of DNA not for identification purposes but in order to infer probable physical or 'ethnic' characteristics of a person (Graham 2008, Kayser and Schneider 2009, M'charek et al. 2011, Prainsack 2010a). In addition, in all cases where authorities are obliged to delete the data stored in the database, the physical samples must be destroyed as well (§ 67.3 SPG).

---

2 A 'dangerous assault' is defined in § 16 [2] SPG as a threat posed to a legal good through the unlawful commission of a crime which is punishable by a court and which has been committed with intent, and not only upon the request of a another person. Furthermore, the criteria of a 'dangerous assault' are met only if (1) the crime is punishable according to the Penal Code [few exceptions]; or (2) it is punishable according to the Prohibition [of Nazi activities] Law (*Verbotsgesetz*); or (3) it is punishable according to the Illegal Substances Law (*Suchtmittelgesetz*), unless the possession or acquisition of the illegal substance is only for the purpose of the suspect's consumption.

3 By means of internal guidelines the Federal Criminal Police Office authorised a list of crimes in the context of which the retrieval of DNA (by means of cheek swabs) should be standard procedure; these are considered to be categories of crime with a particularly high risk of recidivism, such as property and sex crimes, crimes involving illegal substances, violent crimes.

4 This condition is met if the suspect has a criminal record.

Table 2.1 Regulatory characteristics of the Austrian Forensic DNA Database

Year of establishment	1997
Legislation	Austrian Security Police Act (*Sicherheitspolizeigesetz*, SPG, BGBl I Nr 56/2006)
Custodian of the database	Federal Ministry of the Interior (*Bundesministerium für Inneres*, BMI)
Agent responsible for collection	Any police officer is authorised to proceed within measures to identify suspects of serious crimes
Subjects to DNA sampling	Suspects Convicted offenders Volunteers ('persons of happenstance') Victims Unidentified corpses Missing persons if there are concrete indicators for a crime, suicide, or an accident Police officers (the development of a so-called 'police elimination database' is still work in progress)
Informed consent required	No
Use of physical coercion	Yes, with safeguards for the subject's physical integrity. When made by force, an officer performs a skin swab from the forehead or back of neck
Type of sample	Buccal swab or equivalent
Access to DNA data	Staff members of forensic institutes only have access to DNA profile values and reference numbers. Police and judicial authorities have access to full details
Anonymisation of samples for laboratorial analysis	Yes. Samples are bar-coded for laboratorial analysis
DNA dragnets	Only for crimes punishable with five years in prison or more, where no other means to obtain clues are not available, and have to be authorised by a court

Table 2.2 Entry and removal criteria of the DNA profiles and sample retention and destruction

Criteria for entry of profiles	All convicted offenders Crime scene stains Suspects of having committed a dangerous assault, and if, with regard to the deed, or the personality, of the suspect, it can be expected that the person will leave, in the course of committing further dangerous assaults, further traces that enable his or her identification on the basis of the retrieved genetic information
Criteria for removal of profiles	Convicted offenders: indefinite retention Suspects: if acquitted and if retention is not deemed necessary by the authorities (acquitted suspects must perform a written request to the BMI to have profiles eliminated)
Retention and destruction of samples	Whenever profiles are deleted, samples must be destroyed Unidentified samples are retained until corresponding cases are solved Convicted offenders: 80 years of age (if not subjected to identification in the previous 5 years) Minors: after 5 years without another forensic examination Suspects: if acquitted and if retention is not deemed necessary by the authorities (acquitted suspects must perform a written request to the BMI to have samples destroyed)

The conditions under which the data stored in the database must be deleted are listed in § 73.1 SPG: first, when the originator of the DNA has reached 80 years of age, if s/he has not undergone any examination for forensic identification purposes in the previous five years; second, if the originator of the DNA had been a minor at the time of the provision of the material for forensic identification and if s/he was not examined for forensic identification purposes in the previous five years; third, five years after the death of the originator; and fourth, if the originator of the DNA is no longer suspected of having committed a dangerous assault. In these cases, data deletion on the authorities' own initiative is mandatory unless the authorities' retention of the data is necessary due to concrete circumstances indicating that the person will commit further dangerous assaults (two more cases apply only in specific circumstances: see § 73.1, points 5–6). The subsequent paragraph, §74 SPG, pertains to the deletion of stored DNA profiles on request of the originator. This is the case if the original suspicion against the originator no longer exists, or if the deed has been found to be not unlawful.[5]

Austrian law does not specify a minimum age of persons from whom DNA can be taken for forensic identification purposes. In practice, however, police officers typically refrain from taking DNA of individuals younger than ten. Another feature, which has drawn severe criticism from privacy watchdog groups was the legalisation in 2004 of DNA dragnets through revision of the Code of Criminal Procedure (see, in particular, §123.2 StPO). Austrian police representatives countered the criticism by referring to their general policy of restraint, in that DNA dragnets would be used only if deemed to be absolutely necessary (that is, in high profile cases in which no other means of investigation could be expected to render any clues), and only in crimes for which the law prescribes prison sentences of five years or more. Any dragnet would need to be requested by a public prosecutor and approved by a court. So far, no dragnet has been carried out in Austria.

Transnational Exchange of Fingerprints and DNA Profiles

As a member of the European Union (EU), Austria is part of the Prüm regime, an apparatus of regulations and practices granting law enforcement authorities in EU member countries direct access to databases holding DNA profiles, fingerprints, and vehicle information in other EU countries (Prainsack and Toom 2010).[6] The emergence of the regime dates back to 2005, when seven EU countries – Austria, Belgium, France, Germany, Luxemburg, the Netherlands, and Spain, signed a convention in the German town of Prüm (Prüm Convention 2005). Although the convention was open for accession to all other EU countries, it was not part of EU law at that time but had the status of an international treaty which was legally binding merely for the seven signatory countries. These seven countries had initiated the convention in order to intensify collaboration to combat illegal migration, transnational crime, and international terrorism (Prainsack and Toom 2010).

5 In practice, §73.1 accounts for the vast majority of all data deletions and sample destructions. Most of these are due to the expiry of the time limits for profiles storage. § 74, which grants the former suspect the right to request the deletion of the data, is applied in only a small number of cases annually. Most of these cases pertain to suspects who escape conviction due to diminished responsibility at the time of the commission of the deed. Suspects receive an information sheet informing them of this right at the time of the provision of the DNA sample.

6 Also non-EU countries, such as Norway, Iceland, and the US, have signed, or are in the process of signing, treaties with EU member states that lay down provisions for data exchange similar to data exchange within the Prüm regime.

Three years later, in 2008, the EU decided to adopt the Convention into EU law,[7] meaning that all EU member countries who had not yet done so had to set up databases for DNA, fingerprint, and vehicle data, and allow access to their data to relevant authorities in other EU countries (EU Council 2008, for more details see Prainsack and Toom 2010). The rationale behind this was, and is, that the expansion of the EU and the Schengen regime, which abolished border controls between most EU countries, increases the migration of criminals across Europe. Thus, the main function of transnational bioinformation exchange is to facilitate the solution of cases by identifying persons in the DNA or AFIS database of another member country, especially if there is no match between crime scene traces and DNA profiles or fingerprints stored in the databases of the country where the crime was committed. In addition, the Prüm regime also enables law enforcement authorities to link unsolved crimes in their own countries to unsolved crimes in different member countries to the same (yet unidentified) person; to expose individuals who are registered with different identities in different member countries, and possibly establish their true identity; and to search requests for arrests or whereabouts (see Schmid 2010).

The system operates by allowing law enforcement officers (or members of the judiciary, in countries where forensic databases are not held by the police) to search relevant databases of other EU countries for matches to their search request, may it be an unidentified fingerprint, a DNA profile derived from a crime scene stain, or a query related to a vehicle. If there is a match, then the requesting party can liaise with the contact point in the country for which the match is reported, and ask for nominal data – such as the name and address of the person to whom the DNA, fingerprint, or vehicle match was established. In some cases, the requesting party will carry out a confirmatory analysis, such as a re-analysis of a DNA sample to decrease the chances that the automated match was a false positive, which in light of the sheer amount of profiles stored in forensic databases across Europe has become a frequent occurrence (Hicks et al. 2010, Weir 2004, 2007).

With regard to fingerprints, the requesting party must provide the human resources necessary to establish whether two prints should actually be considered a match. In contrast to matching DNA profiles, which consist of discrete data and can therefore be compared in a fully automated manner, in the case of fingerprints the computer can only identify a range of possible matches for a particular print (see also Dror and Hampikian 2011). This is the case because fingerprint matching entails the comparing of full prints (print of the full finger, or fingers and palm, in good quality in the database) with partial or latent prints left at crime scenes.[8] Thus the matching process entails the 'manual' comparison between the patterns

7 The relevant Decisions are 2008/615/JHA and 2008/616/JHA.

8 Within the Prüm network, the following scenarios for comparison are possible: tenprint to tenprint (TP; a TP is a print of all ten fingers excluding the palm); tenprint to latent fingerprint (LT); palm print (PP) to latent palm print (LP); TP to unresolved LT; LT to unresolved LT; PP to unresolved latent PP; LP to unresolved LP (see Schmid 2010).

of the prints (see Cole 2001). This is a very time consuming process which renders it impossible that every possible match between two prints within databases of EU member countries highlighted by the automated process is followed up by confirmatory analyses (that is, more detailed analyses of the prints) at the side of the requesting and the requested country (see also Schmid 2010). Whether a reported possible fingerprint match will be assigned the human, time, and other resources necessary to analyse it further depends on different factors such as the quality of the print, the importance of the case in connection with which it is found, etc.

From an Austrian perspective, the Prüm regime has been very successful so far: by 2 November 2010, Austria had obtained just under 10,000 hits to DNA profiles in other databases alone; 1,333 of them were matches between an Austrian crime scene trace and a subject sample from another country (Schmid 2010). Unfortunately, no data exist regarding the numbers of cases in which these matches have provided investigative clues and/or decisive evidence leading to convictions.[9] With regard to fingerprints, by the same date of 2 November 2010, Austria had received 41,447 matching requests which resulted in 3,770 hits.[10] The identification results led to several hundreds of arrest warrants issued by Austrian courts, by the police, and by international courts; and to 924 uncovered aliases (Schmid 2010).

With regard to fingerprints, Austria exchanges data also via the Eurodac system, which stores fingerprints of asylum seekers and certain kinds of illegal immigrants,[11] as well as the Visa Information System (VIS AFIS),[12] whose main

9 It should be noted, however, that proving causal connections between DNA or fingerprint matches to convictions is a notoriously difficult endeavour. In some cases where DNA or fingerprint matches are obtained, these are not useful for the investigation (e.g. a DNA match in a rape case where both parties agree that sexual relations took place but they disagree over whether it was consensual), and/or the decisive evidence comes from a different source (e.g., eye witnesses). Thus, media or policy reports which attribute conviction rates to DNA or fingerprint matches in a linear and causal manner are likely to be driven by ideology rather than by a sound empirical basis.

10 In November 2010, when the figures were established, Austria exchanged fingerprint data within Prüm only with Germany, Luxemburg, Slovenia, and Spain.

11 The Eurodac system is based on Council Regulation 2725/2000. It is run by a central unit within the European Commission and consists of a central database containing fingerprints as well as particular types of personal information about the originator of the print (EU country of origin; sex; place and date of asylum application, or place and date of the apprehension of the person; reference number; date of taking of the fingerprints; date of transmission of the print to the central Eurodac unit). For more information on Eurodac see EU 2010a.

12 VIS AFIS is based on Regulation (EC) 767/2008. Data recorded on VIS are: information on the applicant and on the visas requested, issued, refused, annulled, revoked, or extended; photographs; fingerprint data; links to previous visa applications and to the application files of individuals travelling together (EU 2010c).

aim it is to aid the implementation of the common visa policy and to prevent 'visa shopping', namely the practice employed by non-EU citizens whose visa applications have been rejected by one Schengen country to apply to other Schengen countries until one will eventually admit them. Finally, data are also exchanged via the Schengen Information System II (SIS II), which does, however, not draw on AFIS; it is meant to merely store ten print images. However it is planned to link SIS II – which will eventually also store photographs – with AFIS, which in turn is expected to significantly improve the functionality of SIS II in identifying individuals using fake identities. SIS II enables authorities in Schengen countries,[13] as well as Europol[14] and Eurojust,[15] to obtain information pertaining to particular kinds of persons and property.[16] Due to both its location in the centre of Europe and its prominent position in transnational data exchange infrastructures, Austria encounters high numbers of search request, as well as hits, pertaining to fingerprints of convicted offenders matching with asylum seekers and illegal immigrants (Schmid 2010). In addition, in 2009, 51 per cent of new identification records in Austria pertained to foreign suspects or criminals (Schmid 2010).

---

13 In 1995, five EU member countries – Belgium, France, Germany, Luxembourg, and the Netherlands – signed the so-called Schengen agreement (named after the town in Luxembourg where it was signed). The aim of this international treaty (just like the Prüm Convention it was not EU law by the time it was signed!) was to facilitate the free movement of persons across borders within the area, which practically meant the abolishment of border controls. Portugal, Spain, Italy, and Austria joined the Treaty in 1997. Two years later, the Treaty of Amsterdam adopted the Schengen agreement into EU law and rendered it part of the so-called *acquis communautaire* (the body of laws, regulations, and rules in the EU that new accession countries automatically take over when they join the EU). However the countries which now implement the Schengen agreement are not entirely congruent with EU member countries: while EU countries Ireland and the UK opted out of Schengen, several non-EU members, Iceland, Norway, and Switzerland, voluntarily opted into Schengen. This means that any non-EU resident holding a Schengen visa can also travel to these three non-EU states without passing any border controls. In addition, three micro-countries that are neither EU members nor Schengen signatories are de-facto part of the Schengen area due to their bilateral agreements with their surrounding countries: Monaco, San Marino, and Vatican City. (At the time of writing this chapter, three EU countries: Bulgaria, Cyprus, and Romania, although being bound by the Schengen regime, had not yet implemented it. For more information see EU 2010d.)

14 Europol is a law enforcement agency supporting law enforcement in EU countries. In particular, its mission is to tackle problems of transnational and European relevance, such as counter-terrorism, organised crime, etc.

15 Eurojust is a judicial cooperation body within the EU. Its function is to aid and help coordinate measures against serious crime which affect the territory of more than one EU member country.

16 The legal foundations of SIS II are Regulation (EC) 1987/2006 and Council Decision 2007/533/JHA. For more information see EU 2010b.

DNA and Fingerprint Analysis: Practices of Law Enforcement Authorities in Austria

Every arrest procedure routinely entails the collection of verbal data, photographs, and dactyloscopic data in the form of whole palm prints from the suspect. Although Austrian law does not restrict the range of crimes in which DNA may be taken from suspects, in practice (and based on a decree [*Erlass*] of the Ministry of Interior), DNA is only taken on suspicion of a limited number of crimes (see above). 'Verbal data' comprises all personal details as reported to the authorities by the arrested individual, including details displayed on legal documents and ID cards. Second, photographs are taken of the face and body of the person as well as so-called 'particular characteristics', such as tattoos. Third, dactyloscopic data are obtained with the help of an automatic ten finger and palm flat-screen scanner, which feeds the data directly into the database(s). Dactyloscopic data, according to our informants at the Austrian police, are the best tool for forensic identification purposes at the time of arrest, because they are 'unique for every individual and relatively cheap to obtain and process'.

About 25,000 cases of evidence taking, as described above, are carried out nationwide per year. Less than half include the retrieval of a DNA sample. In cases where a DNA sample is taken, the officer first checks whether the arrestee's profile is already stored in the database with the help of finger and palm prints. While arrestees could attempt to hide their identity by giving a false name, the dactyloscopic data would betray them: if the finger and palm prints produced a match in the database it could be assumed that the person was not a first time arrestee and might have a DNA profile stored as well. Subject profiles entered into the DNA database stem from two groups of people: either from suspects (from them, DNA may be taken by force, typically from the forehead or from the neck),[17] or from individuals under no suspicion who might have left their DNA at the crime scene unintentionally but for legitimate reasons ('persons of happenstance', *Gelegenheitspersonen*). Typically, these are partners, family members, flat-mates, and neighbours, cleaning personnel, but also victims. Their DNA profiles are used only for elimination purposes: if their DNA profiles match with profiles from crime scene traces, these matches will be known not to refer to the perpetrator (unless a 'person of happenstance' later turns into a suspect, of course). DNA profiles obtained from such 'persons of happenstance' are not entered into the database, which means they are not used for routine searches against profiles from crime scene traces.

Theoretically, elimination samples from 'persons of happenstance' could be lawfully obtained by force. However, according to the representatives of law

17 DNA samples obtained by force are normally not derived from blood but taken in a situation in which one or two officers restrain the suspect and another takes a skin swab from the forehead (if the head of the suspect is being held back) or the neck (if the neck of the suspect is fixed in a forward position).

enforcement authorities whom the authors interviewed for this study, this does not happen very often in practice. This is because, if a 'person of happenstance' is reluctant to provide a cheek swab voluntarily, they are then informed that they could be labelled a suspect; in that case, their DNA profile would be uploaded to the database and used for speculative searches in the future. If, on the other hand, they provided a sample voluntarily they would remain a 'person of happenstance'.

Turning to the transportation of DNA samples to the contracting laboratories, certain barcodes are used for suspects/convicts and then other barcodes for each of the following groups: volunteers ('persons of happenstance'); victims; profiles of unidentified corpses; profiles of missing persons if there are concrete indicators for a crime, suicide, or an accident; and finally, profiles of police officers respectively. Different levels of comparison (routine or *ad hoc*) also apply to profiles held in these different sections of the database.

To reduce the risk of contamination of crime scene evidence with suspect DNA, crime labs are legally required to process crime scene traces and subject samples on different premises. DNA analyses are carried out at three different laboratories, all part of academic research institutions: the Departments of Forensic Medicine at the University of Innsbruck, the Medical University of Vienna, and the University of Salzburg. Contracts with these institutions stipulate a maximum number of crime scene and subject samples to be analysed; at present, the limit is at about 4,000 crime scene traces and 12,000 subject samples per year (excluded from this limitation are DNA samples related to the investigation of particularly serious crimes, for which the courts cover costs). If the actual number of samples submitted for analysis is below the limit in any given year, then the Ministry receives a 'traces credit', which can be carried forward to the following year. Because subject samples are typically uncontaminated with other substances (retrieving and storing DNA from a cheek swab is a relatively straightforward task), they are much cheaper to process than DNA samples retrieved from crime scenes under difficult technical circumstances from various surfaces and in varying quantities. The average cost of the creation of a DNA profile based on a crime scene sample is currently about €255, while a profile based on a cheek swab (the typical 'subject profile') lies at about €90.

The strict limit on the number of crime scene samples which can be submitted for analysis forces crime scene investigators to divide DNA traces secured at crime scenes into two groups: the first comprises samples deemed essential to be submitted for analysis, while samples in the second group will be stored and perhaps analysed later if in the course of the investigation it turns out that a particular sample might bear clues to the solution of the case. For example, if a murder has happened on the third floor of an apartment building, crime scene investigators might secure cigarette butts from the front of the building. For reasons of cost containment, these cigarette butts will not be submitted for DNA analysis but go into storage. But if, for example, a witness indicated s/he had seen a stranger smoking a cigarette in front of the building prior to the crime, the cigarette butts would then be submitted to a forensic laboratory for DNA analysis. Besides these tactical considerations, decisions on what traces to analyse and which ones to store are made also according to the quality of the sample. Blood, saliva, and sperm, for example, are considered 'good' media from which usable DNA is likely to be extracted, whereas other media such as sweat are more problematic. Consequently, for analysis, evidence in the form of 'good' media usually has priority.

DNA profiles established in the laboratory consist of 11 numbers which correspond with DNA typing results for ten genetic loci plus the result from the analysis of the sex chromosome. If the quality of the sample allows it, the profile derived from it is fed automatically into the database. Reinhard Schmid, the Director of the Department of Forensic Identification at the Austrian Federal Criminal Police Office, asserted that the automatisation of this process renders the Austrian database relatively immune to mis-characterisations of profiles, as the greatest potential for mistakes is inherent in manual transfer of results into the database (as is routinely done in Germany, for example). In case a profile matches another one in the database, the Ministry requests a confirmatory analysis from the relevant laboratory (in such cases, a second DNA sample, which had been submitted together with the first but not yet analysed, will be used).

In sum, the practices of forensic DNA profiling and databasing in Austrian reality are, of course, clearly less glitzy and fast paced than usually portrayed in TV thrillers. In addition, our Austrian informants seemed far less enthusiastic about high-tech solutions in crime investigation than their TV 'colleagues'. The arduous, time consuming and often-monotonous nature of their work are often emphasised. In general, those representatives of the police and the Ministry of Interior in Austria (Prainsack 2010a) were generally aware of the benefits of both tight regulation and monitoring of forensic DNA technologies. Public support for the existing laws, as well as for investigative police work in general, was recognised as a necessary precondition of the smooth functioning of their work.

Public Trust in the Criminal Justice System

Public trust in criminal justice agencies, however, was challenged in the context of several famous cases where suspicions were raised about issues during the police investigation and/or trial. Although the German terms *Polizei-* (police-) or *Justizskandal* (judiciary scandal) are unsuitable as denominators for these cases as in most of them, no wrongdoing on the side of the authorities was ever proven, the notion of a 'scandal' captures well the wide public repercussions that some of these cases had. Several such cases in the more recent past have arguably had particular impact on the way in which the conduct of criminal justice agencies and governmental authorities more generally, are perceived in wider publics. In contrast to other countries such as the US, forensic science and technology do not feature very prominently in the plots of these 'scandals'. Instead, what emerges from these stories is a narrative that articulates feelings of powerlessness on the side of 'normal' people towards alleged networks and schemes of those who are considered parts of the political, business, and societal elite. The enemy of the 'small man' (*kleiner Mann*; the gender-bias is present in the original term) is not as much a particular governmental authority as a general alleged lack of transparency in the way that high-profile cases are handled, paired with the assumption that key players in politics, business, and media have invested interests in them.

This narrative pattern integrates two characteristics of Austrian society: first, networks of power that are organised, to a large extent, in terms of non-transparent or semi-transparent syndicates of (mostly) men whose allegiance reaches back into their student or even high school years, when they became members of so-called *Kartellverbände* (cartels, which often have a Catholic and conservative orientation), student organisations, or other elitist and/or esoteric groups (e.g., Kreisky 1992). For outsiders – which includes women, for that matter, these networks are very difficult to enter, and thus certain processes of political or business bargaining remain not only inaccessible to them but also unobservable and therefore incomprehensible. The second characteristic is connected to, yet different from, the first: although systematic surveys have shown that perceived levels of public-sector corruption are comparable to those in Germany, the UK, Ireland, and Japan (all of these countries reside within the twenty countries with the lowest perceived corruption rates, see Transparency International, n.d.), there is growing public sentiment that political and business elites in Austria are becoming increasingly corrupt (see below).[18]

No hard data exist on what publics perceive to be the biggest judiciary scandals in recent years. In addition, some cases – although it would be an exaggeration to call them 'miscarriage of justice' because there was either no court trial or no miscarriage could be proven – have been particularly prominent in the public debates: one of them concerns a woman named Natascha Kampusch, who was abducted at the age of ten and held captive in a tiny room in the basement for eight years. Police had given up the search for Natascha relatively soon after her disappearance because it was considered highly unlikely that she could still be alive. Aged 18, Natascha Kampusch managed to escape. Her captor, Wolfgang Priklopil, could not be charged as he committed suicide when he found out that Ms Kampusch had escaped (Hall and Leidig 2006, Kampusch 2010).

Natascha Kampusch's story led to a heated public discussion not only because contrary to public sentiment Ms Kampusch refused to vilify her captor, but also because witnesses stated to have seen *two* suspects being involved in Natascha Kampusch's abduction (Seeh 2010). Suspicions were heard that authorities had 'covered up' the truth about additional people involved in her abduction, and refused to carry out a proper investigation (Kraske 2008). Nothing to this effect, however, was proved.

Other instances that have negatively impacted public trust in criminal justice agencies are found in the realm of politics and business (Mayr 2010). An illustrative

---

18 For up-to-date information on global corruption indices etc, see Transparency International (n.d.).

example of such a case concerns a former Federal Minister of Finance and former ally of the deceased right-wing politician Jörg Haider, Karl-Heinz Grasser, with whom he later broke and instead was appointed Minister of Finance on a ticket of the conservative Austrian People's Party (*Österreichische Volkspartei*). Grasser left politics and started a career in business in 2007, after he had already been in the centre of public attention on multiple occasions including scandals involving the alleged taking of gifts from companies, and the alleged sponsorship of Mr Grasser's personal website by the Federation of Austrian Industries, while he was still in office as Minister of Finance (see e.g., Mayr 2010, Simonian 2007). Grasser attracted the attention of the courts due to his alleged involvement in the so-called 'Buwog affair', where he was accused of having made personal profits out of the sale of state housing to a real estate company in 2004 (Bryant 2010). Although the court case was still pending at the time of writing this chapter, it has already had an impact in the sense that it contributed to the increasing perception of Austria as being an 'oasis of corruption', as Mark Pieth, chairman of the Working Group on Bribery in International Business Transactions at the OECD is quoted as saying (cited in Bryant 2010).

In 2010, then Federal Minister of Justice, Claudia Bandion-Ortner, committed 40 out of 300 state prosecutors to the investigation of white-collar crimes (Bryant 2010), to signal that the government takes the problem seriously. A few months later, in April 2011, Bandion-Ortner was replaced as Minister of Justice, corresponding with increasing criticism from judges and state prosecutors in the country of her allegedly inacceptable conduct (e.g., she criticised judges for not working fast enough, and imposed deadlines on state prosecutors) and her inability to effectively tackle the problem of corruption. However, public perceptions of Austria as a country where members of the powerful class can often escape prosecution, and where governmental authorities and agencies collaborate with other members of the societal elite to 'cover up' affairs, continue to exist.

In a sense, the case of Jack Unterweger which we encountered at the beginning of the chapter, who was released from prison due to the intervention of a number of celebrity allies pulling strings on his behalf, can be seen as a template for the story of such a 'scandal': a 'bad guy' is protected by his powerful friends and, in ways that are not entirely transparent to the public, relieved from serving his rightful sentence. Once released, he continues to accrue profits for himself and at the same time represents a threat do innocent citizens.

The feeling of powerlessness vis-à-vis a partly intransparent 'deep state' is also reflected in statements and views of convicted offenders, as will become apparent in particular in Chapter 8.

Public Attitudes Towards Genetic Technologies

It is another discourse, however, which has had, and continues to have, a significant impact on attitudes towards genetic technologies in particular. In the 1990s, Austria was dubbed 'Europe's biggest critic of genetic engineering' (Wagner et al. 1998). Throughout the 2010s, Austria ranked consistently high in terms of opposition to 'gene food' (ORF Science 2004) in public opinion surveys carried out across the European Union: opposition rates in Austria were consistently above the European average. This pronounced scepticism towards genetic technologies is noteworthy also in a comparative perspective, as it seems to be entirely absent in Portugal (see also European Commission 2006, 2010). In Austria it is expressed not only in opinion polls but it regularly becomes a topic of prominent public debate: for example, in 1997, a public petition against the legalisation of importation of genetically modified food and the release of genetically modified organism in Austria attracted 1.2 million signatures, which is a considerable number in a country with a total population of only eight million.

The initiative became the second-largest people's initiative in Austria since 1945. The 'fear of the genes' continues to influence the current political debate and accounts for regulatory restraint in liberalising legislation and regulation pertaining to genetic technology: 'Potential groups of activists (political parties, feminist groups, disability rights groups) would rather not touch a biopolitical issue than risk another anti-technology mobilization of the masses' (Prainsack and Gmeiner 2008: 388). Moreover, although genetically modified food features prominently within anti-gene-technology activism, resistance and scepticism are certainly not restricted to food. As the most recent Eurobarometer survey showed (European Commission 2010), not only did Austria have the lowest level of public support for genetically modified organisms of all EU countries, but it was also among the countries with the lowest levels of support for human embryonic stem cell research, for sharing and exchange of personal data and biological materials, and even for nanotechnology. Overall, Austria was the only country in the EU where declared pessimists towards biotechnology outnumbered the optimists (European Commission 2010: 6).

It is difficult to assess what factors account for this particularly pronounced rejection of genetic and biotechnologies in Austria. While a strong tradition of nature romanticism certainly plays a role (Prainsack and Gmeiner 2008), it is certainly not a sufficient explanation. While we cannot find an answer to this question within the scope of this chapter, noting the very high levels of scepticism towards genetic and biotechnologies in Austria is of crucial importance in interpreting understandings and attitudes towards DNA technologies among stake holder groups and publics also in the realm of police and forensic practice. It is arguably the same public imageries pertaining to genetics in the medical realm – namely that it often entails 'meddling with nature', and with the very essence of life – that shape attitudes towards the use of genetic technologies in policing and forensics. While the underlying science is trusted to be accurate (see also Chapter

4 and Chapter 5), it is seen to expose something about humans – their essence? – that should not be exposed. While it is acceptable, in the cases of those who are seen as criminals, to infringe this principle, it is certainly not acceptable to do in relation with 'innocent' people.

We found this attitude expressed among convicted criminal offenders, and also among members of the police force. For example, after cases of contamination of crime scenes by members of the police force had become recognised as a notorious problem (Schmid and Scheithauer 2010), in 2009 the Federal Ministry of Interior proposed the establishment of a police elimination database. Such databases, as they exist, for example, in Switzerland, England and Wales, and Australia, contain DNA profiles of members of the police force. DNA profiles obtained from crime scene traces in the context of a particular investigation can be compared against the profiles in that database. In case of a hit, investigators can assume that the match results from an instance of contamination during or after the process of securing the crime scene and/or collecting evidence, and they can avoid the unnecessary costs of looking for an unknown suspect, as it was the case in the famous case of the 'phantom of Heilbronn'.[19]

When the plan to establish such a database was released by the Ministry, it encountered immediate resistance from the union of police officers, who called the plan to build such a database expensive and unnecessary, and, interestingly, as being 'against the protection of personal freedom on the side of the police officer' (ORF noe 2010, see also ORF news 2010). The issue became so controversial that it made it into prime time national television news shows.

Conclusion

This chapter started out with a discussion of the history, the legal framework, and the common practices pertaining to the use of fingerprints and DNA profiles for criminal identification and criminal investigation. It was argued that these two practices and technologies respectively represent the core material pillars of criminal identification. Fingerprints and DNA profiles also play important roles in European infrastructures to prevent and combat crime.

We argued that Austrian police officers and representatives of police authorities have played a leading role in establishing closer European and international cooperation in bioinformation exchange. Moreover, rather than treating forensic

19 The case of the 'phantom of Heilbronn' comprised a large-scale multinational police search for an unknown female offender, until it finally turned out that the DNA found at the crime scenes had come from a female factory worker packaging the cotton swabs that were used for the securing of crime scene traces (BBC News 2009). Schmid and Scheithauer (2010: 24) report that a pilot study in which 202 volunteers among the police force had submitted DNA samples and fingerprints showed that 55 of them had unknowingly left DNA traces at crime scenes in 72 instances, and fingerprints in 26 instances.

technologies – and DNA profiling in particular – as 'truth machines' (Peter Neufeld quoted by Lynch et al. 2008), that is, as infallible sources of 'true' evidence, the police officials that the authors spoke to displayed high levels of awareness of the possible problems inherent in the use of these technologies (contamination, human or machine errors, complexity of statistical calculations, etc. See Prainsack 2010a). Also public confidence and trust in the work of criminal justice agencies was seen as a necessary condition for the smooth functioning of their work.

While there is no indication to assume that public trust in the criminal justice system in Austria is lower than it is normally the case in EU countries, some cases in recent history reflect raising levels of discontent with transparency and accountability within the criminal justice system. This discomfort, however, is not directed towards the criminal justice system specifically but instead it takes the criminal justice system as an illustration of what is wrong within the political system as a whole: assumptions about political and business elites as having invested interests in protecting and helping each other, even if it comes at the cost of law, coincide with public criticism of parts of Austrian elites being corrupt. Both circumstances – that overall, public trust in public authorities is relatively high, and that recently instances of corruption and sentiments about Austria being a 'deep state' have started to erode this trust – provide an important context for our interpretation of the convicted offenders' negative views about the work of police and the criminal justice system (see Chapter 8). These collective narratives, of both trustworthiness and corruption, provide tacit frames of references for their accounts.

Another such frame of reference is the particularly wide and pronounced scepticism towards genetic and biotechnologies in Austria. These are arguably due to a combination of collective memories of the fateful marriage between science and government in the Nazi period, and a certain kind of nature romanticism, which provides a frame in which all 'interference' with nature is seen as objectionable. Such interference is not restricted to tangible events such as pollution but it also pertains to ontological interferences such as the opening up of the genetic 'black box', which is seen as (one of) the repositories of human essence.

Both public trust in authorities and the widespread scepticism towards genetic technologies, are relevant in another respect: they contribute to the conviction among policing authorities that strict adherence to rules and guidelines in the use of forensic – and in particular, genetic – identification technologies is of utmost importance. In order to avoid falling victim to the Austrian hostility towards genetic technologies, coupled with low levels of scientific literacy (European Commission 2010), the information about the DNA database that is fed into public media is very limited. Furthermore, the Austrian Bioethics Commission at the Federal Chancellery in Vienna, which would be a public body which could, in theory, want to raise broader societal discussion about DNA databasing for forensic and policing purposes, is prevented from doing so by the explicit limitation of its remit to medical dimensions of technology.

Chapter 3
Setting the Scene: Portugal

Introduction

In May 2007, a British couple – Gerald Patrick McCann and Kate Marie Healy – were in the *Ocean Club* holiday resort in the Algarve in Portugal, together with their three children (Madeleine, aged 3, and twins Sean and Amelie, aged 2). On the evening of 3 May, Madeleine was reported missing from the bedroom where she was supposedly sleeping with her siblings while their parents were having dinner in a nearby restaurant. The initial investigation by the *Polícia Judiciária* (the Portuguese criminal investigation police) was based on the assumption that she had been abducted. On 15 May, a man living near the *Ocean Club* was identified and declared an official suspect (*arguido*);[1] the reasons for this had been his pronounced enthusiasm in assisting the police in their investigation during the days following Madeleine's disappearance, and his volunteering to act as an interpreter during the investigations. However there was never any firm evidence against him.

The disappearance of the British three-year-old Madeleine McCann in Portugal in 2007 was a high-profile criminal case that attracted a level of global media attention unprecedented in any previous missing person case. The disappearance of the child has remained in the public memory and become a cultural reference that may have affected long-term representations of crime and justice (Altheide and Devriese 2007, Jewkes 2004, Reiner 2002, Surette 1998), police practices (Cavender and Deutsch 2007, Huey 2010, Innes 2001, Jackson and Bradford 2009) and public understanding of forensic technologies in Portugal (Machado and Santos 2009, 2011). The combination of the public's exposure to this highly mediatised criminal case on the one hand, and low level of confidence in the law enforcement authorities and courts on the other (see Chapter 3), is an important factor for the understanding of the nexus between technology, crime and criminal

1 According to Article 57 of the *Código de Processo Penal* [Code of Criminal Procedure 2007], *arguido* [official suspect] is the status of an individual against whom a formal accusation has been made or inquiry procedures instigated. Article 58 states that a person may be made an *arguido* on the basis of a justifiable suspicion of crime. *Arguido* status is designed to provide individuals with certain rights, such as knowing the details of charges or the right to remain silent during interrogations and to have a lawyer present at all times, together with obligations that may range from a simple statement of identity and residence to detention on remand, even if no formal accusation has been made and an investigation is still underway.

justice in Portugal. Mass media play a fundamental role in these interrelations, as the use of DNA technologies in high-profile cases bolsters arguments in favour of developing applied forensic technologies and widening the scope of DNA databases. Media pressure may encourage law enforcement agencies to adopt measures that develop the application of forensic technologies in criminal investigation, as it seems to be the case in Portugal: the mediatisation of the Madeleine McCann Case was an additional element that may have spurred the establishment of a forensic DNA database (Machado and Santos 2011).

This chapter begins by providing a detailed description of the legal provisions pertaining to fingerprinting, the forensic DNA database, and to the practices of DNA profiling. We then proceed to outline some of the main stages in the process of constructing a Portuguese forensic DNA database, which began with initial government plans to construct a database for the whole population. Later, a law was passed that compared with other European countries took a restrictive approach to data inclusion and retention (Machado and Silva 2010).

One of the specific features of the Portuguese justice system is that over the years there were continuous attempts to align civil identification more closely with criminal identification procedures. Another particularity of the Portuguese justice system is its inquisitorial orientation and the coexistence of informal police databases containing various types of data (from biological samples and DNA profiles to more descriptive data on the character of the offender, their criminal history and habits, distinguishing physical features, aliases and any record of suspected activities) with official criminal registers which contain fingerprints and data on all criminal convictions by Portuguese courts and convictions issued by foreign courts relating to Portuguese citizens.

In the final section of this chapter we discuss the implications of the Madeleine McCann case for public understandings of forensic technologies and criminal investigation work. The analysis of this criminal case is important since it shows that although forensic evidence plays an increasingly prominent role in criminal investigation work, their use is still ridden with problems. In addition, the McCann case – not least because of the wide attention it received – may have provided social and political conditions favourable to public support of the creation of a forensic DNA database (Dundes 2001, Gamero et al. 2007, Hindmarsh 2008) in Portugal (Machado and Santos 2011).

Laws and Regulation

The Legal and Regulatory Background to Fingerprinting

As in various other countries throughout the world (Cole 2001), the bureaucratic development of the modern Portuguese state was accompanied by the creation of modern criminal identification systems. The identification of criminals has been a matter of concern for states since the mid nineteenth century, when biological sciences were first used systematically for this purpose. As described in detail in Chapter 2, from that time onwards various forms of individualisation were used, involving observation and measuring of the body, using what were considered the most refined scientific techniques available at the time, such as anthropometry and dactyloscopy.

Portugal was no exception with regard to the development of criminal identification systems to accompany the expansion of the bureaucratic apparatus of the modern state. From the beginning of the twentieth century the anthropometric system was used to measure the length of bones (in male prisoners and in corpses), and fingerprinting as a means of establishing individual identity became increasingly popular. In 1902 – four years after its adoption into the Austrian system – anthropometry became the official method for identifying prisoners in Portugal. All male prisoners were subjected to an examination in which their bodies were measured with millimetric precision, and their physical characteristics recorded with scientific rigour (Madureira 2003: 284). It would not take long before fingerprinting would overtake anthropometry also in Portugal from the time when the first corpse was identified with the help of fingerprinting techniques in 1904.

Similar to the situation in Austria (see Chapter 2) and in other European countries, fingerprinting developed more quickly and extensively in Portugal than anthropometry. The most plausible reason for this are the lower costs of a fingerprint-based criminal identification system, and that it required less skilled personnel to operate it (Cole and Lynch 2010: 111). While anthropometry was considered a task to be performed by scientists, or at least by extensively trained staff, fingerprinting rapidly became part of daily police practices and was also used for civil identification purposes. The first attempt to create an archive of citizen data for civil identification dates back to 1912 and resulted from the initiative of the Republican government, which had abolished the monarchy in Portugal two years earlier. The government planned to introduce identity cards to be held by all state employees, which would include fingerprints taken from the five fingers of the right hand, a photograph, and a description of distinguishing features. In other words, the aim was to use the scientific knowledge and techniques employed in criminal identification for the purposes of civil identification.

This first attempt at systematically collecting and storing civil identification data from the whole population failed. But in the following decades, additional attempts to expand the fingerprint database were successful. These attempts to create a universal fingerprint database for forensic and civil uses in Portugal were paralleled by developments in countries such as Argentina in the 1910s and in US in the 1930s and early 1940s (Cole and Lynch 2010: 112). However, contrary to what happened in most other countries, where efforts to include non-suspect citizens in databases were a failure, in Portugal, after an initial resistance, civil uses of fingerprint databases continued to expand in a relatively uncontroversial way. The identification of individuals no longer served strictly criminal purposes but instead both civil-administrative and forensic goals, and it was reframed as a matter of collective security that required the fingerprinting of all the citizens (Madureira 2003).

In 1927 (Decree 13254 of 9 March) regional identification archives were created which combined both criminal and civil competences. In the same year, compulsory identity cards were introduced for all professions and for those seeking admittance to any secondary school or university. Identity 'cards' were in fact four-page documents including the holder's name, parentage, birthplace, date of birth, and profession, as well as details of any distinguishing features, a photograph, fingerprint and signature (for those who knew how to write).

In the following years, civil and criminal identification were aligned even further. In 1944, Decree 33555 of 21 February created the Department of Identification Services (*Direcção dos Serviços de Identificação*) which would include the Criminal Register and Police Records General Archive (*Arquivo Geral de Registo Criminal e Policial*) and the Civil Identification Archive (*Arquivo de Identificação Civil*). In an article published in a legal journal in 1960, a famous law professor, Adriano Moreira, wrote that 'it can only be advantageous for a small country to possess a general dactyloscopic file for civil and criminal identification purposes' (Moreira 1960: 234); and he continued:

> Although not everyone will be convicted or imprisoned, everyone will need an identity card and therefore within a few years we will have a dactyloscopic file for the whole population. We could also adopt the system of compulsory fingerprinting for this purpose, for example, for individuals of school age. (Moreira 1960: 234)

Official procedures for criminal identification were transposed to civil identification and the identity card appears to have entered into the everyday life of the population without contestation. As Catarina Fróis notes, since around 40 per cent of the Portuguese population were illiterate until the 1960s, the identity card became a useful document for providing proof of identity, as a fingerprint could replace a signature for those who could not read or write (Fróis 2008). Unlike the situation in other countries where the practice of taking fingerprints was associated with criminal identification (Cauchi and Knepper 2009, Cole 2001, Cole and Lynch 2010, Finn 2005), citizens in Portugal appear to have accept this 'double use' until today, without questioning its mandatory nature.

In 2008, the so-called citizen's card replaced the traditional identity cards. Carrying a citizen's card, which now was available in smart card format, remained compulsory. In addition to replacing the previous identity card, it took on also the functions of the previous taxpayer card, social security card, electoral registration card, and National Health Service card. The citizen's card also bears a photograph, fingerprints taken from the left and right index finger, address, and a digital signature.

Portuguese law allows fingerprints to be taken from all Portuguese citizens for the purpose of issuing a citizen's card or passport, and for it to be cross-referenced with fingerprints found at crime scenes. Equally, criminal police investigating bodies can take fingerprints, photographs or other items of a 'similar nature' for use in identifying a suspect. However, the law does not specify what is meant by evidence of a 'similar nature', and it is therefore not clear whether the collection of samples for DNA profiling can be included in this category (Moniz 2009: 3).

Another important identification technique for criminal investigation are the databases for criminal identification held by the General Board of Administration of Justice (*Direcção-Geral da Administração da Justiça*) which contain criminal registers (*Registo Criminal*), with information on all criminal convictions of Portuguese citizens, and fingerprints of convicted individuals. These databases are governed by Law 57/98, of 18 August 1998, which defines the general principles regarding the organisation and functioning of criminal identification. In order to apply for particular jobs, for example as a state employee, it is obligatory to submit a criminal register clearance certificate. A criminal record is deleted five years after the sentence or detention order has expired, provided that there have been no other criminal convictions in the meantime. The law on the DNA profile database stipulates that the DNA profile is removed at the time of the definitive cancellation of the decisions cited in the criminal record (Article 26.1f of Law 5/2008).

Plans for Creating a Universal DNA Database

On 21 March 2005, the newly elected government announced the intention to create a genetic database of the entire population for civil identification purposes, which could also be used in criminal investigation work. Although this plan never passed into the law, this political intention resonates with a long social history of the state collecting personal identification data with the citizens' acceptance.

The plan to create a universal genetic database announced by the government was announced in conjunction with strategies to improve justice in Portugal, more specifically as part of a series of measures designed to 'make the fight against crime and criminal justice more efficient, whilst respecting the right of defence' (Portuguese Government 2005). The announcement stated that the establishment of an 'integrated criminal information system' was needed that would allow for links to be made between the various existing public databases, to which the universal genetic database would simply be added.

This objective was framed within what the government programme called the intention to reinforce 'methods and programmes to prevent and combat organised crime, corruption and economic and financial crime in general, with a particular emphasis on the fight against terrorism and the trafficking of drugs, human beings and weapons' (Portuguese Government 2005: 142). The announcement also stated that the criminal police would not be the custodian of the genetic database. On various occasions during the two years that followed, representatives from the Ministry of Justice emphasised the idea that the police would not have direct access to genetic information for the purposes of criminal investigation, to ensure adequate protection for citizens with regard to possible abuses of the DNA database.

Press reports discussing the government's intention to create a genetic database stated that the Portuguese government intended to implement a universal DNA database by bringing together the DNA data with other existing police databases. In addition, it was proposed to make use of the blood samples that had been collected, on a mandatory basis, from all newborn babies in Portugal under the so-called National Early Diagnosis Programme (*Programa Nacional de Diagnóstico Precoce*) in order to detect congenital diseases using the Guthrie test since 1979.[2]

If this plan had been implemented, Portugal would have been the first country in the world to have a centralised DNA database of its entire population for civil and criminal identification purposes. However, the idea of creating a universal database was eventually transformed into one of the most restrictive laws in Europe in terms of the criteria for DNA profile inclusion and removal for criminal investigation purposes (Machado and Silva 2010).

Law 5/2008, which approved the creation of a DNA profile database, stipulated that the body responsible for its operations was the National Institute of Forensic Medicine (*Instituto Nacional de Medicina Legal*), which processes the DNA samples (Article 16 of Law 5/2008). The Institute is accountable to the Ministry of Justice (the custodian of the DNA database) and is responsible for forwarding results to the competent judicial authorities (Article 19 of Law 5/2008).

The government's intention to create a universal DNA database seems to have aroused little interest amongst the public. Also the media coverage of the subject was mainly neutral and descriptive in tone and limited to presenting regular updates on the draft bill, the Parliamentary debate and the setting up of the database (Águas et al. 2009, Boavida[3] 2005).

The Legal Background to the Forensic DNA Database

Law 5/2008 combines separate purposes within the same law, namely civil identification and identification for the purposes of criminal investigation. As described in the previous section, there were historical reasons for unproblematic way in which attempts to combine civil and criminal identification could proceed without any public resistance, and even without a significant public debate.

The law establishes the principles for the creation and maintenance of the database and regulates the collection, processing and storage of human cell

2 The Guthrie test is a medical test performed on newborn infants to detect a wide range of congenital diseases. A drop of blood is usually obtained by pricking the heel of the baby.

3 The well-known Portuguese biologist commented online on 7 April 2005 that '[d]espite the threats that such a universal system poses to citizens' liberties, the country does not seem alarmed enough. So far, there has been little public debate' (Boavida 2005).

samples, their respective analysis and the obtaining of DNA profiles. It also determines the methodology for comparing DNA profiles and defines the rules for processing and storing the respective information in computerised files. The use, analysis and processing of any type of information from the database for any other purpose is expressly forbidden.

The custodian of the DNA database is the Ministry of Justice. The National Institute of Legal Medicine is the institution responsible for processing the data (Article 17 of Law 5/2008) and for communicating the results of analyses to the competent judicial authorities (Article 19 of Law 5/2008). All the activities developed by the National Institute of Legal Medicine pertaining to the forensic DNA database are supervised and controlled by an independent Supervisory Body (*Conselho de Fiscalização*) with powers of authority, nominated by the Portuguese Parliament.

In Portugal, as in most European continental judicial systems (Toom 2010), judges are supposed to function as impartial fact finders. They play a prominent and active role in the examination process and in the imposing of the rules of evidence and court procedures. This inquisitorial orientation of the Portuguese criminal justice system is reflected also in the DNA database law: the collection of samples for criminal investigation purposes requires a judge's order, or a request by the defendant (Article 8.1 of Law 5/2008). The inclusion of DNA profiles in the database always requires the order of a judge (Article 18 of Law 5/2008). Finally, DNA evidence is only admitted in court if requested by a judiciary authority (the judge or the Public Prosecution Service – *Ministério Público*) (no. 1 of Article 154, Portuguese Code of Criminal Procedure 2007).

Regarding profile entry criteria (Article 15 of Law 5/2008), the Portuguese forensic DNA database can include a) profiles from volunteers, b) profiles obtained from samples collected from corpses, parts of corpses, objects or places where collection is undertaken for civil identification purposes, c) reference samples from missing people or their relatives, d) profiles obtained from samples collected from crime scenes, e) profiles from convicted offenders receiving a sentence of three years or more, and f) profiles from professionals who collect and analyse samples.

In the case of volunteers, relatives and professionals (whose profiles are intended for elimination purposes), Portuguese law establishes that DNA profiles as well as the corresponding personal data can only be included in the database with the free, written and informed consent of these individuals (Article 18.1a–b of Law 5/2008). Samples originating from formal suspects (*arguidos*) and convicted offenders can be collected without their consent. Nevertheless, the law states that individuals have the right to be informed about the content and possible uses of their genetic information. Samples can also be collected from convicted offenders receiving a sentence of not less than three years (Article 8.2 of Law 5/2008). DNA profiles from official suspects are never included in the forensic DNA database used for criminal purposes and samples cannot be collected from mere suspects; they are only included upon conviction and if ordered by a judge (Article 18 of law 5/2008).

Table 3.1 Regulatory characteristics of the Portuguese Forensic DNA Database

Year of establishment	2008
Legislation	Law 5/2008 of 12 February Deliberation 3191/2008
Custodian of the database	Ministry of Justice and the National Institute of Forensic Medicine (*Instituto Nacional de Medicina Legal*)
Agent responsible for collection	Collection of samples can only be carried out at the request of the official suspect (*arguido*) or ordered by a judge. Only adequately trained experts in forensic sciences can collect samples
Subjects to DNA sampling	Convicted offenders receiving a sentence of three years or more Official suspects (*arguidos*) can be sampled but their profiles are only included in the database upon conviction Volunteers (anyone who wishes to be included in the database) Unidentified corpses or parts of corpses Missing persons or their relatives Professionals who collect and analyse samples
Informed consent required	Consent is necessary for volunteers, relatives of missing persons and professionals (who collect and analyse samples)
Use of physical coercion	Yes, with safeguards for the subject's moral and physical integrity
Type of sample collected	Buccal swab or equivalent
Access to DNA data	Only authorised staff has access to the database, limited to the exercise of professional duties. Forensic staff and members of the Supervisory Council of the DNA database are obliged to professional secrecy, even after termination of duties. The INML provides information, upon request, to police authorities and the Public Prosecution. Other requests for information are subjected to appreciation by the data protection authority. Portugal can exchange information with other countries under ratified international agreements.
Anonymisation of samples for laboratorial analysis	Not specified by the law

Profiles are eliminated from the DNA database in the following situations: profiles derived from crime scene samples that do not match the profile of the accused are eliminated 20 years after collection of the respective samples (Article 26.1 of Law 5/2008), and profiles from convicted offenders are eliminated at the time of the definitive cancellation of criminal records, a maximum of ten years after the sentence has been served. The profiles of volunteers and relatives of missing persons are retained for an unlimited period of time unless they revoke their previous consent, and profiles from corpses are eliminated after identification (Article 26.1 of Law 5/2008).

Table 3.2 Entry and removal criteria of the DNA profiles and sample destruction

Criteria for entry of profiles	Convicted offenders receiving a sentence of three years or more, if insertion is ordered by a judge Crime scene stains Volunteers Unidentified corpses or parts of corpses Missing persons or their relatives Professionals who collect and analyse samples
Criteria for removal of profiles	Convicted offenders: profiles are deleted along with the expungement of the criminal record (maximum 10 years after serving the sentence) Volunteers: profiles are retained indefinitely or until consent is revoked Relatives of missing persons: retained until there is a positive identification or until consent is revoked. Unidentified crime scene stains: deleted 20 years after collection Unidentified corpses or parts of corpses are retained until identified Crime scene stains: deleted when the case is closed or at the maximum period of prescription for the crime Professionals: 20 years after termination of duties
Retention and destruction of samples	Samples of volunteers and convicted offenders are immediately destroyed after the profile has been obtained Unidentified crime scene samples are destroyed after 20 years Unidentified samples of corpses or parts of corpses are retained until identified Samples of professionals are destroyed 20 years after cessation of duties No regulation regarding destruction or retention of samples collected from official suspects

Portuguese law stipulates that all samples from volunteers and convicted offenders are to be destroyed immediately after the DNA profile has been obtained (Article 34.1 of Law 5/2008). In addition, the law states that the preservation of samples covers only the analysis and counter-analysis needed for civil identification and criminal investigation purposes (Article 32 of Law 5/2008). Samples collected from corpses, missing persons and relatives of missing persons are to be destroyed when the missing person has been identified. If identification is not possible, the samples are to be destroyed 20 years after collection. Samples collected from forensic professionals must be destroyed 20 years after cessation of their official duties (e.g. on retirement, Article 26.1 of Law 5/2008).

The destination of official suspects' samples collected during criminal proceedings currently lies in a legal limbo, since there is no specific regulation regarding their destruction. In other words, if the profile extracted from an official suspect is added to the database as that of a convicted criminal, the sample is destroyed after the profile has been obtained (Article 34.1 of Law 45/2004). However, if there is no dispatch from a judge ordering the profile to be added to the database or if the individual is acquitted, an omission in law in this area leads to the assumption that the biological samples are to be destroyed at the end of the proceedings, or two years later, in compliance with the law which regulates forensic evidence (Article 25.2 of Law 45/2004). The destruction of samples was envisaged in the draft law but was not included in the approved final law (Moniz 2009: 8).

Furthermore, variations in legislation and regulation between different EU countries can raise potential problems with regard to the exchange of information between Member States (as discussed in detail in Chapter 2). Insufficient harmonisation of the inclusion criteria, sample preservation and profile retention is likely to lead to potential situations of inequality and conflict, since the regulations for the transfer of genetic information require compliance with the rules of both the providing and the requesting states, which can vary from one country to another (Moniz 2009: 11, Prainsack and Toom 2010).

There are not yet any official data regarding the number of samples and DNA profiles held by the NILM. In 2011, Portuguese press reported that less than 100 profiles were included in the DNA database. Apparent causes for this modest start were associated with the restrictive nature of the legislative framework, and with the considerable financial investments required for the establishment of the database. The fact that judges do typically not order the inclusion of DNA profiles of individuals receiving prison sentences of three years or more, apparently due to insufficient information on how the forensic DNA database operates, was reported by the press as the main cause of this delay. In addition, the financial crisis currently affecting the criminal justice system in Portugal may also be a contributing factor (Machado 2011).

The high costs associated to DNA analysis when compared to other European countries have also been a matter of concern regarding the development of the Portuguese DNA database. Prices were stipulated by the Ministry of Justice on 28

April 2011 (Decree 175/2011) and depending on the degree of complexity of the analysis (which is used as a step to increment costs, but not properly defined), a DNA analysis for the purpose of inclusion in the database can cost between €204 and €714 per sample.

Legal Regulation for DNA Profiling Operations

On 3 December 2008, the legal regulation of database operations was approved by the Medical-Legal Council (*Conselho Médico-Legal*) of the National Institute of Legal Medicine with the publication of Deliberation 3191/2008. This document contains the legal provisions governing database operations and includes rules for collecting and analysing samples, DNA profiling and the inclusion of DNA profiles in the forensic genetic database, and the types of informed consent.

The Portuguese Code of Criminal Procedure (*Código de Processo Penal*) establishes that 'all evidence obtained by means of torture, coercion, or general offence against an individual's physical or moral integrity is null and void, and cannot be used' at court (Article 126.1 of the Code of Criminal Procedure 2007). The Portuguese law which regulates the functioning of the DNA database only safeguards the principle of free, informed and written consent in cases of sample collection involving volunteers or relatives of missing persons (Article 4 of Deliberation 3191/2008). In the case of official suspects and convicted offenders, the protection of human dignity and individual physical and moral integrity appears to be connected to the method of sample collection, as established in Article 8 of Deliberation 3191/2008, which stipulates the following: 'Samples are gathered from individuals in duplicate, by collecting cells from the buccal mucous membrane or by other non-invasive methods that respect human dignity and individual physical and moral integrity.'

Official suspects and convicts only have to provide authorisation for their photograph to be taken and for personal data relevant to the investigation to be recorded, with submission to biological sample collection being mandatory. The following personal data is collected from citizens: name; home address; telephone number; personal identity card number; date of birth; civil status; profession; ethnic group and place of birth; father's ethnic group and place of birth; mother's ethnic group and place of birth.

It has been argued that the inclusion in DNA databases of information on an individual's ethnic group can lead to discrimination. Moreover, the inclusion of information on the ethnic group of the individual from whom the DNA sample is collected will regularly be based on the personal judgement of the forensic technician, or the individual's self-classification, and may thus not correspond with the classifications used in population genetics research (Machado and Silva 2009). In addition, since the use of such classifications is not universal, these labels may vary greatly over space and time and are rarely with consistency (Nuffield Council on Bioethics 2007: 80). Furthermore, it has been argued that the information on ethnic background in forensic DNA databases may allow researchers to explore links between race and genotype information, leading to attempts to identify relationships between genetics and criminal behaviour (Duster 2006b, 2008, Nuffield Council on Bioethics 2007: 77–88).

The inclusion of the ethnic group category in the information collected from individuals whose DNA profiles will be added to the database contradicts the trend that has prevailed until now in Portuguese legislation of preventing discrimination or the 'racialisation of society' evident, for example, in the fact that crime statistics only record nationality, not ethnicity or phenotype (Cunha 2010). It has been argued that the inclusion of the ethnic group of those convicted of crimes represents a new trend in terms of criminalising particular minority groups in Portugal, henceforth based on genetic-criminal identity (Machado, Silva and Amorim 2010).

Organisation of Criminal Investigation

The Portuguese justice system establishes that the investigation of crimes and their punishment is carried out by the state through the Public Prosecution Service (*Ministério Público*) and the courts. In the first phase of criminal investigation, known as the inquiry phase, in which the aim is to determine whether a crime has been committed and who the perpetrator might be, the Public Prosecution Service is the authority which conducts the investigation and may be assisted by criminal police bodies such as the *Polícia Judiciária*, the *Polícia de Segurança Pública*. or the *Guarda Nacional Republicana*. The primary function of the *Polícia Judiciária* is to carry out criminal investigations, whilst the main mission of the *Polícia de Segurança Pública* is to safeguard internal security and provide a public service on behalf of the community. The *Guarda Nacional Republicana* is military in nature but is involved, above all, in neighbourhood police work, intervening in areas such as domestic violence and the protection of nature and the environment.

The organisation of criminal investigation work is determined by Law 49/2008 of 27 August. This law stipulates that criminal police authorities have autonomy in carrying out the activities deemed necessary to the success of a criminal investigation, although the police always work under the authority of the *Ministério Público*. The latter may supervise the progress of police work, check that it complies with the law and issue specific instructions concerning actions (Article 2 of Law 49/2008).

All three types of police forces, the *Polícia Judiciária*, the *Polícia de Segurança Pública*, and the *Guarda Nacional Republicana*, may be involved in criminal investigation work, but more serious crimes can only be investigated by the *Polícia Judiciária*, which is considered the prime criminal police force as it has more experts, resources and past history of developing criminal investigation work. It was created by Decree-Law 35042 of 20 October 1945, and in 1957 the Police Forensic Laboratory was founded. This laboratory, together with the

National Institute of Legal Medicine laboratories, can analyse samples from the National Forensic DNA Database.

The Criminal Investigation Police is involved in transnational cooperative criminal investigation activities in the fight against terrorism, cross-border criminal activities and illegal migration. It has an International Cooperation Unit, responsible for the operations carried out in collaboration with Europol, and an office that works with Interpol.

The beginning of international cooperation in police investigation in Portugal dates back to 1924, when Portugal joined the International Criminal Police Commission, founded in Vienna, Austria, in the previous year, and the predecessor of Interpol. In December 2006, Portugal officially stated its intention of signing the Prüm Treaty.

According to informal conversations with representatives of law authorities in Portugal, there appears to be a consensus on the advantages of engaging in the cross-border exchange of national digital fingerprint files, DNA and car registration data. Portuguese legislation pertaining to the forensic DNA database provides the obligation to comply with its national rules regarding international cooperation in the domains of civil and criminal investigation using DNA profiles, and states that the cross-border exchange of biological material is not permitted (Article 21.2 of Law 5/2008).

Finally, police records are another essential instrument in criminal investigation. Decree 27304 of 8 December 1936 provides the basis for the establishment of a criminal register and police archive in Portugal; this is despite the fact that records had been used by police since the end of the nineteenth century at least. The law stipulated that the criminal register would record data on convictions and detentions of all citizens. Police records would be more informal, containing data on the character of the offender, their criminal history and habits, their distinguishing physical features, aliases, and any record of suspected activities. Information could be added to the police records regardless of whether they had been brought to trial or not, convicted or acquitted: it was sufficient for them to have had any real or notional connection with a crime. In the past, courts made extensive use of police records, often asking for the respective files and including them in proceedings (Durão 2008, Marques 2005).

Nowadays the *Polícia Judiciária*, the criminal investigation police, still retain files from police records, which contain fingerprints collected from suspects and convicted individuals, as well as biological samples and DNA profiles,[4] but the use of this information has not yet been legalised: the Portuguese law 5/2008 remained silent on fate of the samples and profiles collected in the

4 There are no official figures about the size, the sort of data, or any other details held, in police databases. In January 2011 Portuguese newspapers reported that the Laboratory of the Criminal Investigation Police (*Polícia Judiciária*) currently was holding 2000 DNA profiles collected from crime scenes as well as suspects and convicted individuals (Fontes 2011).

course of criminal investigations before the establishment of the DNA database. These samples and profiles can not be used in criminal proceedings because of the lack of legal framing of their collection and storage. The Portuguese Data Protection Authority (*Comissão Nacional de Protecção de Dados – CNPD*) is an independent body, with powers of authority to supervise and monitor compliance with the laws and regulations in the area of personal data protection. CNPD has recently announced that the police records held by the *Polícia de Segurança Pública* contain information violating the law on personal data, namely files with data regarding ethnicity, behaviour in private life, religion, political or trade union affiliation (Marcelino 2011). In the words of a former director of the Criminal Investigation Police interviewed for the purpose of this book, 'there has not been the political ability to resolve this matter and all the inefficiency it implies. The problem of police information and the sharing and control of this information is nowadays one of the most sensitive issues in the sphere of justice and security in Portugal'. Negotiations are now taking place between the Criminal Investigation Police and the Supervisory Board (*Conselho de Fiscalização*) that controls all the activities related to the forensic DNA database, to decide if and how these profiles hold by the police will be uploaded in the national database.

Returning to the Madeleine McCann Case

The Madeleine McCann case was a landmark for the public understandings about criminal investigation, police practices, justice system and uses of forensic technologies in Portugal. The dramatic potential of the case, allied with the current cultural context in which television crime series with a focus on forensic science are becoming increasingly popular, contributed to the Portuguese media's paying increasing attention to the details of the practices of the forensic scientists and the probative value of the scientific evidence (Machado and Santos 2011). The leading Portuguese tabloid *Correio da Manhã* published 384 articles relating to the Madeleine McCann case between May 2007 and July 2008 alone (Machado and Santos 2009). Police work received greater coverage in these items (100 articles – 39.7 per cent) than news on the McCanns themselves (95 articles – 37.7 per cent). Forensic science was highlighted in 54 (21.4 per cent) of the articles published (Machado and Santos 2009).

The McCann case quickly became international news and remained the focus of extensive media attention during a relatively long period of time. Two photogenic white doctors were the centre of a story that could be told in simple terms and was thus accessible to a broad range of audiences. It also involved children and the threat of an unknown sexual predator or international paedophile ring. This is the story that best-selling crime novels are made of.

The public spectacle provided by the involvement of celebrities in a public campaign to help find the missing girl also helps to explain the fame that the disappearance of Madeleine McCann acquired within the media. The Portuguese footballer Cristiano Ronaldo launched, together with other football stars such as John Terry, Wayne Rooney and David Beckham, an appeal on 9 May 2007 for anyone with any information on the whereabouts of Madeleine McCann: 'I was very upset to hear of the abduction of Madeleine McCann' … 'I appeal to anyone with information to come forward. Please come forward' (Sky News 2007).

Only a few days after the disappearance of young Madeleine the Portuguese and English press reported that various celebrities, entrepreneurs, friends, and anonymous individuals had offered large sums of money as a reward for anyone offering information that might lead to the child being found. Football clubs such as Manchester United and Chelsea joined the appeals to the public to help 'find Madeleine'; videoclips with that very title were screened football stadiums across the UK for months following the disappearance of the child.

The parents of Madeleine McCann suddenly found themselves being public figures. They used their new celebrity status to keep public attention focused on the disappearance of the child. An official site for the search was set up and a fund-raising company, *Madeleine's Fund: Leaving no Stone Unturned*, was launched.

A particularly striking episode in this portrayal of the McCanns as living examples of painful victimisation by an alleged unknown abductor (Peelo 2006) was their audience with Pope Benedict XVI on 30 May 2007. The image of their agony merged with the image of two relentless crusaders dedicated to the cause of abducted children, for whom Madeleine became an icon (Griffin and Miller 2008, Machado and Santos 2009: 157).

The case took an unexpected turn in July 2007 when the British police brought in dogs trained to detect the scent of tissue putrefaction and blood. The dogs were reported to have discovered biological traces in the McCanns' holiday apartment, as well as in their rented car. These traces were collected and sent to a British laboratory (the Forensic Science Service lab in Birmingham). On 7 September 2007, after questioning by the Portuguese Criminal Investigation Police, the Portuguese Public Prosecution Service (*Ministério Público*) decided to make Madeleine McCann's parents official suspects (*arguidos*) under the alleged pretext of suspected murder and concealment of the body. On 21 July 2008, however, the investigation was closed due to lack of evidence. Despite all the extraordinary resources mobilised by the police investigation, the evidence that was gathered proved inconclusive and the actual fate of Madeleine McCann remains unknown to this day.

Throughout the course of the investigation, the work carried out by the Portuguese police became the target of critique by experts cited in the British media. These experts claimed that the crime scene had not been properly secured and preserved, and that there had been technical errors and a failure to recover traces from the crime scene. They also criticised that no detailed information had been provided to the border and maritime police authorities immediately after her disappearance, that officers had not been seen making extensive door-to-door inquiries, and that the police had failed to ask for surveillance pictures of vehicles leaving Praia da Luz (where *Ocean Club* was located) at the time of Madeleine's disappearance.

As British criticism of the *Polícia Judiciária* grew harsher, the *Correio da Manhã* newspaper sought to counter it by giving high visibility to the Portuguese police's investigations and opinions in the press, and by seeking to refute the main points of criticism: 'There is no such thing as a perfect police force, and before casting stones, the British should take a look at themselves, at their own failed cases and incomplete investigations' (Dâmaso 2007).

However, although the Portuguese popular press supported the *Polícia Judiciária*, it also commented on the need to extend new investigation methods, specifically through the use of databases containing information on paedophiles and DNA profile databases. In an article entitled 'Police on the kidnapper's trail' published on 6 May 2007, the *Correio da Manhã* stated:

> In 2003 the National Society for the Prevention of Cruelty to Children (NSPCC) defined Portugal as a 'paradise' for paedophiles, together with Holland, Austria, Germany and Ireland. This was due, above all, to the fact that the country has a 'poor child protection system' and no database containing a register of sex offenders like there is in the United Kingdom. (Eusébio et al. 2007)

On various occasions the same newspaper lamented the lack of a DNA database in Portugal, acknowledging that if such a database had existed it might have been easy to identify a suspect and solve the case.[5]

The McCann case rendered Portugal the epicentre of a crime drama which put the positive image of the Portuguese authorities and the country to the test. The considerable human and financial resources devoted to this case could only be justified by the disproportionate internal and external media attention and the high-level political interest in both Portugal and the UK. Many commentators saw this criminal case as an example of the problematic nature of the work of criminal investigators in Portugal, in particular with regard to isolating and preserving crime scenes and collecting forensic evidence (Machado and Santos 2011). In addition, this type of case is illustrative of the media's capacity to pressurise judicial institutions into actions that may also suggest a need to expand the use of forensic technologies to catch criminals (Brewer and Ley 2010, Cutter 2006, Innes and Clarke 2009), while reinforcing punitive visions and reinforcement of surveillance on the basis of highlighting the benefits of forensic technologies to fight and prevent crime (Duster 2004, Hindmarsh 2010, Neyround and Disley 2007, Williams 2010b). The McCann case also helped to legitimise the creation of a DNA database for criminal investigation purposes, which eventually occurred in 2008.

5 There are several references to this in news articles on the Madeleine McCann case in the *Correio da Manhã* online editions of 3 June 2007, 24 August 2007 and 26 September 2009.

Conclusion

Similar to what is happening in many countries across the world (see also Chapter 2), there is a growing public sentiment in Portugal that corruption is on the rise. According to an international survey, the majority of respondents in Portugal considered the anti-corruption efforts of the governments to be ineffective, or even extremely ineffective. The institutions considered to be most affected by corruption in Portugal are politics, business, police and the judiciary (Transparency International 2010). These data are corroborated by national opinion polls that indicate that Portuguese citizens see the justice system as being vulnerable to pressure from powerful people and affected by corruption (Cabral et al. 2003, Santos et al. 1996). According to these polls, Portuguese citizens have little trust in the confidentiality and security of the information generated in the course of criminal investigations (Costa 2003). This aspect is important for our understanding of how 'prior histories of public experiences with government and law enforcement … influence policies for managing DNA databases, including rules of access and accountability' (Jasanoff 2010: xxiii). In the Portuguese case, lack of trust in institutions and authorities might provide an important context for our interpretation of the convicted offenders' narratives, as we will describe in the following chapters.

So far, in order to present a comprehensive picture of the ways criminal investigation is carried out in Portugal, we described the organisation of criminal investigation in Portugal and the legal and regulatory framework and practices regarding the collection and storing of DNA samples and fingerprinting. A historical background regarding the development of identification systems was presented to demonstrate the efforts into combining civil and criminal identification. The intention to establish a universal fingerprinting database endorsed by Portuguese policy makers was discussed, including its public perception as a relatively uncontroversial fact. This particular development of a fingerprinting system in Portugal will probably set the path to the future development of the DNA database for criminal investigation.

In order to understand the historical and cultural context of the development and management of forensic technologies and its application in criminal investigation in Portugal it is important to take into consideration the interrelations between the different actors in the criminal justice system. The inquisitorial orientation of the Portuguese criminal justice system creates tensions between the more informal way in which criminal investigations are typically carried out by the police on the one hand, with the more hierarchical and formal procedures followed by the Public Prosecution Services and the courts on the other. In addition, the coexistence of official identification systems with more informal databases held by the Criminal Investigation Police illustrates the extent to which uses of forensic techniques and technologies are deeply conditioned by cultural and historical trajectories.

Crucial for the present understanding of the nexus between crime investigation, the justice system, and public assessments of those activities, is the role played by the media. Public opinion data on the extent of corruption in Portugal indicate that public media are seen as less affected by corruption than politicians, the business sector, the police and the judiciary system. This could indicate that media reports are considered a relatively reliable source on the workings of the crime justice system, and criminal investigation work in particular. Against the backdrop of the nexus between public trust in state institutions and the role of public media, this chapter ended with an analysis of a high-profile criminal case that was a landmark for the public's understanding of criminal investigation, police practices, the justice system and the use of forensic technologies in Portugal. We also explored the contribution that public media made to preparing the ground for the establishment of the Portuguese national forensic DNA database, by providing reasons why an expansion of forensic technologies was necessary to fight crime.

Chapter 4
Inside Jobs: How to Avoid Crime Scene Traces

Introduction

A substantial part of the information that members of the public receive about criminal investigation and the uses of forensic technologies is conveyed by the media, in particular by high-tech crime television series, such as *CSI*. Prisoners, however, are more than just ordinary viewers of TV crime drama. In their conversations with us, convicted offenders[1] – who of course are only a sub-set of all those who plan to commit, or have committed, crimes – compared what they saw on television with their personal experiences with the criminal justice system.

In the focus of this chapter are prisoners' reflections on media representations of forensic technologies. The latter were referred to by prisoners as scripts of cultural meaning that sometimes sat uncomfortably with their own experiences and narratives. Yet, at the same time, media portrayals were in some respects seen as practical sources of information and knowledge about criminal tactics. The role of the mass media as a source of information about crime scene management has been discussed in the criminal sociology and criminology literature as one variant of the *CSI* effect. Are the mass media, and television crime shows in particular, indeed educational vehicles for criminals or potential criminals? Beauregard and Bouchard (2010) have used the notion of 'forensic awareness' to refer to the employment of detection avoidance strategies of criminal offenders (in their case: sex offenders). Is such forensic awareness on the rise in the era of *CSI*?

As the following discussion will show, we are in need of a more empirically grounded approach, and greater sensitivity for the situatedness of the 'education' of criminals in this context. For a more situated understanding of the possible effect related to our interviewees' contact with forensic science fiction TV we need to look into how the prisoners in our study made sense of what they saw on television.

Existing literature on the *CSI* effect – which we have briefly touched upon in our Introduction, and which will be discussed in more detail in Chapter 5 – suggests that the dramaturgical fusion of melodramatic elements with the objective of crime fighting and solving, in which forensic science is the protagonist, tends to render the line between reality and fiction increasingly difficult to draw for the common

1 We use the term 'convicted offenders' with the reservation that although all of our interviewees were convicted, we do not know whether all of them had actually committed the crime in question. As we will see in the following chapters, some of our interviewees claimed to have been wrongfully convicted.

viewer (Deutsch and Cavender 2008, Huey 2010). While representations of crime scene work in popular media often lack nuance to accommodate the uncertainties and ambiguities of crime scene work in 'the real world',[2] convicted offenders have often experienced this reality, or they have had access to real-world knowledge of crime scene practicalities via the experiences and stories of accomplices or other inmates. Prisoners have their own expertise (Prainsack and Kitzberger 2009): they are people who either have committed crimes, and/or who were convicted of having committed a crime. In both scenarios, they are likely to have had their fingerprints, DNA profiles, and various other kinds of data taken and stored in centralised databases.

Sources of Knowledge About Forensic Technologies

The prisoners in our study articulated a complex repertoire of sources of knowledge about criminal investigation and forensic technologies that could not be simply explained by reference to the consumption of crime shows on television. Although a large majority of our respondents mentioned television as the main source of knowledge about the management of crime scenes and criminal investigation, crime drama was not the exclusive media genre that provided useful information on these matters. Some inmates referred to other TV formats such as news broadcasts and documentaries describing the application of forensic genetics in criminal investigation, which indicates the importance of considering how multiple forms of media use are related to perceptions of DNA evidence among the general public (Brewer and Ley 2010: 99). Others mentioned conversations with other prisoners and the mere fact of living in prison, or with certain people 'outside' – that is, other offenders – prior to their imprisonment, as the main sources of knowledge about crime scene work.

At the time of our conversation with him, Daniel was a 36-year-old former bar bouncer sentenced to 24 years in prison for murder, which he admitted to having committed. Daniel was one of only two interviewees with a higher education degree (in his case, psychology), which he had taken while in prison. Daniel's statement that 'whatever television [networks] sell, people like, and [they] demand life sentences, death penalties, and microchips inserted into children because of the abductions', resonates with Hughes and Magers' (2007: 262) diagnosis of the emergence of a new culture fostered by a cultural industry that reinforces punitive visions of criminal policies and typically highlights the benefits of forensic technologies to fight and prevent crime. Daniel also emphasised the educational effect that crime television allegedly had; he thought that it taught criminals or potential criminals how to eliminate traces from crimes scenes (Durnal 2010) and

2 We continue to use the term 'real world' not with the intention to signify a 'truer' reality than the one that is shown on television, but to refer to non-fictional and non-mediated settings of crime and criminal investigation.

helped them to develop more sophisticated tactics. In other words, crime shows and documentaries on television can enhance or feed into criminals' informal expertise on how to avoid detection (Prainsack and Kitzberger 2009). This is how Daniel put it:

> [Upon watching] *CSI*, even an illiterate prison inmate will know that he cannot leave a hair, he knows that if he leaves any blood, even if he washes [the stains] off, there is a chance that the evidence will stay there anyway … he knows that if he gets into a fight and the other person scratches him, that person will probably get pieces of his skin under the fingernails … *CSI* gives a lot of hints and anyone who watches the series will remember to be more careful when committing the next crime.

Daniel differentiated between the educational effect that he attributed to TV series like *CSI*, and the educational effect of TV documentaries and news coverage of real cases. He felt that '*CSI* is not that scientifically rigorous. I have heard [police] investigators say that there is some scientific rigour to it, but that things aren't [really] done at the speed of light like they do it on TV'. This view of *CSI* as at least partly 'unrealistic' – which was shared by other prisoners in Portugal and in Austria – led Daniel to consider that media coverage of real cases was more reliable and, therefore, that news media could teach criminals *more effectively* about how criminal investigation operates than television drama could.

Daniel also explicitly commented on the disappearance of Madeleine McCann, the young child who disappeared from a holiday resort in Portugal, which we encountered in the previous chapter. He referred to the fact that in the McCann investigation, the British police had used two sniffer dogs trained to detect the scent of blood and dead bodies, and expressed admiration of the progress of forensic science, while at the same time emphasising that the media coverage of the case had provided details that could be quite useful for would-be criminals:

> With the Maddie case we almost took a degree in criminal investigation while watching the news. There were references to several investigation techniques, the use of dogs, how long will a scent, or a stain, stay … well, we – or any other mere mortal – learned a lot. Obviously, if I were to commit a crime now, I would be more careful, and certainly I would remember that!

These excerpts from our exchange with Daniel – which reflect the tone of conversations with other prisoners on the same topic – illustrate the need to debunk the simplistic variant of the claim that crime television educates offenders in a linear manner. Although the convicted offenders in our study admittedly represent only a small fraction of those who have committed, or intend to commit, crimes and criminal offences, it was clear that they held rather nuanced views regarding the trustworthiness of television as a source of information. Our informants compared what they saw on television with what they or other people whom they knew had experienced themselves. While they dismissed certain aspects of crime drama as unrealistic and fictional – especially with regard to how well, and how fast, crime scene technologies are put to work in television when compared to real life – they took useful clues from TV drama especially in terms of what kinds of technologies existed, and how technologies worked *in principle*. For example, Ernst, 30, serving three years for fraud, said that although he had never broken into a property or committed any violent crimes, he knew from television shows that it was not possible to do that without leaving 'hundreds of thousands' of minuscule biological traces which would then be analysed 'in a computer' and lead to identification, if one had the misfortune to 'be in that computer'. Twenty-five-year-old Quentin, who was serving eight years for arson, found the speed at which forensic technologies deliver results on television as particularly unrealistic. The fictional content of television shows, in his opinion, did not stem primarily from the need to keep the audience entertained and alert, but they were attributed to a deliberate decision on the part of the producers to *prevent* the TV show from being *too* educational for potential offenders:

> Quentin: I can't get enough of this forensic technology stuff. I watch every episode of *CSI*. And it continues with *Autopsy*, and so on. It's plenty of fiction, but also lots of facts.
>
> Interviewer: Where is the fiction?
>
> Quentin: Well, the fiction is: first [the crime scene investigator] finds a corpse, then he finds [the murderer's] traces, and eight hours later, he's got the criminal. No – that's a bit strange, this entire thing. But I guess they are not disclosing everything that is really being done [in real life]. (cf. Prainsack and Kitzberger 2009: 60)

Quentin's quote also points towards the importance for some offenders of outsmarting the police, which was something that appeared significant for some of the prisoners we interviewed. This competition is largely a battle over access to relevant knowledge, whereby the police and the general criminal justice system were considered to have a competitive edge over everyone else, partly because they had had easier access to privileged knowledge on how technologies worked. Offenders, on the other hand, had relevant knowledge on how to deceive or trick the police. Bernhard, a 28-year-old man serving a three year prison sentence for a series of break-ins, suggested that pouring milk over blood stains left behind at crime scenes made it more difficult for crime scene investigators to analyse the blood (see Prainsack and Kitzberger 2009), and many other inmates explained the ways in which one would need to dress these days in order to minimise the risk of leaving biological traces; recommendations ranged from wearing hats and gloves to wearing diving suits or cover oneself in latex. Others mentioned that in order to minimise the risk of detection, burglars who did 'jobs' in posh neighbourhoods should always wear expensive suits, so that they would not stand out and would thus be less likely remembered by potential witnesses. Some prisoners even referred to the possibility of altering fingerprints, like Nelson, 35, serving nine years for sexual abuse of minors: he stated that 'nowadays, fingerprints can be forged. There is a gel that we can put on our fingers that can falsify fingerprints.' Gil, 33, serving six years for drug trafficking, said that it would be very easy for him to adopt a new identity if he underwent surgery to alter his facial features[3] and fingerprints. Altering his DNA, however, was something that he thought could not be done:

> Gil: In Portugal people do not talk about it very often, but I know that it is very easy to change fingerprints, I think. If I want to have a surgery – it will cost around 2000 euros – I can totally change my face and my fingerprints.
>
> Interviewer: And what about DNA?
>
> Gil: DNA you cannot change. It is impossible. [That is why] DNA it the most effective tool to fight crime.

The reasons for why police and criminal investigators were seen as having an advantage over criminal offenders were related to different levels of access to public resources – such as, as mentioned before, easier access to sophisticated and expensive technologies. However prisoners also assumed that criminal investigators had 'better' knowledge about forensic technologies, which gave them a competitive advantage over the criminals. The knowledge of criminal investigators was seen as superior in the sense that they had a better grasp of the allegedly 'high science' underpinning these technologies. High science (see also Chapter 5) was seen as the realm of elite knowledge, where truth is regularly produced not by humans but by machines; and machines were seen as far less prone to error than humans (see also Mnookin 2008). This association between forensic technologies – and DNA technologies in particular – with high science became explicit in the accounts of some prisoners, who shifted the focus of our conversation away from DNA technologies to scientific achievements in general, as soon as our discussions had moved to information about management of crime scenes.[4] For example, when asked what he knew about crime scene traces, Ludwig, 29, serving 15 years for murder, described that he liked watching science documentaries featuring DNA technologies, but also emphasised that the reason for this was merely his wanting to keep up to date with progress of science:

---

3 Variants of this theme feature not only in crime television but also in movies such as *Face Off* (1997), or television series like *Nip/Tuck* (2003–2010).

4 See Tyler (2006), who argues that people expect more from forensic science because of the rapid advances in the field of science and technology in general.

> Ludwig: Very generally, what one sees on TV… reports, and so on… I watch *Welt der Wunder* [*The world of miracles*, a nature documentary] every now and then. Sometimes they show something about DNA traces, what the percentage is to which they show whether somebody has done it. But nothing special, [I watched] just a little bit. I don't remember a lot, I just watch it out of interest.
>
> Interviewer: Why are you interested in it?
>
> Ludwig: I always watch such shows, unless they are boring. Then I switch off the TV. But [DNA] is as interesting to me as shows about outer space. There's a broad range [of interests that I have. About what science] can do. How technologies advance, and so on.

Also Manuel, aged 27, who had been convicted to 14 years in prison for drug trafficking and murder, after – accidently, as he insisted – crashing against a vehicle carrying eight passengers when driving under the influence of alcohol, mentioned that both scientific documentaries and conversations with other prisoners had taught him what he knew about crime scene technologies: 'I have heard about DNA technology on television … I remember watching a scientific documentary about these matters and something about it on the newscast.' Later in our conversation, Manuel distinguished between what he considered 'legitimate' sources of information about crime scene work and forensic technologies, namely scientific documentaries on the subject, which he said he had a vivid interest in; and the source of information that, in his opinion, was the most frequently used by prisoners to learn about forensic technologies: living and learning in prison. In reference to the latter Manuel described prison as a 'school for the good and for the bad' (Clemmer 1940, Toby 1962) which can teach a lot about how to commit crimes without being caught:

> Prison is a school where you can learn a lot, for the good and the bad. It depends on the perspective that people have and the way they face it [life in prison]. One can learn how to be part [pause] of the world of crime and one can obtain all the necessary tools for … understanding certain things [how to commit a crime] that I, for example, did not know when I got here [to prison].

Although the prisoners' main source of information about forensic technologies was apparently television – both in the form of crime shows as well as documentaries and news coverage – other sources of knowledge about crime scene work were the press, conversations with other prisoners, internet, radio, school training and personal experience from dealing with the criminal justice system. The number of those who mentioned conversations in prison and personal experience as sources of knowledge, however, was relatively small. This might be explained by the fact that most cases leading to the current imprisonment had not, or not centrally, involved DNA evidence: among our informants in Austria, DNA evidence had played a role in nine out of twenty-six investigations and trials respectively; in Portugal, only one inmate referred to the fact that in his case DNA evidence was presented in court. For the majority of the inmates, a DNA sample was taken either upon arrest or when under pre-trial custody. Daniel, one of our Portuguese informants, described how a DNA sample was collected from him while already under pre-trial custody:

> I came to prison in 1997, at the time there was no database, but it was already a known practice, right? They [criminal investigation police] came and collected my DNA with my consent – at the time they needed my consent – and I gave it, of course, so they collected a sample for the investigation and ... they used it in court [silence].

Among the few who mentioned personal experiences with DNA technologies were the aforementioned Austrian prisoner Bernhard, who suggested that pouring milk over blood stains could mislead investigators, and his fellow inmate Gert, a 30-year-old convicted to three years and six months for rape which he insisted he had not committed. Interestingly, despite most of our informants having been exposed to biological sample collection upon arrest or while in custody, the taking of DNA during arrest or in custody was rarely addressed. Whenever it was brought up, it appeared in the context of the stigma stemming from having one's profile included in the forensic DNA database, and in connection with the hope that a stored DNA profile would counteract possible wrongful allegations in the future, whereby the DNA profile would prove the person's innocence (see Chapter 7).

In the cases of virtually all Austrian prisoners, DNA samples were routinely taken at the time when they had become a suspect.[5] The DNA profile would then be uploaded to the national DNA database. In the case of a later conviction, the DNA profile would remain there; in case of no charges being pressed, or the person being acquitted, the former suspect could apply for the removal of the DNA profile from the database. In the cases of ten of the Portuguese prisoners, where the inclusion of DNA profiles of convicted criminals in the national DNA database is not standard procedure, DNA samples were also taken after the individual had been identified as an official suspect (*arguido*).[6] Thus, prisoners

5 This was the case because legal provisions in Austria authorise police to take a DNA sample (in addition to fingerprints) at the time of arrest if the arrestee is suspected of having committed a dangerous assault, and if with regard to the deed or the personality of the suspect it can be expected that the person will leave further traces that enable his or her identification in the course of committing further dangerous assaults (for details see Chapter 2). With the exception of the aforementioned Ernst, a fraudster, all Austrian prisoners in our study were convicted of crimes that meet this requirement; thus DNA was taken from them at the time of arrest.

6 In Portugal, Law 5/2008, published on 12 February 2008, approved the creation of a DNA database for civil and criminal investigation purposes. The Law established

in the two countries were faced with different contexts of use of DNA profiles: in Austria, DNA profiles were used for two different, partly overlapping, purposes; they were used during the investigation, where DNA traces found at crime scenes were compared with the DNA profile of the suspect and in the case of a conviction they remained in the database which also assumed the role of a registry of DNA profiles of all prisoners in the country.[7] In Portugal, at the time of the interviews, the forensic DNA database was still not operational, but it was common practice for police to use DNA profiles for investigative purposes; that is, they collected biological material at crime scenes and compared it with the DNA profile of an official suspect (which had not been uploaded to a database). Alternatively, they collected a DNA sample from a suspect to compare it against the police database[8] or to facilitate a confession, a method which is currently used in many countries (Williams and Johnson 2005, 2008). At present, however, the collection of a DNA sample from a suspect can not be done by the police's own initiative but instead a judge has to issue an order for that purpose. In the past the police compared the DNA profile obtained from a suspect with the DNA profiles they had in their database. Since the creation of the national DNA database (which is not hold by the police and the police does not have direct access to that database), this is no longer allowed; Law 5/2008 – the law by which the Portuguese DNA database was established – provides that DNA samples from suspects can only be collected upon the order of a judge, and the resulting DNA profile may only be compared with profiles already stored on the national database. It should be noticed that

that the collection of samples for criminal investigation purposes can only be carried out at the request of the defendant or ordered by a judge. The law also stipulates that DNA profiles from official suspects (*arguidos*) are included to the central database only upon conviction and if ordered by a judge, and that samples cannot be taken from mere arrestees. In addition, profiles are removed from the database with the expungement of the criminal record (maximum ten years after serving the sentence).

7 The routine storage of DNA profile of all convicted offenders in the centralised DNA database (as well as the retrospective DNA-sampling of the entire prison population, see NECN 2001) has an investigative purpose as well, of course, as it can turn out that a newly uploaded subject profile from a convicted person matches a crime scene profiles in the database. This would be a 'cold hit' which could be followed up by a separate investigation and trial.

8 As described in Chapter 3, the Portuguese criminal investigation police has files that contain fingerprints collected from suspects and convicted individuals, as well as biological samples and DNA profiles, but the use of this information in criminal investigation has not yet been legalised; no arrangements were made in the law to include and centralise information from already existing databases.

There are no official numbers about the size, sort of data or any other details about police databases. Nevertheless, in January 2011 some Portuguese newspapers announced that the Laboratory of the criminal investigation police held about 2,000 DNA profiles collected from crime scenes, suspects, and convicted individuals (Fontes 2011, Marcelino 2011).

Law 5/2008 did not mention the fate of the samples and profiles collected by the criminal investigation police until the DNA database was created.

As mentioned above, conversations with other prisoners were only rarely referred to as sources of useful information on how to commit crimes without being detected; a possible reason for this is the likely reluctance of our informants to give the impression that they could be planning their next crime while still in prison. Explicit lack of interest in the practical workings of DNA profiling, for example, was often very pronounced. Some of our informants emphasised that although they had a strong penchant for crime television, this was merely due to a fascination with science, and not to any instrumental value that such knowledge would have for them. This raises the important methodological question of veracity. Did our informants tell us the 'truth'? Even if they did not strictly lie to us, did they disclose everything? These questions have been discussed in literature about conducting qualitative research in prisons (e.g., Schlosser 2008) and it is impossible to give a general answer to this, as it is clearly dependent on each individual setting and situation.

In this particular instance, it could be suspected that the relative scarcity of references on the side of our informants to conversations they had with other prisoners about crime scene work could be justified by the brief period of contact between the inmates with the interviewers, which was not sufficient to establish a trust relationship that would make them more willing to report backstage prisoner interactions (Waldram 2009). This does, however, sit squarely with some prisoners' open admission that they would never want to go back to leading a 'normal' life anymore. As 37-year-old Paul, serving a 15-year sentence for a series of armed robberies, called it, 'if you have licked blood once it's impossible to stop' (cf. Prainsack and Kitzberger 2009: 71); and also other prisoners referred to themselves explicitly as criminals (in some instances even as 'career criminals'). Thus, the most plausible conclusion is perhaps that prisoners did indeed not have frequent discussions with each other about crime scene work; unless, of course, the relative scarcity of references to 'DNA talk' with fellow prison inmates was (also partly) caused by an attempt to create a virtual distance from the 'criminal world' (Machado et al. 2011: 17), which we will discuss in the next section.

Managing Knowledge

As we have seen, an important dimension of the relations that prisoners established with forensic technologies concerns the ways in which individuals can make use of such knowledge. To display robust knowledge about how to avoid leaving traces at crime scenes, to show interest in TV crime dramas, or even to talk about TV crime series, appeared to be seen by some of our informants as something that could raise suspicion. This 'law abiding stance' was represented by 22-year-old Joel, who had been an industrial weaver operator before his five and a half years' imprisonment for aggravated rape. Joel did not approve at all of the fact that prisoners could use crime television to learn about crime scene work and technologies. He distanced himself personally from the alleged educational impact that crime television had, by laughing about it; yet at the same time he expressed concern about how others might make use of this knowledge. The following quote also echoes other prisoners who used our conversations about the instrumental value of knowledge obtained from television as an arena in which they distanced themselves from criminal life, and from other prisoners:

> *CSI* is fiction, but it teaches you how to commit a crime … [One day] we were watching *CSI* and my mate even said: 'Look, they're teaching how we should kill a person.' We laughed and joked about it, but it's actually true … *CSI* teaches you a lot … how a person can be protected from incriminating evidence … That is what I don't agree with.

In stating that TV series can teach criminals to avoid leaving DNA traces at crime scenes but that they personally 'aren't interested in that', the interviewees seemed to display what they believed to be a socially accepted identity (Goffman 1959, 1986 [1963]). These are instances of the normalisation processes through which the imprisoned individual is disciplined into appearing to conform to legal norms (Irwin and Cressey 1962). A few prisoners seemed to talk about criminals with a sense of 'otherness' which rendered them righteous citizens in comparison. Hence, they expressed support towards measures that may help to combat crime, e.g., retaining DNA profiles in forensic databases and broadening the scope of inclusion. This stance represents prisoners' attempts to align themselves not only with the moral authority of the law, but also with the authority of science – perceived as the language of truth.

Such an attempt to create distance from the realm of the 'criminal' was apparent also in the words of David, 42, an ex-manager of a construction company with six years of formal schooling. David was serving a sentence of three years and ten months for attempted murder and told us that he did not really enjoy watching *CSI* and other similar TV series; he much preferred to be left alone, and did not appreciate conversations with other prisoners. He saw himself as a law-abiding citizen who had the misfortune of having accidentally run over a woman while driving under the influence of alcohol. David's explicit insistence, however, that he did not know much about crime scene work, was contradicted by his relatively specific knowledge about the work carried out by the criminal investigators: 'They go to crime scenes, look for blood, traces of pieces of clothing, sometimes little scrapings from under the fingernails or skin … there must be many more things that they do, but I don't pay attention … I'm not really into that sort of thing …'.

Literature on the 'educational' variant of the *CSI* effect has emphasised both the positive and the negative impact of crime series consumption. Cole and Dioso-Villa (2007, 2009) described as the 'police chiefs' version' of the *CSI* effect the assumption that *CSI* educates criminals on how to avoid detection (see also Durnal 2010), while the 'producer's version' holds that the show is educational because it leads to better knowledge of forensic science on the side of juries and 'the general public'. These authors describe the existence of both positive and negative *CSI* effects in 'educational' terms as a 'hypothesis swapping' (Cole and Dioso-Villa 2009: 1346), in which evidence supporting one supposed effect was used to support claims about the existence of a different effect.

Consequently, the educational version of the *CSI* effect could be seen as having a twofold impact: first, it could have a deterrent effect on criminals, who refrain from committing certain – or all – further criminal activities due to the increased risk of detection because of their knowledge of the intensive use of sophisticated forensic technologies. As Evan Durnal of the University of Central Missouri's Criminal Justice Department stated, '[t]he smarter the criminals become, the more and more investigators and attorneys must dig in order to find that tiniest shred of evidence that may make or break their case' (Durnal 2010: 3).

Second, the educational variant of the *CSI* effect could be seen as potentially rendering crime more attractive, as *CSI* allegedly teaches criminals valuable things about how to decrease the risk of detection and conviction. This additional knowledge could make them confident enough to feel that they could adequately assess the risk of detection in a given context and make a calculated decision of whether or not it would be worth pursuing a certain gain (Beauregard and Bouchard 2010). The latter scenario was mentioned explicitly by 37-year-old Sigi, who was serving 18 months for battery. Due to the use of forensic DNA technologies in particular, Sigi said, fewer and fewer 'jobs' were still worth the risk:

> One needs to consider carefully what to do and what not to do. If somebody tells me: 'Let's do this and that!', then I say I will look into it. If it's interesting, then I say: 'Look, 90 per cent that we will get caught'. Forget it. (cf. Prainsack and Kitzberger 2009: 73)

This second variant of the argument quickly loses plausibility, however, if we do *not* presuppose that some sort of rational assessment of costs and benefits underpins the commission of crime. In our view, access to knowledge is not a sufficient explanation for the potential 'educational' effect of TV crime series on would-be or convicted criminals. What also matters are the ways in which such knowledge manifests itself in practice. While some of the prisoners in our study supported the view that knowledge about forensic technologies and crime scene work deterred many criminals or made their lives harder, others argued that most crimes were committed by people who did not consider the consequences of their actions, and who certainly did not carry out a cool-headed analysis of risks and benefits. We believe that both perspectives are correct: while 'career criminals', who see their criminal activity as their way to make money, would soon be out of work if they did not assess the likely consequences of their actions, others commit crimes on impulse, or in a state of rage or intoxication (see Chapter 8). Thus, the 'education' provided by techno-centric crime TV affects both groups differently. It seems plausible to argue that the second group would not be deterred by increasing knowledge about efficient crime scene work or technologies. While among our prisoners the latter was particularly true for murderers and sex offenders, it was not restricted to them: even 40-year-old Christoph, serving a ten-year sentence for the kidnapping of a young woman, whom he had kept locked in the boot of his car while waiting for the victim's family to pay ransom, claimed that he had never worried about traces:

> Interviewer: What would you have done with the car if [your plan] had worked out? Were you worried about leaving traces anywhere, about somebody finding out it was you [who had taken the ransom]?
>
> Christoph: No, not at all. I was so 100 per cent certain that it would work. You have no idea. I wasn't even nervous. …
>
> Interviewer: And you were totally sober, right?
>
> Christoph: Yes, I was sober. I had had a few drinks the day before, but nothing [on the day of the kidnapping. …]. I knew exactly what I was doing, in inverted commas. But perhaps that's why I took it easy, because I knew I would not do anything [to physically harm her]. In inverted commas. I think. Because [people who] beat or even kill [their victims], that happens as well.

Christoph's explanation that he did not worry about traces because he was sure he would exchange the woman for the money and leave her physically unharmed does not make sense within a rational paradigm: if he had 'returned' the woman to her family and ran off with the money, police would certainly have searched for him. Given that the victim was very likely to have been able to describe both her kidnapper and his car, Christoph would have faced a very high risk of detection. In this situation, traces of the victim or her clothes in the car would have been very strong evidence of his guilt.[9] Christoph's story illustrates very clearly that the separation between those who commit crimes for financial gain and those who do it for other reasons is not straight-forward at all; with respect to most crimes, the motives are probably mixed (Agnew 1992, Cloward and Ohlin 1960, Dobash and Dobash 2011, Hamlin 1988, Jacobs 2010, Jacobs and Wright 1999, Minor 1980, Putniņš 2010). The sliding scale between premeditated and coldly calculated

9 Later in the conversation Christoph added that another reason why he did not worry about detection was that his fingerprints were not in any police database, thus any fingerprints that the police could find on the victim or on her clothes would be useless. For the aforementioned reasons, however, this does not fit into the rational paradigm either; it is plausible that this explanation represents an ex-post rationalisation of why he had not been worried about traces in the first place once he had heard from other inmates in prison that fingerprint and DNA evidence was useful only if there was a reference print or profile in the police database.

crimes on the one hand and crimes out of impulse on the other also came up in our conversation with the aforementioned Portuguese prisoner Joel:

> If I wear a hood, put on some gloves, if I take every precaution not to leave DNA behind, it will be very hard for the police – even having all those technologies – to figure it out, right? But there are many robberies that are done on impulse or opportunity, right? For example, if I was a thief and saw someone withdrawing money from an ATM right in front of me … I would probably neglect all those precautions. But if it is a planned robbery, that doesn't happen.

Although this statement of Joel's could be interpreted as a reiteration of the notion that crime is opportunistic (Cavender and Deutsch 2007, Jewkes 2004), this situation also seriously complicates the claim that more knowledge about crime scene technologies has a deterrent effect on prospective offenders (see Chapter 6).

Reintegration

Overall, the prisoners in our study could be divided into two groups: first, those who, as discussed earlier, identified themselves as criminals. Xaver, 27, a 'recidivist' serving 18 months for battery, is an example: he said that he regarded the advancement of forensic technologies as something negative, because, as he added, 'I'm a criminal, […and we criminals] bond together.' The other group consisted of those who articulated their readiness and eagerness for reintegration into 'normal' society. Some used our conversations on crime scene technologies, as we showed in the previous section, to demonstrate that they had so little interest in committing crimes in the future that knowledge about crime scene work had no instrumental value for them. With respect to this second group of those who insisted on their readiness for reintegration, we can distinguish further between men who had engaged in premeditated criminal activity for personal gain ('career criminals'), and those who were convicted – mostly, but not exclusively – for sexual or violent crimes that they had committed 'in the heat of the moment'. In this latter group, nobody self-identified as a criminal, or articulated any intent to engage in criminal activities in the future.

Most of these men did not see themselves as criminals even after their conviction; their crimes were often referred to as 'accidents', as something that had happened to them, and that was an exception to the rule of how they led the rest of their lives (see also Hochstetler et al. 2010, Maruna and Copes 2005, Sykes and Matza 1957, Topalli 2006). As Christoph, the kidnapper, stated: 'I am basically a completely honest and truthful guy'. Before he had had the 'crazy idea' – as he called it himself – to kidnap a woman, apparently he had indeed been a law-abiding citizen; Christoph had no prior convictions of any sort, and he already had a concrete plan for the time after his release, which involved starting a family and buying a particular kind of furniture for his flat, all by legal means.

To Conclude: Fiction and Reality of Crime Scene Work

As we have seen, prisoners' representations of DNA technologies and their uses in criminal investigation cannot simply be explained by the *CSI* effect (see also Prainsack and Kitzberg 2009: 53). Many of our informants assessed crime television in a way which could be described as a mix of science enthusiasm and taking a critical distance from the high-tech scenarios projected by *CSI*. Some prisoners asserted that the portrayals of criminal investigation supported by forensic genetics in television crime shows belong to the realm of fiction; other prisoners thought that it might correspond to some extent with reality. This seeming contradiction can be overcome by differentiating, as we argued earlier, between portrayals of how technologies work in principle, and depictions of how they are used. While the former were regularly seen as useful information by our interviewees, the latter were encountered with a high dose of scepticism, both in Portugal and in Austria.

An example of the how *CSI* and other science-focused crime shows represent 'forensic realism' (Deutsch and Cavender 2008) was mentioned by Valter, a 25-year-old man sentenced to 18 years in prison for kidnapping, rape, and aggravated burglary. Making explicit reference to *CSI*, Valter talked about crime series on TV as a mix of fiction and reality: 'Perhaps in those series they exaggerate a little. But there must be some [true] basis to what they do, right?' Valter also said that before coming to prison he had thought that the high-tech scenarios projected by *CSI* were all 'rubbish', but that he had changed his mind once he had spoken to other prisoners. He explained that what he saw on TV became meaningful and 'true' only if it was confirmed by what he had learned about real cases:

> Before coming here [to prison] we had the idea that: 'Hey, that's television, it's all rubbish. [The criminal investigator who found] only a hair will never know that he is guilty.' But then I came to prison and started hearing things like 'this one was because of a drop of blood that he left in a window, and that one was because of a blood spot on his trousers'. A guy starts to become more up-to-date, right? By listening to more information on the subject.

Valter's biography fits perfectly the stereotype of a poly-criminal. Like many poly-criminal persons, he had had a difficult childhood: when he had been four years old, he had been taken from his family, considered dysfunctional by the child protection services, and spent the rest of his childhood and his adolescence in institutions for teenagers at risk, and for juvenile delinquents. He referred to these institutions as schools of crime (see also Foucault 1975): 'People think that a guy will take the straight path [at the institution for teens at risk] but [instead] it is the school of life and a guy starts going down the wrong path and that's why I got into a life of crime.'

Earlier in the conversation, Valter had said that because of all the practical knowledge that a prisoner obtained while behind bars, it would be unlikely for him to be caught if he committed other crimes after his release. This is another articulation of prisons as schools of crime. It was particularly interesting to note that as a result of what he learned about crime scene work and forensic technologies in prison, Valter's assessment of the credibility and value of TV shows such as *CSI* had changed: what he had dismissed as mere fiction prior to his incarceration he now saw as an – at least partly – accurate depiction of reality. Valter's example is a reflection of the particular perspective that many prisoners have when discussing media portrayals of crime scene work; it is one in which the very term 'crime scene work' represents a combination of two different communities of practice: the one related to the commission of the crime, and the one revolving around investigation, detection, and conviction. The boundary between the two does not neatly correlate with the distinction between offenders on the one hand, and investigators and prosecutors on the other. It is vital for offenders to obtain knowledge about the inner workings of protocols, technologies, and rationalities on the side of investigators and prosecutors, and vice versa.

Our study necessarily comprises a particular sub-set of those groups who commit crimes – namely those who were caught, as well as possibly also some of those who were convicted of crimes that they did not commit. Some people were explicitly situated in between the two communities of practice described before: namely those prisoners who either said that they had been wrongfully convicted and insisted on their innocence, and those who referred to their crime as an isolated incident which was external to their being. These two groups did not consider themselves 'insiders' on the side of those who committed crimes, for whom knowledge about crime scene work had instrumental value for the commission of future crimes. Such knowledge did have instrumental value for them only insofar as they had been affected by police investigations and evidentiary procedures at court; crime scene work and forensic technologies had thus entered their sphere without their having intentionally contributed to it. In sum, although for all of the 57 prisoners in our study, knowledge about crime scene work had relevance, the contexts in which it was relevant differed greatly, and so did the intended future uses of this knowledge. Thus, crime TV, in both its fictional and documentary form, does engage prisoners in reflections about crime scene work and, in some respects, also 'educates' those who watch it. The difference between most consumers of crime television and prisoners is, however, that the latter have practical experience with the topic that yields a rather nuanced assessment of the allegedly truthful and fictional dimensions of these media representations.

Also the physical and cultural 'proximity' (Jewkes 2004: 51–53) of prisoners to events depicted on television had an effect on their assessments. Prisoners seemed to be more aware of cases that had occurred in a location close to their own, and they could gather more information on the actual capabilities of the local police from these sources, for example, on the basis of real-life cases heavily publicised in the media, from the testimonies of fellow prisoners who had been connected to, or known details about, the case, or occasionally from their own experiences. Probably because details about crime scene work and forensic technologies were topics which were not discussed in isolation but instead embedded in thick narratives of the commission and detection of (alleged or actual) crimes, very few prisoners referred to conversations with fellow inmates as important sources of instrumental knowledge about crime scene work. This is probably the biggest difference between crime scene work and technologies portrayed in TV series such as *CSI* when compared to perceptions of those in real life: while on television the technological tools tend to overshadow other aspects of the story, in real life they do not.

Our informants made sense of what they saw on television by merging certain elements of the fictional representations of high-tech crime scene work with their own experiences in dealing with the criminal justice system as well as their particular perceptions about criminal activities and the work of crime investigation authorities. This set of interactions between the media's cultural images of criminal investigation and the ways in which the prisoners in our study interpreted them provide the basis for a more 'grounded assessment' (Duster 2006a) of the fictionalised portraits of forensic science and criminal investigation circulated by TV series.

Popular and scholarly discussions on how the media portray criminal investigation and forensic identification technologies have been based on the assumption that it is mainly television crime dramas such as *CSI* which play a prominent role in shaping public perceptions about crime scene work and DNA evidence in particular. However, there is no consensus in the literature regarding the directions of the expected impacts (Schweitzer and Saks 2007, Tyler 2006, for an overview, see Cole and Dioso-Villa 2009, Durnal 2010). Findings from our study further complicate the picture by indicating that not only are there multiple sources of information about crime scene work and forensic technologies but there are also diverse ways of making sense, and managing, that knowledge.

Chapter 5
Biological Traces: 'The Evidence Doesn't Lie'

Introduction

The hero of the TV crime series *Crime Scene Investigation* (*CSI*), scientist and crime lab supervisor Gil Grissom, personifies a near-to ideal image of science: brilliant, earnest, and always seeking to remain objective, yet at the same time sensing that his human nature sometimes tempts him into bias. While Grissom himself fights this temptation to the point of leading a life virtually devoid of what most of us consider the pleasures of human existence, such as family life, social activities, or sex, he is aware that he cannot turn himself into a fully disinterested, objective, infallible servant of science. The lack of trust his own machinelike qualities renders him suspicious of his fellow human beings: as he famously said in one of the series' first episodes in 2000: 'I tend not to believe people. People lie. But the evidence doesn't lie' (episode 3: 34–40, see also Kruse 2010a).

This quote of Gil Grissom has become so famous that it has entered many realms of popular culture (e.g. one can buy it printed on – non-*CSI* merchandise – T-shirts, see Cafepress 2011). For some social science observers, it has become a symbol of one of the variants of the so-called '*CSI* effect', a tendency prevalent among stake holders and publics to assess the inferences that can be made on the basis of DNA evidence as higher than inferences made from other kinds of DNA evidence (e.g., Briody 2004a, *The Economist* 2010, Nance and Morris 2005). The *CSI* effect, whose alleged 'educational variant' we encountered in the previous chapter, articulates itself, for example, in jurors or judges refusing to convict a suspect if no DNA evidence is presented; or in jury members insisting that all available evidence must be analysed for DNA traces, irrespective of the investigative clues that can be reasonably expected from them (*The Economist* 2010, see also Cole and Dioso-Villa 2007).

Kim et al.'s (2009) finding, based on a study carried out in Michigan, that *CSI* watching had no independent[1] effect on juror's verdicts, could be seen as

1 Frequent exposure to CSI watching was found by Kim and colleagues to have no direct effect on the willingness of jurors to convict. It did, however, have an indirect effect insofar as it raised jurors' expectations about scientific evidence to be presented by the prosecutor ($p<.004$). These raised expectations in turn significantly lowered jurors' willingness to convict defendants on the basis of circumstantial evidence alone ($p<.001$) (Kim et al. 2009: 457; the study was carried out in Michigan, $N= 1{,}027$). Interestingly, frequent exposure to a range of other crime and justice-related TV shows other than *CSI* dramas were also found to correlate with jurors' raised expectations about scientific

challenging the existence of a *CSI* effect (see also Podlas 2006). However it could also indicate that the *CSI* effect has found entrance into shared public representations of forensic science to such a large extent that it has become part of collective tacit knowledge (Polanyi 1966). Cole and Dioso-Villa (2009: 1371) regard the ample attention paid to the allegedly raised expectations of DNA and other evidence on the side of jurors and judges as indirectly working in the favour of prosecutors: because prosecutors are seen as confronted with increasingly unfair and unreasonable expectations regarding the presentation of scientific evidence, publics and stake holders sympathise with them, and regard their positions more favourably. Cole and Dioso-Villa also introduced the term '*CSI* effect effect' to signify the tangible realities that discussions about the impact of technology-intense crime dramas have created on the ground. Indeed, regardless of whether or not one agrees with these authors on the point of the *CSI* effect working to the advantage of prosecutors, it is evident that media representations of forensic technologies have had an impact on how powerful, reliable and (in)dispensable the latter are perceived to be (Baskin and Sommers 2010, Brewer and Ley 2010, Holmgren and Fordham 2011, Huey 2010).

Truth Machines (Lynch et al. 2008)

The fact that, as Kruse (2010a) notes, Grissom's use of the term 'evidence' includes only physical, not other (e.g., narrative) kinds of evidence, does important work to establish and maintain a boundary between those types of evidence that lend themselves to measurement and quantification (DNA, chemical traces, lie detectors, and, to a lesser extent, fingerprints) and those types of evidence that are less easily quantifiable, such as eyewitness testimonies, bite mark analysis, or graphological expertise. Evidence of the latter kind is thus seen as more prone to human error. Human error could take place within the sphere of those who testify, or contribute to the production of the evidence (which is assumed to have existed previously and is only rendered visible accessible by, for example, the eye witness through her statement), or it could be situated within the sphere of those interpreting the evidence. The crucial point is that it is assumed that in general,

evidence ($p<.01$), and it had the same effect as *CSI* drama on their willingness to convict on the basis of circumstantial evidence alone ($p<.001$) (however see also Ghoshray 2007 who found that *CSI* watching did *not* lower the assessment of the value of circumstantial evidence). Moreover, unlike exposure to *CSI* drama, the consumption of other crime series was found by Kim and colleagues to have also an independent effect on willingness to convict: 'The more jurors were exposed to those programs as a whole, the more they were willing to convict defendants without any scientific evidence ($p<.01$), even after controlling for expectations about scientific evidence and various individual characteristics' (Kim et al. 2009: 458). The age, race, gender, education, and political views of the participants in Kim et al.'s study significantly correlated with different expectations about scientific evidence.

the lower the level of involvement of human beings in the production of forensic science evidence, the smaller the risk for error (see also Mnookin 2008, Dror and Mnookin 2010). This also becomes apparent in the ways in which both Austrian and Portuguese prisoners referred to DNA and fingerprint evidence, where DNA evidence was regularly seen as the more 'reliable' form of evidence (see also Prainsack and Kitzberger 2009: 66). Feliciano, for example, aged 34, and serving a 12-year sentence for murder, described DNA evidence as 'totally infallible': 'If there is a drop of blood at the crime scene, that is irrefutable evidence, it's almost a confession to the [commission of] crime.'

It is arguably not genetic determinism or essentialism in the traditional sense of the word that underlies such reasoning, but instead the fact that forensic DNA evidence is carried out in a scientific laboratory and that it is typically expressed in discrete numbers. In contrast to fingerprints, which even in their digital form appear as a complex patterns of lines and dots which rely on human interpretation to become 'legible', a DNA profile is a set of discrete numbers which can be digitally stored and automatically compared. Feliciano thought that DNA was more powerful than other types of evidence exactly because it is readily digitised and stored on searchable databases. This, he argued, could not be done with fingerprints (see also Cole and Lynch 2010: 107):

> The matching [of DNA profiles] is almost like [with] a fingerprint. You look at a fingerprint and see if it matches with the ones you have. [But with DNA] you just need to input the data, right? And, automatically, the database carries out an instant search – I think – and a few minutes later, or less, it will confirm if [the profile] really matches that individual or not.

Arguably, also because forensic DNA evidence is understood to be more easily quantifiable, it is more strongly associated with 'high science' (Lynch et al. 2008: 309) than fingerprint analysis. As Dorian, 60, who was serving 15 years for murder, put it, DNA represented 'safer' evidence than fingerprints because 'it was produced in a lab; that's something very different from somebody sending your fingerprint up and down through the scanner'.

While the large majority of our informants in both countries articulated the idea that DNA was the most robust form of evidence to be obtained and used in criminal investigation, some prisoners in Portugal emphasised that Portuguese laboratories might lag behind in the adoption of developments in forensic science internationally. Interestingly, the television show *CSI*, again, served as a standard against which they compared the situation in Portugal. The glitzy surfaces, futuristic tubes, and slim computers shown in *CSI* symbolised sophisticated, cutting-edge science, and the characters of the TV series embodied the objective, disinterested, dispassionate (yet not infallible!) ideal of scientists or law enforcement officers.

Emílio, a 32-year-old man serving 15 years for murder and sexual coercion, thought that in comparison to the police officers and crime scene investigators on television, Portuguese law enforcement was not particularly well resourced:

'While on *CSI* the use of DNA is trivial, this is not the case in Portugal. Not even the *Polícia Judiciária*, the Criminal Investigation Police, who runs a number of laboratories, has the resources to use DNA in all cases.'[2] Emílio also said that although the science underlying DNA typing could not be 'tricked', mistakes could happen due to DNA contamination in Portuguese crime scenes or crime labs: 'It is possible to swap samples in the laboratories, but it is not possible, for instance, to forge your own DNA.' Also Feliciano, whom we encountered earlier in this chapter, mentioned the possibility of contamination due to human negligence or error:

> Sometimes, even in *CSI*, the investigators make mistakes ...; they know who the criminal is and can't secure a conviction ... because the evidence was flawed – but that is caused by human error – because the evidence was contaminated, because the police unintentionally left fingerprints because they didn't wear gloves.

It is noteworthy that although both Austrian and Portuguese prisoners mentioned the possibility of contamination of crime scene samples, the source of it was always described in terms of wrongful human action at the crime scene; contamination was never seen as something that happened in a laboratory. The close association between DNA and high science was also expressed by some of the prisoners by drawing an explicit link between DNA evidence and science documentaries on the one hand, and what they called 'a general interest' in the progress of science on the other.[3] The association of DNA evidence with scientific achievements also contributed to the 'inversion of credibility' (Cole and Lynch 2010: 107) by which dactyloscopy was seen as something similar to DNA technology in one respect – namely in the sense that fingerprints were unique in each individual – while it was seen as different from DNA technologies in terms of its technological sophistication. In the words of Rúben, a 31-year-old former computer analyst sentenced to six years imprisonment for aggravated fraud, document forgery and illegal access to a computer system, fingerprinting was losing credibility due to the

2 The argument about badly resourced law enforcement agencies or police labs was not mentioned by any of the Austrian prisoners.

3 The insistence on the side of our informants that their watching *CSI* was due to a general interest in science may also have stemmed from desire to assure the interviewer that knowledge about the avoidance of biological traces at crime scenes had no practical utility for them, who, in most cases, emphasised that they would never want to engage in any criminal activity anymore in the future (for exceptions see the stories of Xaver, Sigi, Paul and Daniel in Chapter 4). At the same time, however, expressions of enthusiasm about the advancement of science seemed genuine; in our view it is plausible that the prisoners' assurance about their purely non-instrumental interest in forensic technologies served more than one goal. For a more detailed discussion of this aspect see Chapter 4.

allegedly old methods of their storage and comparison. His is the story of paper file meets computer archive:

> Rúben: Fingerprints, although unique, have many things that can interfere with them. There is probably a lot of manual work being done regarding fingerprints. And that might affect the reliability of results.
>
> Interviewer: By influence of human error?
>
> Rúben: Not just by human error, but because of the circumstances of the taking of the fingerprints themselves. Because of the comparison procedures, which I honestly don't know how they are made, and I haven't the slightest idea. But I can imagine the archives, and the 50-year-old papers, and going there and comparing a sample and using that material that is probably degraded. I don't know… right?

Thus, while the production of DNA evidence in a laboratory was see as 'safe' and unproblematic, this applied less to the process of taking fingerprint evidence, which was referred to as an outdated technology. Rúben compared the 'objectivity' obtained by means of computer analysis with the allegedly subjective character of 'manual' comparison of fingerprints. This aspect was relevant also to his own case, as the decisive incriminating evidence against him had come from a forensic handwriting examination. Rúben played down the importance of the results of this examination by emphasising that what had 'really' led to his conviction was that he had ultimately confessed to the crime. He asserted that graphological analyses were not very reliable in general, making explicit reference to the lack of 'proper' quantification of the results of this technology:

> DNA evidence is more scientific than fingerprinting or handwriting tests. I am quite familiar with handwriting tests and I know that the result is expressed on a scale that goes from 'not likely' to 'highly likely' and nothing more [beyond that scale]. DNA, being a computer analysis, will never provide just a 'highly likely' answer. DNA results are not qualitative but quantitative. And I believe that it provides greater reliability.

Theodore Porter (1996) famously used the term 'mechanical objectivity' to refer to the greater authority bestowed upon 'impersonal numbers' in many spheres of our political, economic, and social realities than on human experience and judgment. It is, to a large extent, the attribution of this kind of 'mechanical objectivity' to forensic DNA technologies which helps us to understand great trust in the scientific accuracy of DNA evidence on the side of our informants.

However it is also the 'physical and ontological location of DNA' (Prainsack 2009: 144) which contributes to the image of forensic DNA evidence as being a 'truth machine' (Lynch et al. 2008). Because it is in the centre of our cell, and because it has a history of being described as being the 'book', 'blueprint', or 'code' of life, it is unsurprising that it has assumed a symbolic place as the bearer of (at least part of) the essence of individuals, and the essence of humanness, in collective imageries (Nelkin and Lindee 1995). As one of us argued elsewhere,

> This physical and ontological location bestows on forensic DNA relevance in a larger societal context which has become suspicious of exteriors: dangerous elements, 'strange subjects', cannot be easily spotted from the outside anymore, but the enemy now lives among us and looks like one of us: the nice student from next door who suddenly turns into a dangerous terrorist; the gregarious parliamentarian who secretly exploits allowances, and the friendly neighbour who turns out to be a convicted sex offender. In all of these examples, the danger is invisible to the eye. DNA assumes a comforting voice in this discourse because it bears the promise not to be distracted by exteriors; it claims access to the 'essence'. DNA grants an undistorted view of the body from the 'inside'. (Prainsack 2009: 144)

Yet another reason for the perception on the side of many of our informants that DNA technologies are more 'dangerous' to them than fingerprint evidence pertains to the way that the evidence is left at the crime scene. Ernst (30, convicted of fraud, with a three-year prison sentence) said that:

> … a DNA trace is more dangerous than a fingerprint because the perpetrator cannot control what he leaves behind and thus he leaves traces. Because fingerprints, that's easy. [Leaving] a fingerprint I can avoid every time, but a DNA trace one cannot avoid. That may be the advantage [!] about DNA traces. I mean, there's definitely a disadvantage. If someone has a prior conviction and [police] look at how the burglary was committed, for example, then the *modus* [*operandi*] tells them whether it's him. And perhaps he has no alibi.

What is striking in this quote is that it reflects the interconnected nature in which different kinds of evidence, and different forensic technologies, work together to produce the 'story of the crime' (Kruse 2012). DNA technologies are not put to work in isolation from other technologies, neither at the crime scene, nor at court. However, as discussed earlier in this chapter, the *CSI* effect is seen as doing exactly that, namely isolating DNA technologies from the cluster of forensic technologies; it remains to be seen how effectively it will do that in the longer run. Ernst started out by – quite accurately – describing how difficult, if not impossible, it is to avoid leaving biological traces at crime scenes. However when he then talked about how in the cases that were familiar to him people were *actually* caught, he suddenly referred to police analysing the perpetrator's *modus operandi*. In Ernst's account, DNA played no more than the role of an ancillary technology in this process; after police had identified possible suspects on the basis of other evidence or investigative clues – such as the analysis of the *modus operandi* – DNA testing could corroborate the involvement of a particular suspect or exclude him from the investigation.

This exculpatory capacity of DNA was mentioned by the majority of our informants (for more details see Chapter 7). However, the way our interviewees phrased this exculpatory potential of DNA evidence, again, conveyed absolute trust in the infallibility and truthfulness of the technology, and therefore, in DNA evidence. The most illustrative example in this context is the case of Gert, 30, who was convicted to three years and six months in prison for raping a colleague from work, a crime which he persistently denied having committed. The decisive piece of evidence in Gert's trial had been a DNA match between Gert's profile and a profile obtained from a sperm sample found on the outer wall of the house in which the crime had been committed. The victim had never seen the face of the perpetrator because he had worn a mask; however she had identified Gert as a potential suspect on the assumption that he had an axe to grind with her due to conflicts at work. Gert, convinced of his innocence and thus not having felt that he could be in any danger of remaining a suspect, had volunteered a DNA sample during the investigation. He reported to have been absolutely shocked when he heard that the DNA sample had matched the DNA from the crime scene:

> They've got [the sample] from the outer wall of the house, they took three swabs from there and one was useless, and about another one [the file] says that they could identify sperm but no DNA. And there is one where they say it's a [*sic*] sperm, and it's my DNA. I don't understand why.

Gert kept insisting that he was innocent, but it did not occur to him to dispute the reliability of the scientific process: '[T]he DNA, it is unique among 10 billion or million, or something like that. … I agree, if they found [my DNA], it's going to be mine, I do believe that, I am not as dumb as not to know that.' Nevertheless, how could he then square his insistence that he was innocent with the 'fact' that the DNA test 'proved' it was his? Gert, who overall struck us as an intelligent and articulate person with no leaning to conspiracy theories, resorted to a rather bizarre explanation of what he thought must have happened:

> It must have worked very simply, very simply. I think [the victim] took sperm from her husband, she must have done this in quite a simple way, so that they don't see it, and she mixed it with my saliva. I wonder whether that works. … I am not a biologist, but it must have worked like that.

Rather than questioning the scientific process that led to the – in Gert's mind – false evidence, he suspected that the victim had planted it. That this rationale may be more common became apparent also in the famous case of the English 'Night Stalker', a man who had brutally assaulted and raped a number of elderly women between 1992 and 2009. When a combination of investigative methods including phenotypic DNA profiling and the analysis of CCTV footage led to his detection,

DNA samples were taken and found to match the DNA profiles obtained from semen found on the victims. The defendant, Delroy Grant, denied his involvement with the crimes and instead blamed his ex-wife of having planted the evidence against him: he accused her of 'having stored various samples of his body fluids and over the subsequent 31-year period planted them at the crime scenes to frame him' (BBC 2011). Like Gert in our study, Delroy Grant did not attempt to challenge the scientific nature of DNA analysis, or any other activities that were carried out by machines and computers. Despite his pleas of innocence, Grant was convicted of 29 counts of rape, robbery and assault on 24 March 2010.

Gert also mentioned, albeit very briefly, the possibility of human error within the sphere of the police: 'Perhaps they confused [the samples]. Because [the victim's] brother in law, or someone like that, they took him for a DNA test as well, he had to give a sample as well.' Gert did not, however, follow up on the possibility of confusion of samples in the laboratory in the remainder of the conversation. Instead, he went into great detail about the process by which the victim could have gotten hold of his bodily material. In addition, also the insinuation that police might have confused the samples of two different suspects does, if at all, challenge the quality and reliability of the police investigation, but not the truth-producing capacities of the DNA 'machine'. In other words, the narrative 'told' by the DNA evidence was seen as so strong that it could not be challenged, and the prisoner's story had to settle around it. Gert's agency was thereby 'overruled' by the agency of his DNA; in making truth claims about the course of events, his own body was his competitor (see also Prainsack and Kreissl 2011).

The conviction that the DNA machine, as opposed to humans, is not prone to error was expressed very explicitly also in Hubert's account. Forty-one-year-old Hubert was serving seven and a half years for the sexual abuse of two minors, and DNA evidence had not played a decisive role in neither of the trials:

> The DNA trace … does not only prove that I am guilty, and I think that's a good thing, because it can also prove my innocence. Talk is cheap …: like it is these days with eyewitnesses, they [describe the perpetrator as] between 25 and 50 years old, [the hair colour] ranging from light blonde to black. I think it's a good thing, to give my DNA trace [*sic*] when I know it wasn't me [who committed the crime].

Hubert's fellow inmate Quentin (25 years old, sentenced to eight years for arson) agreed with this assessment, and he put it in words that are reminiscent of the TV character Gil Grissom: DNA evidence 'is a good thing … . Because much more comes into the light. [The suspect] can't say, a hundred times, no, it wasn't me. If the DNA says it was you, then it was you. I think it's a good thing. The DNA does not lie' (see also Prainsack and Kitzberger 2009: 64).

Despite the belief in DNA as a truth machine some prisoners emphasised that human actions could lead to biased uses of this sort of evidence. Rúben, whom we encountered earlier in this chapter, explicitly mentioned that his computer science background enabled him to discern some technologies displayed in *CSI* as unrealistic: 'I don't believe that it is representative of reality. I think it is light-years away from reality.'

Also Frederico, 54, sentenced to 20 years for drug trafficking and leading a criminal organisation, thought that television crime drama did not depict investigative practices in a realistic manner: 'Of course in movies everything is much easier. In order to capture people's attention, a movie has to have some fiction.' Frederico also said that the judges might 'undervalue' DNA evidence if the defendant has a past criminal record: 'The judges often don't really seek the truth to 100 per cent, because if the defendant has a past record, if they had been arrested for this or that, the judges become convinced that the defendant committed the crime. And that's just not true.' Henrique, 37, sentenced to three years imprisonment for burglary and forgery, also mentioned the power of interpretation of evidence, while referring that the key to avoid a prison sentence was a good lawyer:

> [For example] you rob a café and you're not caught. But they accuse you of robbing the café, which is a public place. If your fingerprints are behind the counter, you might be accused. If the fingerprints are outside of the counter, then this is not possible. Because, [the bar] being a public place, anyone can go there. However, if the fingerprints are behind the counter, you can find yourself incriminated. What you need is a good lawyer for the evidence to be interpreted. ... A good lawyer might save [a criminal].

Personal experiences clearly play a fundamental role in the prisoners' assessment of the value of forensic technologies (see Chapter 4). As described in this chapter, the large majority of our informants considered DNA the 'gold standard' (Lynch et al. 2008) of identification. However, three Portuguese informants stated that fingerprinting was a more robust kind of evidence than DNA, either because they considered it to be the most commonly used method of the identification – not detection! – of suspects; but also because they thought that some crimes which featured prominently in the media – such as the Madeleine McCann case (see Chapter 3) – showed that real science has its limitations. Artur, a 38-year-old former electrician, sentenced to 12 years of imprisonment for aggravated burglary and theft, effectively illustrated this argument:

> I think fingerprints are more effective. They also say DNA is effective. I don't know because I am not familiar with it. But I have gone through fingerprinting, right? I don't know about DNA. If DNA were to be more effective they would have solved Maddie's case, right? They had a drop of blood there and the analyses were carried out in England. I think that if it was effective they should be able to say whose blood it really was.

The Madeleine McCann case was covered by the Portuguese tabloid press in such a dramatic way that it could well be mistaken for a *CSI* plot. Nevertheless, while science was portrayed as the (only) solution for the crime, the absence of a scientific explanation for the known facts placed the capabilities and limitations of real science against fictionalised representations of forensic science (Machado and Santos 2011). In this sense, the scepticism or general mistrust that some Portuguese inmates showed when talking about DNA evidence was an example of 'grounded assessment' of forensic technologies as described by Troy Duster for the USA context (Duster 2006a).

Besides rendering the limits of forensic technologies – and DNA evidence in particular – more visible in the public sphere, the Madeleine McCann case also provided a concrete point of reference for the perception of some Portuguese prisoners that DNA technology may not be used fairly and accurately during the investigation and in court.[4] Artur, for example, compared the Madeleine McCann case with another highly prominent criminal case: the disappearance of the Portuguese 8-year-old Joana Cipriano Guerreiro in 2004, from her home in the village of Figueira (region of Algarve), seven miles from where Madeleine was last seen:

> In my opinion, Joana's mother's prison sentence is unjust. There was no body, no murder weapon, nothing, but the court had to give her a hard sentence because she had already been convicted by public opinion, before standing trial, she already had been convicted by the media. Given that Joana's mother was convicted, the McCanns should also have been convicted, in my point of view.

Artur's quote referred to the debate launched by both the Portuguese and the British media immediately after the McCanns were given the *arguido* status. A substantial part of the public criticism of Portuguese police practices in the Madeleine McCann case was related to the conduct of Gonçalo Amaral, at the time a senior police officer and head of the regional *Polícia Judiciária*, who coordinated the search for Madeleine's alleged abductor. Amaral had also been in charge of the investigation of Joana Cipriano's disappearance, in which no body had been found, but which had ended with the conviction of Joana's mother and uncle.

---

4 In the Austrian context, the case of Peter Heidegger – a young man who was wrongfully convicted of robbery and murder on the basis of false eye witness evidence – provided a similar reference point for prisoners to suspect that police misconduct and unfair trials were a frequent occurrence (the Heidegger case is discussed in detail in Chapter 7). Interestingly, despite the fact that Heidegger was neither convicted nor exonerated on the basis of DNA evidence, the planting of DNA evidence featured prominently in the scenarios of possible misconduct by criminal justice authorities drawn by Austrian prisoners. This was the case despite the fact that Austrian prisoners were neither asked about the possibility of planting DNA evidence, nor about any other scenario of misconduct involving DNA technologies.

When in February 2008 Amaral and other Portuguese police officers were accused of forging evidence and covering up for other investigators who had allegedly tortured Joana's mother to coerce a confession, it was accompanied by a heated public discussion over injustices and wrongdoings within police investigations and the criminal justice system (Brown 2007).

In sum, based on the accounts of the prisoners in our study one could argue that there is indeed such a thing as a *CSI* effect, albeit not necessarily in the more narrow meaning of the term. Recent empirical studies (e.g., Kim et al. 2010) found no correlation between greater exposure to *CSI*, or similar techno-centric crime drama, and greater trust in forensic technologies. Although our interview study did not set out to explore this question specifically, we did find – as shown in the previous chapter – that television was mentioned by our prisoners as the main source of knowledge about crime scene traces; and trust in the infallibility of forensic technologies seemed to correlate negatively with the extent to which human expertise and judgment was involved in it. However we had no indication to conclude that those informants who referred prominently to crime shows held different beliefs about the power of DNA technologies than those who did not speak (much) of crime TV.

Inmates' representations of forensic DNA technologies reflected the impact of watching TV crime drama but they also showed the critical distance that many prisoners took from the portrayals of forensic science and crime scene work on television. This critical and reflexive stance was articulated, for example, by some interviewees stressing the discrepancies between TV fiction and reality. Some – particularly in the group of prisoners in Portugal – also pointed out the contingencies of the use of forensic DNA technologies due to possible human errors or abusive uses by authorities. As we saw in Chapter 4, rather than as an entirely accurate representation of reality, *CSI* was referred to as a mix of reality and fiction; it was seen as a repertoire of wishful-thinking science (Kruse 2010a), creating a fictional 'better society' in which crime is eradicated with the help of science. Science, in turn, had a clear hierarchical structure, according to how 'truthful' and reliable it was considered to be. With DNA technologies representing the 'gold standard', other techniques and technologies such as dactyloscopy or handwriting analysis were seen as potentially more fallible because they allegedly relied more strongly on human interpretation.

One factor which arguably contributed to the lack of trust in human judgment among our interviewees was their experience with, and perception of, societal, state, and sometimes also parental authorities, which was portrayed as mostly negative. The prevalent feeling of disappointment or anger towards – mostly human – representatives of these authorities, who many of our informants saw as having deceived them and let them down, was certainly not conducive to their trust in the action of authorities, and perhaps of human action in general. Overall, however, we believe that it was primarily the association that prisoners saw between forensic science – and DNA technologies in particular – with 'high science' which accounted for the dominant understanding that '(DNA) evidence does not lie'. The role of *CSI* and similar TV series in this dynamic was that they solidified and enhanced understandings of machines and technologies as reliable and stable, in opposition to humans who were regularly depicted as unreliable and unstable (and for most of our interviewees, also as untrustworthy). Such understandings have permeated public imageries of the working of the criminal justice system, and the role of technologies and humans in it, to the extent that it is no longer necessary for individuals to personally spend long hours watching TV crime shows to share these collective images.

Control, Human Error, and Planting Evidence

It is possible that there is a connection between the way in which people relate to the authority of high science and their status in society. For example, with regard to people who have had access to higher education, would it be plausible to assume that they are less easily intimidated by claims to scientific authority that is bestowed on forensic science applications with the outer signs of high science? Moreover, is there a connection between how much one feels in control of one's own life on the one hand, and one's willingness to accept the authority of science over an entire functional field, in the sense that it assumes a more intimate relationship to truth than other ways of relating to the world?

Both in Portugal and in Austria, overall, the higher the level of formal education of a prisoner was, the greater was his willingness to talk about the scientific underpinnings of forensic technologies. At the same time, in terms of enthusiasm for the use of forensic science there was no difference between prisoners with more and fewer years of formal schooling.

If it is indeed the case that the feeling of control over one's own life is related to one's acceptance of claims of scientific authority, then this would be an interesting dimension to explore in further studies in this field. Control over their own lives is a very central issue for prison inmates, as the lack thereof is one of the distinctive characteristics of imprisonment (Sykes 2007 [1958]). The feeling of a lack of control over their lives also prior to their imprisonment, or the fear of losing control, respectively, featured prominently in the accounts of many of our informants.

In the context of the crime that lead to their imprisonment, forensic technologies, – and in particular, DNA technologies – belonged to the realm of things that were considered beyond their control; they were portrayed as much less controllable than other factors, such as confessions, witnesses, and even the conduct of jurors or judges. Forensic technologies were beyond their control for two main reasons: first, many inmates felt that it was impossible to 'control' one's body substances (see Chapter 8) well enough to not accidentally leave biological traces at the crime scene (with the exception of fingerprints, which were described as relatively easy to avoid leaving). Second, because of the association between – particularly – DNA technologies and 'high science', many prisoners in our study did not even dare to start to comprehend the underpinning scientific principles and practices. This pertained particularly to those with fewer years of formal schooling. DNA technologies symbolised 'the other': not only 'the other side' of the crime game – the side of law enforcement authorities – but also 'the other side of life', which by most of our interviewees was seen as unattainable for them. It was the side of life where white coats, professorial habitus, and fancy computers belonged to. DNA technologies were within the realm of the people inhabiting another life for virtually all of our informants.

DNA technologies were also seen as tools which helped to police the border between the spheres of 'normal life' on the one hand and the criminal realm on the other. The existence of a national forensic DNA database, for example, was seen as a 'good thing' by many of our interviewees because it helped to maintain order in society (Prainsack and Kreissl 2011). As Oliver, 34, serving an open sentence for attempted murder and rape, put it: 'I'd say, to protect society, it's a good thing.' Dorian, another Austrian prisoner whom we encountered earlier in this chapter, even stated that that 'if society didn't catch the criminals then everything would sink into chaos' (cf. Prainsack and Kitzberger 2009: 68); while Feliciano, whose statements we have also discussed before, argued that 'personally … as a … criminal – criminal in commas – that word is a bit… but that's what we are, that's why we are here… I think it's sort of a good thing, in my opinion, it is an advantage for criminal investigation and to fight future crime.'

At the same time, however, the same authorities that – literally – policed the boundaries between the criminal realm and the realm of 'normal life' were also suspected of abusing their power at the cost of the inmates. Inmates very frequently expressed the feeling of stigma, being 'marked for life' (Machado et al. 2011), and of being helpless against the power of authorities, especially when they were wrongly accused – which some of our interviewees claimed had happened to them, while others referred to it as a possible future scenario. In this context, DNA technologies were perceived as a tool that could, in theory, empower them as it could prove their innocence, or force police to carry out a proper investigation instead of simply going after who they thought was a suspect because the crime fitted their *modus operandi*. DNA technologies were a 'truth machine' (see Lynch et al. 2008) against which even the police were powerless. In an interesting way, technology assumed the role of becoming an ally of prisoners against abusive authorities (Chapter 8): even the police could not trick it.

Although police were not seen as having the power to interfere with the 'DNA machine' itself, however, they were seen as able to 'play' the system by planting evidence. Many of our informants both in Portugal and in Austria mentioned this possibility. Norbert, 50, serving a life sentence for three counts of attempted murder, represented a typical example of this fear (see also Prainsack and Kitzberger 2009: 68):

> Hair and saliva can be abused. … Due to pressure from the media, if [the police] do not have a [suspect], and then there is somebody who would make for a good

> conviction because he might have had a murder [conviction] in the past, then [they might say:] 'we go get him.'

Oliver, another Austrian prisoner we encountered earlier, referred to his own case as an instance of DNA evidence planting: when he had been charged of the rape and strangling of a young woman, a crime which he emphatically denies having committed, no physical evidence had been found to corroborate his involvement at first. Relatively late in the investigation, however, a hair from the victim had suddenly turned up in his flat, after the flat had already been examined multiple times. Oliver claimed that it had been planted by the investigating officer, either unintentionally or intentionally: 'If I'm polite I say that what had happened there was an unintentional trace transfer' (the topic of DNA planting is discussed in more detail in Chapter 9).

It is noteworthy that most examples pertaining to the planting of evidence referred to the planting of DNA traces at crime scenes. Although some prisoners did mention other kinds of evidence in connection with wrongful convictions, the 'problem' with other evidence was not so much the intentional planting of that evidence by the police, but instances of human negligence or error. Some prisoners thought that DNA was different in that it was much more prone to being deliberately abused by the police than other technologies. The following is an excerpt from our exchange with Norbert, who was serving a life sentence for three counts of attempted murder:

> Norbert: I think DNA is easier to abuse than fingerprints, because [of the latter] every person has only one. But the DNA one can get from saliva, hair, sperm, and so on. I think therefore it's easier to abuse.
>
> Interviewer: How do people talk about DNA traces in here?
>
> Norbert: Yes, they say that there are many cases [of abuse]. For example, one guy went in [to the interrogation room] and the policemen didn't say anything but pulled out one of his hairs: 'We found that at the burglary [scene].' That's just an example.
>
> Interviewer: They pulled out his hair and the planted it at the scene?
>
> Norbert: That's what he says, I can't know for sure. That's what he said, I can't judge whether or not it's true. But I say one thing, fingerprints are certain [*sic*], but DNA one can abuse.

Jürgen, 29, serving five years for aggravated battery, however, told us about how worried he was not only about his DNA profile, but about his fingerprints being stored in a centralised database. This was the case because of his profession as a waiter, which meant that he left his fingerprints in many places:

> Then they are stored and everything, and then [the police] know ok, it was him [who had committed a certain crime]. But then, perhaps, he wants to change. [He] leads a good life, and so on. And after five years, [another crime] happens. And his fingerprints pop up, although he had nothing to do with it, he is linked to the case although he's innocent.

A few minutes later in the conversation Jürgen made it clear that what he was worried about his own future after leaving prison, fearing he could become a notorious suspect:

> For example I don't know what will happen when I get out. For example I could be in a bar and there I could have a row, but I don't hurt anyone. … As a waiter you leave your fingerprints on the glasses or on the food, I've got my hands everywhere. And all it takes [for me to become a suspect] is for one person to say it was me. Although I am innocent.

Here, the fault on the side of the police was that they did not, or even could not, establish that in this particular instance the originator of the fingerprint had not committed the crime, but that his fingerprints were at the crime scene for a perfectly legitimate reason. Although the same scenario could just as well happen with DNA evidence, very few of our informants explicitly mentioned this possibility. When Frederico, the former leader of a criminal organization, for example, complained that criminal investigations could be 'biased', he referred to how the police

> … managed to place my fingerprints in [connection with] a crime I did not commit. The investigator may, or may not, be an honest person. They can collect fingerprints here, take them, and say that they were taken over there. They can present them in court as if I had entered the house next door.

Some prisoners, rather than drawing up concrete examples or scenarios of how police could plant evidence, expressed the feeling of powerlessness against police authorities, or the criminal justice system as a whole, in broad and general terms. Ingo, 43, for example, who was serving a life sentence for murder, said that in general, a universal DNA database could be a good thing because it would help to solve many crimes. Yet he did not have a good feeling thinking about what the authorities could do with the data stored there: '[the authorities] can do so much. ... We're already transparent. And now, with [reference to] terrorism and security, everything can being justified. [Authorities and politicians] are greater criminals than we are.'

Conclusion

Our informants perceived DNA technologies as having almost absolute power in terms of identification and uniqueness; the majority of our interviewees considered it a technique far superior to fingerprints in this respect. However, while much of the power ascribed to DNA technologies was attributed to the fact that DNA evidence was seen as being produced by machines and not by humans, both in the Austrian and Portuguese groups of prisoners, the infallibility of DNA technologies was not taken to be absolute in connection with the possibility of human error or deliberate wrongdoing. In other words, while none of our interviewees mentioned the possibility that the scientific processes associated with DNA analysis could be fallible in some respect, the one reason for why DNA analysis could yield wrong results was human action. Human factors – the police, courts, and people with bad intentions – were mentioned by some interviewees as possible causes for abusive and improper use of DNA evidence against them, or simply as the cause of involuntary contamination. Our interviewees expressed strong suspicions regarding police or people with malicious intentions deliberately 'planting' biological traces at crime scenes in order to incriminate them, or with regard to authorities using false information on the availability of DNA evidence to elicit confessions.

Our informants frequently emphasised that while one could control or forge anything else (especially also fingerprints!), one could not eradicate or forge one's DNA. DNA assumed the role of the immutable and truthful result of a reliable technology associated with 'high science'; DNA, as one of our interviewees put it, 'did not lie'.

The function of forensic DNA technologies as 'truth machines' (Lynch et al. 2008) does not remain without effects for prisoners' understandings of contingencies in the accounts of the crimes for which they were committed. Many of our interviewees told us that once DNA evidence had entered the scene, they realised that the game was 'over', that it would not make any sense to insist on one's innocence – regardless of whether or not they had committed the crime. In this sense, DNA technologies assumed a unique role among forensic technologies; although fingerprints were also seen as strong evidence by many of our informants, they were deemed less powerful because they were relatively easy to avoid leaving, because they were not matched fully automatically but with the help of human fingerprint experts, or because they were simply seen as an 'old' technology. It is noteworthy that references to human error, or human misconduct, which were mentioned both in relation to DNA technologies and fingerprint comparisons, did not seem to detract from most prisoners' assessment that DNA evidence did not lie. In other words, although some prisoners mentioned that both fingerprints and DNA analyses were prone to errors due to contamination at crime scenes, or the deliberate planting of evidence, with regard to DNA evidence this conviction did not 'trickle down' to the end point of a general assessment of the reliability of these technologies, where DNA was seen as the gold standard.

The powerful way in which our informants saw forensic DNA technologies did arguably not remain without effects on their self-understandings either. Because DNA evidence was seen as hard, truthful evidence, the story that it told took precedence over alternative stories that prisoners may have had to offer. These dynamics were apparent in the prisoners' accounts, where the link between the person and the crime had been replaced by the link between the body and the technology (Prainsack and Kreissl 2011). This arguably constrains prisoner's agency even further than it is already constrained by the nature of captivity (Sykes 2007 [1958]). As opposed to, for example, techniques of interrogation producing a guilty plea, DNA evidence require no active participation of the suspect. The mere fact of his bodily existence forms the basis of evidence. Whether this body is strong or in good shape is meaningless. All aspects of outer appearance lose their significance and hence the individual's control over his body is irrelevant. Physical strength, endurance, intelligence and self-control, attributes of the dominant male personality highly valued in hegemonic male discourse, do not play any role in the realm of DNA, curtailing the options for identity management and presentation of the self. The self is reduced to an abstract pattern of marks plotted on paper and bear no significance with regard to the social body or person. No account of innocence, no defence can be brought forward against these marks since they are the product of a process involving mute biological matter and incomprehensible technological manipulation (Prainsack and Kreissl 2011) by potentially abusive authorities (Machado et al. 2011).

This creates a new regime of (forensic) truth based on the assumption of an infallible biological identity. Confronted with this regime, our informants felt that they had no possibility to refute the claims brought forward against them. In other words, because of the scientific power ascribed to forensic DNA technologies, the space for 'alternative narratives' pertaining to culpability was seen as shrinking drastically in light of incriminating DNA evidence. In this sense, in the accounts and views of our informants, DNA evidence became a 'truth machine' (see Lynch et al. 2008) for those on whom it was used in a very particular way: it locked them into a state of objectivity (Prainsack and Kreissl 2011).

Chapter 6

In Everybody, 'There's Always a Bug Inside': Does DNA Profiling and Databasing Deter Criminals?

Introduction

Around the world, the collection and use of bioinformation has become an important instrument of contemporary state efforts to detect crime, monitor offenders, and predict the risk of criminal activity (McCartney 2006b, Williams and Johnson 2008). In many jurisdictions the establishment and successive expansion of centralised DNA databases for forensic and police uses has been largely based upon efforts and aspirations of key criminal justice and forensic science stakeholders to ensure that more offenders are prosecuted and deterred from re-offending. Central to these developments is the belief that scientific and technological knowledge make a clear and substantial contribution to crime investigation and prevention.

Although fingerprinting remains the most commonly utilised method of forensic identification (Bradbury and Feist 2005: vi, McCartney 2006a: xi), portrayals of DNA identification as an infallible tool to identify perpetrators are common in popular culture. Such imaginaries are also prevalent in the work of journalists, lawyers and legal scholars (Lynch et al. 2008: xi) (see also Chapters 4 and 5). The imagery of DNA as the 'gold standard for individual identification' techniques has given DNA profiling and databasing an unrivalled status among the tools for crime detection and deterrence. As some commentators argue, the expectation is that DNA technologies and DNA databases will be used to solve every crime – for instance, from burglary and criminal damage, to car theft and other examples of volume crime (Asplen 2004, Bradbury and Feist 2005).

This chapter starts by discussing how the adoption of scientific and technological devices for corroborating or inferring identities based on forensic bioinformation – DNA profiles and fingerprints – has become an important feature of modern state surveillance to ensure public safety and security, and how contemporary societies are currently witnessing a trend to expand forensic DNA databases. We balance the arguments put forward by some governmental actors and forensic scientists in support of expanding the sizes and the uses of DNA technologies in the criminal justice system, with the ethical and political considerations raised by academic researchers, advisory bodies, and civil organisations (for a detailed overview of this line for argumentation consult McCartney, Williams and Wilson 2010, Nuffield

Council on Bioethics 2007). In this latter group of 'expansion sceptics', many argue that the expansion of forensic DNA databasing creates new risks, including function creep (see below). We then go on to analyse prisoners' assessments of the value of the DNA databases in crime prevention and deterrence. Here, we will look particularly at how prisoners evaluate the scenario of a wider use of forensic DNA technologies, including the establishment of universal DNA databases.

Expanding the Uses of Forensic Bioinformation

DNA profiling and DNA databasing have been presented as the solution to the problem of crime in policy documents, but also public imaginaries. The supporters of more inclusive forensic DNA databases have consistently appealed to various strategic arguments, such as that the inclusion of a broader range of profiles in forensic DNA databases would eventually improve police effectiveness and the targeting of criminals, and consequently bring down investigation costs (Gans and Urbas 2002: 5). Some stakeholders in the area of politics, forensic sciences and the justice system sustain that the benefits in increasing the uses of DNA identification in criminal investigations are manifold: DNA databases help to reduce the need for costly alternatives such as the use traditional investigative techniques (McCartney 2004), help prevent miscarriages of justice, and DNA evidence may also prompt confessions (Garrett 2010). Some authors also claim that with the creation and expansion of forensic DNA databases, some offenders may be deterred from further criminal activity because of the increased risk of detection (Beauregard and Bouchard 2010, Gans and Urbas 2002, Home Office 2009, Weiss 2004).

The DNA Expansion Programme in UK, launched in 2000 with the purpose of increasing the growth of the NDNAD until the entire 'known active offending population' are on the database (Home Office 2003, 2005, McCartney 2006b: 175), is a particularly illustrative example of contemporary governmental and societal concerns with crime control and securitisation that have led to an increasing investment in DNA profiling and databasing. Also in accounts of the history of forensic DNA databases, crime is typically a problem 'that has been created in the social sphere and solved by technological means'. Such stories regularly tell us:

> … that in order to solve severe crimes, we need technology. All the possible problems and ambiguities inherent in the use of technologies – for example, that forensic DNA analysis always bears the risk of contamination, of human or machine errors, etc., and that even a DNA match between a suspect and the crime scene does not automatically prove guilt … – are absent from its narrative. It provides a firm basis upon which the systematic extension of DNA profiling – from its use on an *ad hoc* basis to the systematic storage of profiles in a centralised database – seems like the logical solution to a problem. (Prainsack and Toom 2012)

Although national practices and debates around the costs and benefits of developing DNA profiling and databasing may vary substantially between countries (Hindmarsh and Prainsack 2010), the typical pattern of diffusion of DNA technologies has been to start with limited collections of samples and profiles and then to widen the scope of purposes of its uses ('function creep').[1] While the first databases, emerging in the 1990s, were limited to storing the DNA profiles of convicted rapists and murderers and other serious felonies, over the last two decades many state legislatures have rapidly expanded the scope of the databases to include many or all convicted felons, juvenile offenders and even arrestees (Van Camp and Dierickx 2007, 2008).

Such database expansions were supported by proponents of more expansive uses of DNA identification in criminal investigations and in criminal trials, including in appeals and post-conviction proceedings (see Chapter 8). Thus, the issue of database expansion is far from being black-and-white, where those in favour of expansion are law-and-order types supporting police-state surveillance, and its critics are the only ones concerned about civil freedoms. The situation is more complex than that: some of those supporting the expansion of DNA databases, or the contexts in which DNA data should be used in the criminal justice context, are driven by the same values and concerns as some of those who oppose database expansion: justice, privacy, and the prevention and correction of miscarriage of justice. As Prainsack and Toom (2010: 1124) argued with regard to the implementation of a new EU law (Prüm Decision) which will grant policing agencies and/or criminal justice authorities direct access to DNA databases in other EU countries,

> … the complex of surveillance systems inherent in the Prüm regime also empowers those who demand higher data protection standards, not only by highlighting the topic of data protection in the political and public domain as a valid concern in light of the increasing size and interlinking of databases, but also – and perhaps more importantly – by restricting the amount of personal identifying information that travels across borders. The latter also benefits suspects whose identifying details, in pre- Prüm times, would have been submitted to authorities in other countries while this is no longer the case within the Prüm regime (unless a DNA match has been established).

One of the areas which have received very little critical scrutiny – and attention from the side of empirical social science research – so far is the assumption that DNA databases deter people from (re-)offending. According to the deterrence argument, in many circumstances DNA database expansion is part of national governments'

1 Function creep refers to the observation that technological infrastructures that were set up for a particular purpose often start to be used for wider purposes (Dahl and Sætnan 2009). Once they are set up, it becomes difficult to prevent them from being used more widely.

attempts to ensure that more offenders are prosecuted and that criminals are deterred from offending upon release. Along with the potential deterrent effect, some commentators have also suggested that there is also evidence of changes in criminal behaviour to avoid leaving DNA evidence at crime scenes – offenders are becoming increasingly 'forensically aware' (Beauregard and Bouchard 2010, see Chapter 4).

Research into criminal careers (Piquero et al. 2007, Sampson and Laub 1993), however, make us question the assumption that the larger the DNA databases are, the more 'useful' a deterrent or an investigative tool they will become. Among the arguments for defending the benefits of criminal DNA databases is that its utility theoretically increases as the volume of data it contains continues to expand (Bieber 2006, Briody 2004a: 176, Wilson et al. 2010: 464). In some countries, such as the UK, the national forensic DNA database was extended on the basis that it would target not only violent crime but also volume crime. However, neither was DNA profiling and databasing found to reduce volume crime (Tracy and Morgan 2000), nor did higher trace collection rates at crime scenes scare away offenders fearing higher detection rates (Freckelton and Selby 2002, but see the reference to data by Zamir and colleagues, who state that a research study carried out by the Israeli police showed deterrence rates of 22 per cent when subjects were DNA sampled at the time of their first recordable offence; Zamir et al. 2012). Thus the specific deterrent effects of DNA databases are likely to apply only to a small proportion of offenders (Briody and Prenzler 2005: 81).

Some studies even indicate that the lack of evidence for DNA databases' deterrent effects in the context of volume crime (Bhati 2010) might be explained by offenders' becoming more diligent in avoiding traces, or using drugs or alcohol to overcome inhibitions (Mays et al. 1991: 42, Wright and Decker 1994). Important elements for the understanding of the potential deterrent effect of forensic DNA databases are the views and perceptions of prisoners. In the next sections of this chapter, we will take a look at the narratives of prisoners in Austria and in Portugal, exploring their rather nuanced and diversified accounts of the promise of deterrence inherent in the rhetoric of DNA database expansion.

The Fiction of Deterrence: Prisoners' Perspectives

Overall, prisoners did not believe that the awareness of DNA databases had a significant deterrent effect on offenders. A high number of crimes, they argued, were committed on impulse; and generally, more often than not, they said, offenders do not weigh risks and benefits in a rational manner before the event. For example, as David, 42, sentenced to three years and ten months for attempted murder, argued: 'People who are used to robbing … They are not concerned about [whether or not there are surveillance] cameras, as they will cover their faces and rob anyway'. David also believed that the existence of forensic DNA databases did not prevent murderers or sexual offenders from (re-)offending because, in his opinion, such people are simply evil, or they have psychological or personality problems:

> These are people who do bad things but do not even think about what they are doing, they need not have a notion of what they are doing. A person who is a rapist or a paedophile, or something like that, must be a psychopath. They must have some sort of childhood trauma.

The association between crime and psychological and mental illness that some of our prisoners in Portugal referred to[2] dates back to periods before the eighteenth century (Foucault 1975). Mental illness is one of the most important empirical and theoretical pillars of some approaches to understanding crime and deviance (Silver et al. 2008), such as forensic psychopathology and criminal anthropology and biology.[3] The representation of crime as something endogenous to the individual was reproduced by some of our interviewees in Portugal: the 'real criminals', they said, have crime 'in their nature'. In the words of 49-year-old Joaquim: 'Once they are born crooked, crooked they die.' This prison inmate, who was serving six years in prison for sexually abusing his under-aged daughter, who allegedly got pregnant as a result, also referred to criminals as people with an 'addiction', an uncontrollable drive or impulse. When asked whether he thought that inmates would stop 'messing around' because they knew that there was a forensic DNA database that might lead to their detection if they re-offended, he answered in the negative. He said that they were plenty of people who obtained pleasure from their transgressions (see also Agnew 1990, Brezina and Piquero 2003):

> Interviewer: Do you think that some inmates, when they get out of prison, will stop committing crimes because there is a database with DNA profiles?
>
> Joaquim: No, no, hardly. Sometimes I overhear some conversations between them [silence] ... People who do those things are people with little sense [they don't think before they act]. One of them was talking to me and he told me that he got more pleasure from doing a robbery than from having [sexual] relations with a lady. Imagine the [addiction] of the boy…

---

2 Prisoners in Austria did not mention mental illness as possible 'causes' of criminal behaviour.

3 Forensic Psychopathology focuses on the application of psychological analysis in a forensic and legal context. Essentially, this discipline's role is to perform evaluations of offenders' capacity to stand trial, elaborate a psychological profile, to assess their criminal responsibility (state of mind at the time of the offence) or eventual mitigating factors that can affect sentencing. Criminal Anthropology is the study of the association between human physiological features and appearance and a supposedly 'born' tendency towards criminal behaviour (Howitt 2002).

Lucílio, 34, convicted to two years in prison for driving without a license, also did not believe that databases for criminal investigation worked as crime deterrents. In contrast to David and Joaquim, though, Lucílio did not refer to a propensity for crime as something that some people were born with or had in their 'nature'; Lucílio blamed socio-economic circumstances for facilitating criminal behaviour. Thus the only effective measure to reduce re-offending would be psychological support and behavioural therapy:

> Interviewer: [Can a forensic DNA database] prevent crime?
>
> Lucílio: Not actually preventing crime because these people have a different way of thinking. I have my way of thinking, they have theirs. In here we have kids, actual 18 or 16 year-old kids, who robbed jewellery stores and who are already thinking that when they get out in seven, nine, or ten years from now, they will get back into 'business'. It also depends on the education they received, they are street kids [living in troubled neighbourhoods], and the need creates opportunities. They are really into it, when they get out, if it's not [doing robberies] they will break into everything, they have another way of thinking, another mentality. These are people that should be receiving psychological treatment. But there is no funding for that.[4]

This line of reasoning was also very common among the Austrian prisoners we interviewed, who almost exclusively attributed the cause of criminal behaviour to people's upbringing, bad influence from friends and family, and to other social factors. None of the Austrian prisoners, however, felt that crime was something that people had in their 'blood' or in their nature. This may partly have to do with the strong Austrian tradition of penal welfarism, which offers a relatively high level of psychological and psychotherapeutic support (many prisoners we interviewed in Austria had access to both group and individual psychotherapy, some over many years). Prisoners are expected to reflect on the social and emotional causes for their offending and change attitudes and coping-strategies not only to avoid re-offending, but to become a better person in a much wider sense. In the accounts of prisoners, socio-economic deprivation, parental and familial neglect, and other social factors were often portrayed as independent agents that triggered crime. Christoph, 40 years old and serving ten years in prison, for example, who had

---

4 Later on in the interview, Lucílio identified sex offenders as the group most urgently in need of such psychological support to stop them from re-offending. At the same time he recognised that the stigmatisation sex offenders by the other prisoners did not help the recovery of the former:

> Rapists get out of prison today and they are already thinking of raping again. They are set aside [from the others], because there is a code among prisoners which states that those people do not … other inmates don't mix with them, right? We discriminate against them as much as possible.

kidnapped a young woman to ask for ransom, said that unemployment had made him commit his crime:

> Fourteen days before my 31st birthday: until that shitty [day] I had never been unemployed. On the contrary, I had been an excellent worker, passionate [about my job] with body and soul. And then I did such shit. [Before that I had] not even had a row. Not a [single] criminal offence, or anything close to a criminal offence, and then I did this shit.

Christoph was very clear about the fact that no forensic technology, no matter how sophisticated, would have deterred him from kidnapping the woman, because he had simply not considered the consequences at the time.

'Forensic awareness' – in the sense that offenders think about the possible consequences of the crime before committing it – was mentioned also by Manuel, one of our informants in Portugal. Manuel was a paradigmatic example of the well-adjusted 'model inmate', and he was highly motivated to successfully re-integrate in society after leaving prison. Aged 27 at the time of the interview, he had been convicted to 14 years in prison for drug trafficking and murder, after – accidently, as he insisted – crashing against a car carrying eight passengers. Manuel had been driving under the influence of alcohol. At the time of the interview, he was studying for a degree in sign language interpretation and translation. He said that his aim was to one day be able to work with deaf people. Manuel was very explicit about the difference that he saw between 'professional' criminals – those who prepare in advance in order to avoid leaving traces at the crime scene – and those individuals who act on impulse:

> [If the crime was] premeditated, the person could be at the least prepared [not to leave traces]. If it's a crime of passion and if the person already has a criminal record and information in a database of the police – they can be identified very quickly and then there is no escape possible. Even if the person goes to the end of the world, they will ultimately be identified ...[5]

---

5 The latter part of Manuel's statement, namely that someone who leaves DNA traces could be tracked down even in the most remote parts of the world, if he or she had profiles and data in the database, was contradicted by Paul, 37, serving 15 years for aggravated robbery and armed theft. Paul, who also had a university degree in philosophy, mentioned that the ability of police investigators to utilise the knowledge held in the database hinged on the suspect being part of 'normal' society:

> DNA traces are only useful ... if the police knows that person X is at place Y. [That h]e works at place Z. [That t]his is his social security number, this is his workplace. Then they can arrest me. [If they don't know my whereabouts], they can't do anything other than putting 'wanted' pictures up with my photo. In hindsight, after the arrest, they can prove everything [on the basis of DNA]. But for the manhunt it's relatively unimportant. (cf. Prainsack and Kitzberger 2009: 71)

Manuel also mentioned that any potential deterrent effect of forensic DNA databases on convicts in prison would be counterbalanced by the effects of imprisonment itself:

> A criminal who is a criminal, the real bandit, when he commits a crime he knows well how to do it without [being caught] … if he already did time in prison [where people learn more criminal tactics], it will be very difficult to let himself get caught.

Amaro, another of our Portuguese informants, held similar views to Manuel's. Both distanced themselves from the world of crime and criminals: both Manuel and Amaro talked about themselves as people who ended up in prison due to a stroke of bad luck in life, although they should not really be there (which was a very common feature also in many of our conversations with prisoners in Austria). Like Manuel, Amaro did not believe that DNA databases would have a significant deterrent effect on offenders: when talking about the possibility of a forensic DNA database being capable of dissuading crime, he said that it depended on the type of criminal:

> If it is someone who is into drugs, when they get out of prison, they probably have friends on the outside and they will be back again [back to committing crimes]. I have seen people going out and after a year or two they are back [in prison]. [There are criminals] who don't think, they get the urge [of committing a crime] all of a sudden and they always leave some clues behind. But if it is someone who thinks things over, things will become more rigorous [more thorough].

In Amaro's opinion, the existence of a forensic DNA database would make criminals smarter and more aware of the risk of getting caught; therefore, they would take better precautions to decrease the risk of detection. This amounts to the opposite of a deterrence effect:

> Interviewer: Do you think the forensic DNA database will make people who get out of prison think twice before doing bad things again?
>
> Amaro: I think it will get worse [laughing]. If there are tighter measures put in place they are likely to become shrewder. They will be thinking to themselves: 'This is getting more dangerous.'

Amaro, 40 years old at the time of the interview, was described to us by the prison director as another model prisoner: a generally good person who once made a mistake. He was seen by all the guards as an honest and hard-working man, and he was allowed to leave prison every day to work as a gardener. Amaro had been a farmer, before, at age 20, he shot two neighbours who had stolen fireworks from him. One of his victims died, and the other lost his eye sight. Amaro was sentenced to 20 years in prison; a sentence he had almost fully served by the time of our interview. It was important for Amaro to point out to us that he 'knew nothing' about the criminal world or the criminals' ways of thinking; whatever he said about criminal lifestyles, he insisted, was only what he was 'imagining' about it.

Ernst, the 30-year-old serving three years for fraud, for example, said that the fact that his DNA profile was stored in a centralised database made him worry about the time after his release; not only because his DNA could be planted at crime scenes to incriminate him by his enemies, but also because he did not trust himself. Because he had always had problems controlling his anger, he could not exclude the possibility that he would become violent and then biological traces could incriminate him. The psychological support that he had received in prison, however, he said, helped him control his emotions better and could perhaps help him avoid getting in trouble again.

Sigi, 37, serving 18 months for battery, thought that recent advances in forensic technologies had changed the game significantly for offenders. He did not refer to DNA databases specifically when discussing the risks in a life of a criminal, but he blamed scientific and technological advance in general for having made the life of career criminals, such as himself, much harder. When he had committed crimes in the past – they included burglaries, thefts, and violent crimes – he said he had always thought about the risk to get caught beforehand. He thought that risk analysis skills should belong to the repertoire of everyone in his business:

> Everyone always thinks about [the possibility of leaving traces]. This is how it is. If you planned to commit a crime then you'd need to first make sure you can be certain not to leave any traces. Because of forensic medicine and forensic technology it has become difficult. Because they've advanced so far that nowadays a small piece of lint is sufficient. Everyone who's planning a job should think about this carefully.

Some prisoners mentioned that there were also groups of criminals who did not care about traces because they were driven not by a rational quest for profit-making but by irrational motives and needs they could not control. The most frequently mentioned example of the latter kind was the 'junkie', the drug-addict who would commit consecutive robberies just to get their hands on some money for drugs. Gaspar, 39, sentenced to five years and six months for burglary, theft and drug use, displayed a paradigmatic example of the mental framing of a drug-addict who, on a first glance, proved right the stereotype of the drug addict who is in and out of prison. At the time of the interview Gaspar was serving his fourth prison sentence. However he did not see himself as the typical substance abusing criminal who acted 'without thinking'. On the contrary, he explained in much detail how one could do a burglary without getting caught, and how to employ strategic planning skills to choose a the best *modus operandi* in any given burglary situation. In

Gaspar's view, the most important skill of a career criminal was to keep a cool head:

> Interviewer: Do you think it is easy to leave traces at the crime scene?
>
> Gaspar: It depends on whether the person is smart or not … whether they are skilled or not.
>
> Interviewer: Whoever commits a burglary will be more careful because there is a database and DNA technology?
>
> Gaspar: [Yes] people who keep a cool head – because there are others that do certain things … without thinking, let's say haphazardly. Now, for people who do the thinking it is only logical that they don't leave traces, right? They are equipped for that. With ski masks and scarves, for example. Certain things … saliva, for example … and also [one has to take care that] hair will be attached to headgear, and that there are plastics to prevent hair from sticking.

Gaspar self-identified as a career criminal and said that forensic DNA databases were beneficial for 'those who are on the other side', adding that individuals who had already been in prison were not going to stop committing crimes, because they had nothing left to lose:

> Interviewer: What do you think about the existence of a forensic DNA database?
>
> Gaspar: [It is a good thing] for society. Because it is more [beneficial] for the other side [the side of the authorities] … [But] people who have been in prison – like myself – have nothing to fear. In my particular case there is no benefit [in the existence of a DNA database] .

A small group of inmates even argued that the existence of centralised forensic DNA databases could give rise to serious crimes as a strategy to clear traces from crime scenes. Feliciano, 34, serving a 12-year sentence for murder, mentioned the following scenario:

> Imagine a robbery that ends up with someone dead, and the killer pours gasoline on the [crime] scene and sets it on fire. There are so many traces that he becomes afraid … and in order not to leave any evidence [he sets the crime scene on fire]…

Also Ingo, 43, serving a life sentence for murder and robbery, said that out of fear that his victim could be identified on the basis of hair, fingerprints, or DNA, he and his accomplices had cut off and burned the victim's hands and head after they had killed him.

Before talking about criminals setting crime scenes on fire out of fear of leaving traces, Feliciano had mentioned that the existence of forensic DNA databases was 'an advantage for criminal investigation and for future crime fighting … it will accelerate investigation … even on an international level it's a great thing that it enables sharing of information about criminals'. However, as the interview progressed, he started to change the course of his reasoning and began talking about the 'new risks' that might appear with the increasing expansion of DNA databases for criminal investigation purposes. On the one hand, he highlighted the possibility of privacy violations and the errors that might occur: 'A factor that must always be considered is privacy … [DNA databases] undoubtedly mess with privacy a bit. I hope that if there are any sorts of glitches in that system – which I regard as infallible – they are adequately solved.'

These problems were exacerbated, Feliciano thought, by social inequalities which were reflected and reproduced by the criminal justice system. At the same time, Feliciano believed that there were criminal geniuses who would always eventually outsmart the police:

> The criminal always tries to overcome, or at least to stay ahead of new measures to fight crime … Justice is evolving – and this [DNA profiling and databasing] is a system that brings a rather interesting development – but usually the criminal mind also evolves and it is always thinking: 'They now have a way [DNA technology] of fixing [the crime problem], so how can I manage it [so not to get caught]?'

While the same notion was echoed by a small number of Austrian prisoners as well, Portuguese prisoner Henrique, 37, convicted to three years for burglary and forgery, believed that the criminals' problem was that no matter how careful they were about avoiding traces at crime scenes, they could always be 'framed' by the police. He considered that even criminals who acted truly professionally could get caught by the police on the basis of biological evidence – a hair, or a fingerprint. He referred to his own case as an example for this problem:

> I've been doing [crime] for 20 years, always getting away with it … I have always worn gloves when I was stealing, I had short hair and never took off the balaclavas in a car … but when the police really wants to nail someone, whether it is through fingerprints or DNA, if they really want to screw someone, they will. A lie from them it is worth more than 100 of our truths … I never got caught, you see? I used to sell drugs, I used drugs, I was even a drug-courier … but I was never caught.

Henrique's story was somewhat confusing as to how exactly he ultimately got caught (we did not have access to his case files). He said that the authorities knew that he was an active criminal (he said he had been under surveillance and was subjected to biological sample collection around 2002) but they were never able to link a crime to him. They waited until he was out of the country, filed criminal proceedings, and convicted him in his absence. When Henrique returned, he said, there was nothing he could do because the cases could not be re-opened. Henrique concluded that the existence of a database had no effect whatsoever on crime deterrence, because in his opinion criminals will just learn to be more careful to avoid being caught by the police. He even admitted that after his release, hanging out with his former friends could tempt him to return to the world of crime. The only way to prevent this would be to leave the country:

> Interviewer: With a DNA database, will people start thinking things through before committing a crime?
>
> Henrique: No! They will commit crimes anyway. They will just be more careful … We just have to figure out a way to get out of here [from prison]. And the way I found is to behave – good behaviour, to do work – everything they gave me I took it, to see if I get out earlier. But now, I don't know how it's going to be like on the outside. [What I am going to do after I leave prison] I will not tell my own father, or my mother, or my family. I don't know what I'm going to do, I don't know what tomorrow brings. If I don't [emigrate] I might be back to the same way of life [committing crimes] if I meet my old companions again …

Most prisoners we interviewed did not believe that forensic DNA databases would reduce crime, or have a significant deterrent effect. At the same time, a considerable number of inmates claimed that additional intensive and extensive uses of forensic DNA databases were desirable because more 'scientific tools' might be more protective of their own individual rights, possibly increasing potential for exoneration or at least protecting them from illegal and incriminatory police actions such as planting biological evidence in crime scenes, forcing confessions or using snitches (see also Chapter 7 and 8). Prainsack and Toom (2010) used the term 'situated dis/empowerment' to highlight the simultaneity of both empowering and oppressive effects of surveillance: '[T]he notion of situated dis/empowerment helps us to see the ways in which empowering and disempowering effects of surveillance are always intertwined and often mutually constitutive' (Prainsack and Toom 2010: 1118). The same could be said about the way in which prisoners spoke about forensic DNA databases.

Nonetheless, DNA databases were not only portrayed by prisoners as both oppressive and stigmatising, making their lives more difficult, and at the same time potentially liberating and helping to keep miscarriages of justice at bay, but conversations about them were also linked to prisoners' identities and subjectivities, perhaps in an unexpected manner. As discussed in our earlier chapters, Beauregard and Bouchard (2010) drew attention to certain detection avoidance strategies as part of 'forensic awareness' that offenders might develop in the presence of the increasing use of forensic science and technologies by law enforcement. Data from our interviews seems to highlight the existence of such a 'forensic awareness' among prisoners; discussions revolving around such a forensic awareness were often couched in a discourse on 'professionalism'. The way prisoners spoke about their own knowledge, or lack of knowledge, about forensic technologies was linked to professional identities, self-worth, and power. The stance of not wanting to, or not needing to, know much about how to decrease the risk of detection served some prisoners to distinguish themselves from career criminals. Statements that focused on how criminal investigators used and (ab-) used forensic science and technologies sounded like in a tug of war between two competing professional groups, where one (law enforcement) was better resourced, but not necessarily always better trained, than the other (the criminals). Prisoners who talked passionately about forensic science and how impressive it was (see Chapter 5) demonstrated an almost 'pure' and non-instrumental fascination with science; this is intrinsically linked to power differentials as most prisoners came from households which did not (or could not) send children to university. In all instances, the way in which prisoners spoke about forensic technologies and about avoiding the risk of detection, reflected how they saw themselves professionally, in society, and in relation to their fellow inmates. It is in this sense that forensic DNA technologies are linked to the self-management of prisoners (Ericson and Haggerty 1997: 53, see also Chapter 8).

Who Should be on the Database?

Among the Portuguese prisoners were many who supported the idea of including DNA profiles of wider groups of people in the national forensic DNA database. Some even supported the idea of creating a universal database comprising profiles from the entire population as a mean of improving the efficiency of criminal investigation. This idea of a universal database is similar to the initial plan outlined by the Portuguese government (in 2005) to create a database containing the profiles of the whole population, as described in Chapter 3. However, it should be noted that none of the Portuguese prisoners mentioned that they knew that the government had intended to create a universal forensic DNA database. Austrian prisoners, although many of them generally thought that forensic DNA databases did a great job in helping 'society' to 'catch the truly bad guys' and thus they saw it overall as 'a good thing' (see also Prainsack and Kitzberger 2009), they did not support the idea of a universal database, or of including wider groups (such as suspects) in the database. Only one prisoner, Karl, 50, serving 17 years for murder and attempted murder, found the idea of a universal DNA database initially appealing; when later in the interview he considered possibilities for police to abuse such a national database he changed his mind (see Prainsack 2010b: 168). Thus, what most prisoners favoured in terms of how comprehensively a national DNA database should be set up and who should be included bore striking resemblance to the *status quo* in the respective countries.

Lucílio, as we discussed earlier, was not optimistic at all regarding the utility of forensic DNA databases for deterring criminal offenders, as he thought that crime was part of 'human nature': in Lucílio's words, 'I think [forensic DNA databasing should be] for everyone. Not just criminals … All of us, right? Deep inside we are all criminals.' Yet he also thought that it would help criminal investigation if the criteria for profile inclusion in the database were to be expanded. He added that criminals were well aware of DNA technologies' potential. Everyone knew, he said, that '[DNA is used to prove] things related to crimes, through hairs, pieces of skin, blood, saliva, teeth … fingernails … Everybody is aware of that, but no one is worried about it.' Because criminal leanings were something that people had in their nature, the only way to stop criminal offenders would be to catch them and lock them up. A universal database would be a strong instrument to make this happen:

> Lucílio: I think that it should be applied to everyone. Not just criminals because… We are all criminals on the inside … The whole population [should be included]. Such as myself, my children, my wife.
>
> Interviewer: Everybody?
>
> Lucílio: Everybody, because there is always a bug inside, right? And we never know what we're going to do tomorrow.

Tomás, 28 years old, was convicted of rape and murder. Traces of blood were found on the victim's body, which served as evidence to support the 21-year sentence he was given. Tomás' opinion was very close to the intentions expressed by members of the government to the Portuguese press in 2006 and 2007 when mentioning the possibility of constructing a universal DNA database with blood proceeding from medical tests that are mandatory to be made to every newborn in Portugal:

> We already have a database that contains everyone's DNA from birth. Don't we have that test …[*referring to the Guthrie test*]? The first time blood samples are taken you already have identification and that means you have a register. Portugal should have a nationwide DNA database, because it would be a very efficient weapon against crime.

Tomás discussed the ethical questions raised by the creation of a forensic DNA database that covered the entire population, but concluded that the benefits outweighed the risks of repression and the threat to individual rights: 'I know that a universal database would create a big ethical problem in terms of violating freedoms … but really I think it should be extended – I'm being a bit radical here – to all individuals. It should cover the whole population.'

The fact that none of the Austrian prisoners spoke out in favour of a universal DNA database could be connected to the phenomenon that none of them thought that crime was in people's nature, or that some people had it in their blood. Austrian prisoners were social essentialists in the sense that they held social circumstances, relations, and experiences as exclusively responsible for making somebody a criminal.

Yet we found no difference between Austrian and Portuguese prisoners regarding their assessment that a more systematic and wider use of DNA technology – regardless of whether they assessed it as overall positive or overall negative – could increase the social inequalities inherent criminal justice systems. In spite of many of our interviewees expressing fears of the possible abuse of genetic information in the hands of authorities (see Chapter 8) there was a recurrent notion that the best way to put an end to the different treatment of convicts and law-abiding citizens (particularly the privileged social groups) would be to develop databases with a tendency to include the whole population.

Manuel, the well-adjusted prisoner we encountered earlier in this chapter, was of the opinion that 'those who have power have possibilities, they can escape justice and commit any crimes they want', as he stated that: 'The ones who have power, who have close connections with the government, will they have their DNA profile in the forensic database if they commit a crime? ... There shouldn't be any exceptions.'

Although also for Austrian prisoners, the issue of power differentials and stigmatisation of criminals was a very important one, they did not use it as a basis for arguing for database expansion. This was despite the fact that convict-based forensic DNA databases discriminate between convicted and unconvicted people, as they render it very likely that convicts will be detected in case they re-offend while those who were cleared of charges face a much smaller 'risk' of detection on the basis of biological traces. In addition, certain ethnic groups are notoriously over-represented in police databases (see, for example, Cole 2001, Duster 2006, 2008, Nuffield Council on Bioethics 2007, Williams and Johnson 2008). Thus, several commentators have referred to the possibility that expanding the inclusion criteria for DNA databases may help mitigate the databases' discriminatory potential (Connor 2003, Haddow 2008, Kaye and Smith 2004). These comments have fuelled the debate on the need to reconfigure the issue of the threat to individual rights potentially generated by the expansion of the inclusion criteria, and therefore it appears necessary to continue discussing the matter, whilst ensuring that the debate is, as far as possible, open and accessible to all (Machado et al. 2011, Prainsack 2010a) and by including prisoners and other convicts as stakeholders in the debate about the threats and benefits of the uses of forensic DNA technologies (Prainsack and Kitzberger 2009).

Some prisoners have shown support for expanding uses of DNA databasing because they hoped this would lead to more rigorous criminal investigations and thus prevent the authorities from accusing the innocent. In addition, many of our interviewees also felt that more measures should be undertaken to help lower recidivism rates. Such measures would include the improvement of society's capacity to give job opportunities to ex-convicts; at present, prisoners' expectations of social reintegration are instead associated with issues relating to employment and the kind of social networks they will find on the outside. In the opinion of these interviewees, social reintegration was also made at least 'very difficult' by the prevailing social stigma that convicts suffered from (see also Chapter 8).

Conclusion

The special powers attributed to DNA in linking criminals to a crime scene tend to support some public sentiment that the expansion of DNA databases – both in terms of inclusivity and in terms of the scope of purposes that it can be used for – would almost automatically increase crime deterrence. The narratives of our interviewees in prison do not corroborate the argument that a more expansive and systematic use of DNA technology will have a significant deterrent effect. Most prisoners believed that crime would never cease to exist, either because (some) people had crime in their 'nature', or because people were pushed into criminal lives by difficult social and familial circumstances. Both situations could be remedied easily, and certainly not by expanding police databases.

Although they conceded that DNA technologies were seen as very useful in the identification of the criminal offenders (see also Chapter 5), most of our interviewees said that it was not enough for the police to be able to catch the real 'pros' among the criminals – those who are very intelligent and meticulous when it comes to planning a crime, and careful not to leave traces of their presence in crime scenes. Such stances were embedded in a process of a social categorisation of criminals, by which a hierarchy between 'professional' criminals and 'lower class criminals' was established, measured according to how well someone avoided getting caught. There was a tension between the way in which the 'pros' among the criminals were portrayed by our informants, who described them as being smart enough, and the actual situation of our informants who, of course, were all caught eventually. Thus, did this imply that none our informants did not consider themselves 'real pros'? This tension was solved by either highlighting instances in the prisoners' past where they had committed crimes for which they never got caught, or by blaming circumstances beyond their control that had led to their detection, so that their own getting caught appeared as something out of the ordinary, a 'mistake', really. Those prisoners who self-identified as professional criminals (rather than merely career criminals) attributed their detection to an accident or a conspiracy against them, and not resulting from a mistake that they should be held accountable for.

Some inmates who self-identified as criminals mentioned that their time in prison had helped them to perfect their criminal techniques which they would employ when they got out. Prison was portrayed as a kind of 'academy' for criminals by these informants. Others emphasised that they were basically good and law-abiding people, and they had ended up in prison only due to a stroke of bad luck. This latter kind of prisoners typically went out of their way to emphasise that they had no forensic awareness at all, because for them it would not be of any use. Interestingly, even people in this second group distinguished between the criminal 'pros' who do not get caught, and the 'losers' who were either not smart enough to avoid detection, or who were too 'wasted' to care. DNA databases were seen by virtually all prisoners to mean a greater probability of detection, identification and conviction for the 'losers', who either lacked the experience, or the 'selective gaze' of criminal pros. Even for the 'professionals' among criminals, DNA databases were portrayed as making life more difficult; they were seen as a factor that they needed to consider as part of their risk management in the course of planning and executing a job.

In sum, it is yet to be proven that DNA databases for forensic and police purposes have the effect of preventing and deterring potential offenders from crime (Nuffield Council on Bioethics 2007). Very little published research explores the use of forensic identification evidence and its impacts on the various stages of the criminal justice process (Peterson et al. 2010). An exception might be the study concerning the effects of DNA evidence on the outcomes of homicides cases conducted by Briody (2004b). Briody concluded that cases where DNA was involved were much more likely to reach the court than those without DNA evidence, and that incriminating DNA evidence had a more positive effect on court's decision to convict that on securing guilty pleas from defendants. Whether this situation is an illustration of the *CSI* effect (see Chapter 6) remains an open question.

Nevertheless, although DNA typing represents an important tool in the identification of the perpetrator, as well as an outstanding potential for exonerations (Chapter 7), it is highly unlikely that DNA profiling and databasing will become the cure for the ailments of criminal investigation and adjudication; neither is it likely to become the miraculous tool that will deter people from offending.

The authoritative certainty associated with science is clearly in need to be reviewed, and more detailed independent research on the contribution of bioinformation to crime prevention and crime solving is required (National Research Council 2009, Nuffield Council on Bioethics 2007). As Ulrich Beck (1992) famously argued, in risk societies, science and technology are not the ultimate solution for providing security but they also give rise to new risks. The creation and organisation of forensic DNA databases involves potential threats to a range of individual rights, such as the right to privacy, the right to liberty, the right to moral and physical integrity, the dignity of individuals and the presumption of innocence. The storage of individuals' DNA profiles in a database enables a greater surveillance focus on potential offenders and re-offenders within societies that are less tolerant towards suspect or 'risky citizens'. This notion is often reproduced and supported by public discourses and sentiments (Ericson and Shearing 1986, Hindmarsh 2010). Other new risks associated with the recent growth of DNA profiling and databasing for forensic purposes are the possible increase of deficient criminal investigations because of insufficiently 'forensically aware' police officers, for reasons due to the non-submittal of all materials retrieved from a crime scene, or its poor quality (Saulsbury et al. 1994, Taylor and Hirst 1995), and the tactical use of DNA evidence to 'facilitate' confessions, and the misuse and misinterpretation of forensic evidence as a cause for miscarriages of justice (see also Chapters 7 and 8).

There is yet another set of risks that were pointed out by the inmates: the risk of stigma and the intolerance of society aimed at those who have been in prison. As suggested by many commentators, extralegal variables, such as the victim and the suspect or offender's personal characteristics (ethnic group, age, gender, or economic class), carry significant weight police and court decisions, such as whether or not to make an arrest (Bynum et al. 1982, Gottfredson and Gottfredson 1988). This arguably deepens inequalities in the justice system even further.

A small cautionary note may be due at the end: while it can be argued that the views of prisoners, because of their first-hand knowledge about the criminal justice system, represent a unique perspective on criminal investigation which should be heard in discussions about forensic technologies and surveillance, these views do not automatically apply to all other 'criminals'. Ethnographic studies in Portuguese prisons (Cunha 2002, 2008) have shown that prisoners are as ready to reproduce stereotypical assumptions about criminal populations as any other group. This should be kept in mind when we put the data presented in this chapter in context: prisoners' statements about the behaviour and 'character' of other prisoners does not always derive from in-depth knowledge of these individuals but often also reiterates common stereotypes. Yet this does not mean that for this reason, prisoners' statements about other 'criminals' should be dismissed as biased and informed by dubious motivations; it is impossible to separate the ways in which prisoners speak about others from how they see themselves. The production of the 'I', the 'we' and the 'other' is closely interlinked (Goffman 1986). Looking at our interviewees' perspectives on others and their motivations and plans also allows us to trace what roles forensic technologies play in binding different groups of people together in different contexts: 'good citizens' vs. 'the criminals' in some contexts, 'convicts' vs. 'the criminal justice system' in other contexts, and the stigmatised against those who stigmatise them in almost every respect imaginable.

Chapter 7
Technologies of Innocence: Exoneration and Exculpation

Introduction

In the last two decades, fingerprints and DNA evidence have increasingly been put to use within the criminal justice system not only to convict but also to exculpate and exonerate people. The term exculpation can refer to the presentation of exculpatory evidence at court; but it can also refer to a process that typically takes place during the early stages of criminal investigation, namely when a particular individual is excluded from a group of suspects. Exoneration, in contrast, entails a reassessment of the guilt of an individual who has already been convicted, and is used in numerous criminal appeals, some of which have involved prisoners awaiting execution for capital crimes (Marshall 2004, Scheck 2001, Scheck, Neufeld and Dwyer 2000). Thus, in a nutshell, exculpation typically takes place before or during the trial, while exoneration takes place after the trial.

DNA evidence in particular has played a crucial role in the revision of sentences and the exoneration of convicted individuals. This is because recent DNA technologies have opened up possibilities for obtaining meaningful evidence from materials (e.g., blood-stained clothing) that could not be fruitfully analysed several decades ago. The work of the so-called Innocence Project, a US based litigation and public policy organisation founded in 1992, took a leading role in 'exonerating wrongfully convicted individuals through DNA testing and reforming the criminal justice system to prevent future injustice' (Innocence Project n.d.). The Innocence Project has become an example of how forensic technologies can be used to tackle and sometimes rectify miscarriages of justice, and it has spurred many similar initiatives in other countries.

This chapter opens with a description of the different stages of criminal investigation as well as criminal procedures at court, in order to provide an overview of the circumstances in which individuals involved in criminal proceedings are exculpated and exonerated. Although criminal justice procedures vary from country to country, in most jurisdictions they involve the same core stages of investigation, the pressing of criminal charges, prosecution, and trial. In the second section of this chapter, we will discuss the role of high-tech evidence in the work of the Innocence Project, where post-conviction DNA testing has been used in numerous appeals to overturn wrongful verdicts. The main mission of the Innocence Project (and similar projects) is however not only to exonerate the wrongfully convicted but also to reveal the causes of wrongful convictions and recommend measures and reforms to prevent further instances of injustice.

After an overview of the Innocence Project and a discussion of the most common reasons leading to wrongful convictions in the only country where such data has so far been made collected systematically, the US, we will analyse prisoners' views on the incriminatory as well as exculpatory potential of DNA profiling. In addition, we will look into their assessments of the factors that may contribute towards wrongful conviction.

Exculpation and Exoneration in the Criminal Justice System

The first stage of criminal investigation is usually the initial discovery by the police, or notification by the victim or a witness, that a crime has occurred. The police then go to the crime scene or the location of the victim and arrest the suspect (if known and apprehensible), locate and interview witnesses, and collect and preserve other evidence.

The inquiry phase begins after the discovery or the reporting of a crime and follows the criminal law procedure of the country in question. The inquiry entails a series of investigative measures that aim to examine the crime scene, identify the perpetrators, and find and gather evidence in order to decide on the charge. In this phase, law enforcement officers can interrogate witnesses and question potential suspects. The authorities can make (or order) an arrest if there is a good cause to believe that a crime was committed and that a specific person committed it. Usually there is a relatively short period of time following an arrest in which law enforcement officers must either charge the person with a crime or release them. Law enforcement officers may decide to file criminal charges, either before or after arresting a suspect. Including and excluding individuals from the group of suspects is woven into these activities.

Thus, exculpation is an inherent part of the usual procedures of the first stage of criminal investigation, when different leads are assessed and weighed up and suspicions concerning particular people are established or dismissed. Exculpation is therefore not a clearly bounded activity. In fact, although these very activities and processes (witness interrogation, analysis of potential evidence, etc.) play a prominent role in popular television shows such as *CSI*, *Medical Detectives*, etc.,[1] the term exculpation does not appear regularly in crime shows.

1 Another meaning of exculpation, which literally signifies a process of clearing somebody of guilt or blame, pertains to the successful defence of a suspect (or defendant, as this process can take place in court) on the basis that the person is not culpable. Reasons for lack of culpability could be that the suspect or defendant is a minor, or because they lost their intellectual capacities when allegedly committing the crime (possibly due to drug use, psychosis, etc.). However as this variant of exculpation does not usually involve the use of forensic technologies, it is not discussed in this chapter.

Not all criminal investigations result in a criminal charge, either because it is decided that no crime has been committed or because there is no legal possibility of initiating criminal proceedings against an individual suspected of committing the crime. The authority investigating the crime may decide to simply archive the material gathered in the process of the investigation if the evidence suggests that no crime was committed, or that a particular individual – the suspect – effectively did not commit the crime, or because it is not legally possible to continue the criminal investigation in order to bring forward a formal accusation. Examples for the last scenario are cases where the victim withdraws their complaint, where the legally established period in which a charge must be made has expired, or where it is concluded that there is no indication of evidence that can be used to support a charge, i.e., insufficient evidence to verify the existence of a crime or the identity of its perpetrators. Evidence to support a charge is considered sufficient when it results in a reasonable possibility that it would lead to the accused receiving a sentence or detention order following a trial.

Exoneration, in contrast, entails a reassessment of the guilt of an individual who has already been convicted. In most countries there is no limit on the time when a case can be re-opened with the aim of exoneration; it always takes place after the judgment has become effective (that is, when no further appeals are possible), and in cases where a prison sentence has been imposed it often takes place while the convicted person is still in prison. Cases can also be re-opened after the convicted person has been released, and even after they have died (e.g., to claim compensation, clear their name, etc.).

Although there are great variations with regard to particular details, most jurisdictions allow cases to be re-opened when 'new evidence' has come to the attention of either the prosecution or the defence. For example, when a central witness whose testimony had played a significant role in the conviction retracts her or his statement, the defence can apply for a re-opening. In addition, if new material evidence turns up – such as the wreck of a victim's car found at the bottom of a lake many years later containing evidence that could change a guilty verdict – the defence stands a very good chance of being allowed to re-open the case. Although in most jurisdictions the prosecution as well as the defence can apply to re-open a case, the term exoneration applies only when this is pursued by the defence and leads to the acquittal of the individual previously convicted.

Both in Austria and in Portugal, re-openings can be initiated by both the prosecution and the defence when facts or evidence emerge which are 'objectively new' (*nova producta*). This means that if a particular piece of evidence was not included in the original trial because the prosecution or defence thought it was not relevant enough, this cannot be the grounds for re-opening the case if the party simply changes their mind (for example, if they later realise that they had misjudged its relevance). There are, however, sufficient grounds for re-opening a case if new facts emerge that render it plausible that the same neglected piece of evidence could provide an important lead or even proof relevant to the case. For example, if a DNA profile obtained from a cigarette butt found near the crime scene had not been included in the original trial because it was assumed to be irrelevant and the convicted person or their lawyer simply realise that they should have presented this evidence 'just in case', this would not be sufficient for a re-opening. If, however, a new witness turned up who plausibly testified that he or she had seen a person smoking in the exact place where the cigarette butt had been found, and who could very likely have been the perpetrator (e.g., because the new witness knew that the person he or she had seen had had a secret affair with the victim, which had not been known during the trial), this may be sufficient grounds for re-opening the case. The availability of new technologies or techniques to analyse evidence is an acceptable reason for re-opening. If a semen stain on the underwear of a rape victim could not exculpate a suspect three decades ago (because adequate technologies for DNA analysis were not available), it could now exonerate a wrongfully convicted person if sufficient DNA was available to carry out a DNA test.

According to Austrian law, *nova producta* – which justify the re-opening of a case – are facts or pieces of evidence which were *unknown* or *inaccessible* to the party requesting the re-opening, unless they were unknown due to their own negligence. Thirty-six per cent of all applications to re-open cases in Austria were granted in the 2009–2010 period (i.e. 1,914 out of 5,328, courtesy of the Federal Austrian Ministry of Justice).

According to Portuguese law, cases can be re-opened if new facts or evidence are discovered which, in themselves or combined with evidence previously considered during the trial, 'raise serious doubts about the justice of the conviction' (Article 449.1.d of the Portuguese Code of Criminal Procedure 2007) and the review of the sentence must be authorised by the Supreme Court of Justice.

Representatives of investigation authorities in Portugal who we interviewed for the purpose of writing this chapter said that it was 'relatively common' [sic] to re-open criminal cases that were closed during the inquiry phase before being brought to trial (although there are no official data regarding the number of re-openings). In Austria, re-openings of pre-trial hearings have represented only 17 per cent of all case re-openings between 2001 and 2010 – courtesy of the Austrian Federal Ministry of Justice. Also in accordance with information provided by legal authorities in Portugal, the re-opening of criminal investigation not resulting in a criminal charge is, in their own words, quite a frequent occurrence in this country. The fact that Portuguese law stipulates a period of only ten days after the opening of the inquiry phase in which a charge can be brought against a suspect may help to explain the reason why the filing of criminal investigations is very common in Portugal. Regarding criminal trials, requests have been made to re-open cases on the grounds of new witness evidence (either because a new witness becomes available, or because a witness who testified at the original trial comes forward with new information which is relevant to the case). So far, however, no original verdicts have been overturned in Portugal, and no criminal investigations or trials have been re-opened because of new DNA evidence.

According to one of our informants, an experienced person within the criminal justice system who coordinated criminal investigations in Portugal, 'we are still in the stone age in terms of using DNA and it will be a while before we get cases re-opened or reviewed on the basis of this type of evidence'. This informant also stated that cases of miscarriages of justice were rarely discovered in the Portuguese penal system, in contrast with the situation in other countries. This was not the case because the Portuguese justice system was less prone to errors than other justice systems, but because – by his own admission – there was a corporate mentality that prevented the system from recognising its errors. In the words of this interviewee:

> I believe that this corporate mentality is not conducive to reviews [and the re-opening of criminal cases] and may be one of the obstacles preventing this from happening more frequently. In addition, in countries where reviews are more common, this is not unconnected with the existence of a strong public voice and pressure groups to support those proclaiming their innocence. We should also take into account the fact that neither the police nor the Public Prosecution [in Portugal] has a 'review' culture offering the possibility of reassessing investigations and consequently convictions.

The possibility that DNA techniques may help to correct (or compensate for) errors in the criminal justice system and serve as the basis not only for a more stringent identification and charging of the perpetrators of crimes but also for proving the innocence of individuals who have been wrongfully convicted, has gained a high level of public prominence through the Innocence Project.

The Innocence Project(s)

The Innocence Project was founded in the US in 1992 and provides *pro bono* legal representation for individuals seeking to prove their innocence after conviction (for a discussion of prominent cases that the Innocence Project has taken on, see Krimsky and Simoncelli 2011). For many years only cases in which DNA testing could be used for exonerations were accepted under the remit of the Innocence Project. More recently, however, the Innocence Project has agreed to represent clients in cases where attempts to exonerate were based on another method or technology. As representatives of the Innocence Project state, this underscores the fact that due to the frequent absence of suitable evidence, DNA testing is only possible in 5 to 10 per cent of all criminal cases (Innocence Project 2009a), and thus 'DNA testing alone cannot overturn most wrongful convictions' (Innocence Project n.d.). In fact, as shown by an analysis of the causes of the wrongful convictions of the first 239 individuals the project has helped exonerate in the US, eyewitness misidentification played a role in over three quarters of the convictions overturned through DNA testing; in half of all convictions overturned through DNA testing, eyewitness misidentification had been the main reason for the conviction (Doyle 2005, Innocence Project n.d., see 'Eyewitness Identification'). The criminologist Richard Leo states that eyewitness misidentification 'appears to be the leading cause of wrongful conviction' (Leo 2005: 208). This is hardly surprising, as much psychological, social science, and – to a lesser extent, criminological – research has shown that human recollection is far from reliable, and prone to be influenced by knowledge of the particularities of a case acquired later (e.g., Neuschatz et al. 2007, Wells and Olson 2003). For example, it has been found that some eyewitnesses' recollections of the physical features of a perpetrator change when they learn about the physical features of the actual suspect(s) (Wells and Quinlivan 2009). In 15 per cent of the exoneration cases analysed by the Innocence Project (n.d., see 'Informants/Snitches'), the informants gave false evidence. In addition to genuine errors, the reasons for false evidence included bribes – financial or otherwise, e.g., early release from prison – and attempts to divert attention away from the possibility of their own involvement in the crime (see also Center on Wrongful Convictions 2005).

The problematic use of forensic science was another frequent cause of wrongful convictions. Over 50 per cent of the first 225 wrongful convictions overturned by means of DNA testing involved 'unvalidated or improper forensic science'. Instances ranged from the application of unestablished scientific findings or technologies – such as the visual comparison of bite marks, or simply looking at two hairs and testifying that they looked 'similar' – to outright negligence or misconduct (Garrett and Neufeld 2009, Innocence Project 2009b). Especially noteworthy in connection with improper DNA analysis was the case of Josiah Sutton in Texas, who was wrongfully convicted of raping a woman in the back seat of her car in 1998. Although the DNA test excluded Mr Sutton as a suspect, this was not mentioned in any of the reports. Even worse, the DNA expert witness at Mr Sutton's trial claimed that the 'DNA type of J. Sutton can be expected to occur in 1 out of 694,00[0] people among the black population' (Thompson 2003: 7, cited in Garrett and Neufeld 2009: 65), and that if 'it came from one person, it should have a same exact DNA pattern. No other two persons will have [the] same DNA except in the case of identical twins' (Thompson 2003: 176, cited in Garrett and Neufeld 2009: 65–6). Thus, as Garrett and Neufeld (2009: 66) conclude, the 'jury was left with the mistaken impression that the DNA evidence uniquely identified Sutton as the rapist'.

False confessions seem to be yet another basis for wrongful convictions. Approximately one quarter of all DNA exoneration cases analysed by the Innocence Project involved incriminating statements, confessions, or guilty pleas by suspects or defendants. Whilst in some instances false confessions could be explained by the mental state of the suspect or defendant, they could also have been made due to duress, coercion, fear of violence, the actual inflicting of harm, misunderstandings, or threats (Innocence Project n.d., see 'False Confessions').

DNA evidence seems to be particularly popular in triggering confessions; Williams and Johnson (2005: 11) address the issue of the police using DNA evidence to 'coerce or deceive' individuals. In addition, the report by the Nuffield Council on Bioethics on *The Forensic Use of Bioinformation: Ethical Issues* (2007) discusses the strategic use of DNA to obtain guilty pleas from suspects.

All these factors contribute to the problem of wrongful convictions, which seems to be a problem whose true dimensions we have only started to see.

The Prisoners' Views

One in three of the prisoners we interviewed explicitly mentioned the capacity of DNA technologies in particular to help prove their innocence. In this sense, some forensic technologies can be seen as 'allies' of suspects, which probably also explains that DNA technologies, and even DNA databases, were seen by many prisoners as 'a good thing' (see Chapter 6, also Prainsack and Kitzberger 2009). The fact that all the prisoners referred to the exculpating and exonerating potential of forensic technologies only in relation to DNA is interesting as, in theory, all kinds of evidence (for instance, fingerprints and witness testimonies) could be their allies in indicating or proving their innocence. DNA technology assumed this role more than other forensic sciences or practices arguably because it was generally seen as the least fallible. Even state authorities – and, first and foremost, the police – were seen as having to submit to the authority of the evidence that they have helped to produce.

Valter was a 25-year-old drug addict who had been sent to a centre for juvenile offenders at the age of ten. He came from a family described 'dysfunctional' by social workers. His story was an example of the power attributed to DNA evidence in identifying the true perpetrators of crimes and how agency is effectively attributed to the technology itself, not to those who use it. When Valter talked to us, he was serving a sentence of 18 years for a number of crimes – kidnapping, rape, theft, aggravated burglary, possession of an illegal weapon and forgery. He believed that DNA evidence could prove innocence, since this was what had happened in his case. He told us how, when he had been taken into custody by the police, a saliva sample had been collected from him for DNA analysis, which later 'proved' that he had not had sex with a female rape victim:

> Valter: There was one case with a car that had been used for an alleged sex crime and I was to be included in the crime. The police took saliva to do a blood test for DNA [*sic*], to find out if I'd taken part in the sex crime. It came out negative, it said that I hadn't [raped her], I'd been there, but I hadn't taken part directly… in that. And it was the DNA that cleared me, wasn't it? I got done as an accessory, right? But it cleared me completely.
>
> Interviewer: Of committing [rape]?

> Valter: Exactly … the DNA mattered because I hadn't [had sex] and [the police] didn't believe it… not even when the victim said I was there but I hadn't [done anything]. They said [she had been raped] by a gang. They did tests on me and the others. There were three of us and one was convicted and I got charged as an accessory, for being there and not trying to stop it.

Also the case of Joaquim very clearly indicated the power attributed to DNA as a 'truth machine', but for the opposite reasons than those we saw in Valter's story. Joaquim was 49 years old when we interviewed him, and was serving a six-year sentence for raping his youngest daughter who was 16 at the time of the crime. The daughter became pregnant, allegedly as a result of this incestuous attack. Throughout the interview Joaquim insisted that he was innocent and had never even thought of sexually abusing his daughter. He believed that in order to prove his innocence he should have been given the opportunity to do a DNA test, but did not receive one. In his opinion, the judge had erred in only paying attention to witness evidence against him and the fact that he had undergone a forensic psychology examination which revealed that he had a 'predisposition' to sexual abuse:

> Joaquim: I was hoping they would do tests on [the baby born to] my daughter but [instead] they gave her an abortion … The only thing they did to me was call me in [to a psychiatric hospital] and a psychologist analysed my… deficiency or something… the psychologist who spoke to me sent a report to the court – my lawyer told me about it afterwards – saying I had a tendency to do this. And then I was convicted of this crime. It's wrong because as soon as she was pregnant they [should] have examined her, shouldn't they?
>
> Interviewer: To find out who the father of the baby was?
>
> Joaquim: Yes, to find out who the father was … because my lawyer had witnesses saying that she had lots of boyfriends… But the boyfriends were all saying that it was just cuddles and kisses… Why did [the judge] convict me when I hadn't done a single thing? … I was expecting them to give me some kind of blood test, or analyse some little trace of something … I was hoping and I'm still hoping!

Several prisoners – both in Portugal and in Austria – mentioned that they thought DNA analysis was a particularly robust way of criminal identification, because they knew of many cases in the US in which wrongly convicted individuals had been exonerated after several years in prison. Feliciano, a 34-year-old man serving a 12-year prison sentence for murder, referred to how DNA technologies could be useful in proving innocence and, in his words, fighting the 'corruption' that he said existed within the justice system. Being corrupt, he thought, was part of human nature:

> Feliciano: Human beings are corrupt by nature. And as there are various ways of, of tampering with evidence, this [DNA] is much more reliable … I don't believe there can be errors, because right now in the United States there are lots of cases of prisoners who have spent 15, 20 years in prison using DNA after all that time to prove they are innocent. There was one man accused of raping his daughter, who spent 17 or 20 years in prison and then they re-opened the case because of DNA evidence and in the end they managed to prove that he was innocent …
>
> Interviewer: Right.
>
> Feliciano: The damage had already been done because he'd served [many] years … but between being convicted and then one day, years later, being told 'actually, no, you're innocent after all' – which is a big thing – and the idea that you're guilty forever, [the first option is] still much better.

During our conversations some inmates referred to cases of wrongfully convicted criminals that had not involved DNA evidence, either in the exoneration or the wrongful conviction that had preceded exculpation. In the Austrian context, the so-called Heidegger case was mentioned by several prisoners, although at the time of our interviews, more than three years had passed since Heidegger's exoneration. Peter Heidegger was a 19-year-old floor tiler in the Austrian province of Upper Austria when he was sentenced to 17 years in prison for the murder of taxi driver, Claudia Deubler, in Salzburg in 1993. Heidegger had been arrested on the basis of the statement of two self-proclaimed eyewitnesses who claimed to have seen the young man near the crime scene on the night of the murder. Heidegger had subsequently been submitted to lengthy interrogations during which he had admitted to the commission of the crime, although he had retracted his confession two weeks later. As no evidence pointing to Heidegger had been found at the crime scene, the testimonies of the two self-proclaimed eyewitnesses had been the only evidence linking Heidegger to the murder.[2] Nevertheless, Heidegger had been convicted of robbing and murdering the 28-year-old taxi driver.

Soon after Heidegger's conviction, a young man went to the police to report having witnessed another young man robbing and murdering the taxi driver in Salzburg. The police did not believe him. After ceaseless attempts by Heidegger, his lawyers and his family to prove Heidegger's innocence, the case was re-opened and the other young man was eventually convicted of the murder in 2003.

2 A pen-shaped contraption, which can be used to shoot flares into the air – for example, in emergencies on boats – was found in Heidegger's home, yet the wound on the victim's body did not match the caliber of the signalling pen cartridges. In addition, Heidegger pointed out that signalling pens were very popular amongst young people in his town for shooting flares at parties and in beer gardens during the summer months.

Heidegger, after having spent 2,865 days in prison, was exonerated (Grabher 2007).

For our informants in Austria, the Heidegger case was a frequent reference point when discussing the alleged wrongdoings of the police and the criminal justice system: the fate of Peter Heidegger was seen as illustrative of what can go wrong if the authorities 'have their way'. DNA technologies were seen as a central tool in exculpation and exoneration and this is also interesting in the light of the fact that DNA evidence had played no part in Heidegger's conviction or his exoneration.

In the case of Peter Heidegger, it had been eyewitness misidentification that had led to the wrongful conviction. The main incriminating 'evidence' had come from a waiter in a Pizzeria who had claimed to have given him a lift prior to the murder of a taxi driver. When Heidegger's case was re-opened, it became apparent that the basic characteristics of the waiter's description of the young hitchhiker – such as the colour of his hair – had not matched Heidegger's, and there had been no proper line-up (Grabher 2007) for the waiter to identify Heidegger. Heidegger's false confession had probably been the result of both his mental and psychological state, and his fear and intimidation. Reinhard Grabher, an Austrian journalist who wrote a book about the Heidegger case, surmised that Heidegger, who had suffered from learning disabilities, had felt 'alone and without support, [and] hopelessly overstrained' by being accused of murder (Grabher 2007: 245). One of the reasons why Heidegger's retraction of his confession two weeks later was not deemed credible was that he had not confided his innocence to the psychiatrist during his psychological assessment. When asked why he had not done so, Heidegger said that he had been intimidated 'because I was not familiar with the system' (cf. Grabher 2007: 245). In addition, Heidegger said that one of the criminal investigators had repeatedly 'encouraged' him to confess to the killing of Claudia Deubler, because – so it was suggested to him – he could plausibly claim that it had been an accident and that the bullet from his signalling pen could have released itself automatically. Heidegger was also told that the evidence against him was mounting, so he would not stand a chance to be acquitted anyhow. The latter case – that suspects confess to a crime that they did not commit due to the police investigators' insistence that evidence had been found that 'proved' their involvement in the crime – unfortunately, does not seem to be an isolated incident.

The story of Peter Heidegger was mentioned by Austrian prisoners not only in connection with miscarriages of justice in general, but also with DNA-based exonerations in particular. This seems curious in light of the absence of any significant role that DNA evidence had played in this case. So why did prisoners think about DNA when they talked about Heidegger? The particular position that DNA technologies assumed in this respect are, we argue, not only rooted in their association with high science and infallibility (see Chapter 5), but also the prominent role that DNA evidence plays in exculpation and exoneration cases on TV and in other popular media. Thus, it was probably not the particular case of Heidegger that triggered the association with DNA evidence in our informants, but the topic of exonerations itself was (and still is) inseparably linked with DNA technologies in public imaginaries. More recently, increasing awareness of the important work carried out by defence lawyers in many countries, who donate their time to liberating the wrongfully convicted, has thankfully led to a more nuanced understanding of what DNA evidence can and cannot do. In addition, these initiatives have spurred wider discussions about the robustness and reliability of other forensic and court practices (Saks and Koehler 2005).

Prompting Confessions

Psychological and criminological research (Conti 1999, Gudjonsson 2003, Kassin 2008) has shown that confessions are not always prompted by an individual's actual knowledge or guilt, but they can be conditioned by external influences or adverse circumstances, such as aggressive law enforcement tactics, mental health issues, intoxication or even the defendant's belief, which most people find hard to understand, that they can be released after confessing, and prove their innocence later. The Innocence Project estimated that in 25 per cent of DNA exoneration cases, innocent defendants gave incriminating statements, made outright confessions, or pleaded guilty (Innocence Project n.d.).

In our interviews this phenomenon was mentioned by several prisoners who stated that once the police told them that incriminating evidence had been found, they felt they had to confess to the commission of the crime. Bernhard, 28, for example, who was serving a three-year sentence for a series of burglaries, readily admitted to having committed these break-ins, with one exception: he insisted he had had nothing to do with one particular burglary that he had been convicted of – yet he had confessed to it. Why had he confessed?

> I believe it was a trap by the police … [Burglars] have a scheme – everybody has a different style of breaking in. And this [*modus operandi*] looked exactly like [mine]. They caught me, one year later, with a trap. They said: 'It was you. We found DNA traces.' And I immediately told them that it *was* me [original verbal emphasis]. (cf. Prainsack and Kitzberger 2009: 52)

Quentin, 25, serving eight years for arson, told us the story of his arrest after robbing a bar. Because he had been caught on the way home from the crime scene, with the money still on him, he also confessed to a crime that he had not committed:

> Quentin: And I [also confessed to] another attempted robbery that I hadn't even done.
>
> Interviewer: You didn't do it?

> Quentin: No, I didn't do it, but I told them instantly that it had been me. [I said I confess, and then] 'Leave me alone'.
>
> Interviewer: Why did you say that?
>
> Quentin: Because I wanted to be left in peace. There was that one policeman I can't stand. When I see him, my pocket knife opens in my trousers. I tell you, I start shaking when I so much as set eyes on him.

Although this alleged practice by police investigators of 'encouraging' a confession based on half-truths or outright lies concerning the nature of the evidence is probably not limited to DNA evidence, the readiness of our informants to confess to a crime once the existence of incriminating evidence was mentioned to them was most pronounced when DNA was involved. This was closely related to their assessment of DNA technologies as the most reliable of all forensic technologies; some even argued that while it was impossible for the police to forge DNA, they could forge fingerprints to incriminate a suspect. The following excerpt stems from our exchange with 42-year-old Anton, who was serving three years for aggravated sexual abuse of minors (cf. Prainsack and Kitzberger 2009: 66):

> Anton: You can forge a fingerprint. Not DNA.
>
> Interviewer: How can you forge a fingerprint?
>
> Anton: Well, you see a lot of movies. You can make a copy, and voila, you have a fingerprint. [But] DNA, that's 100 per cent foolproof. The DNA trace [*sic*] is mine only, nobody else has it.

Many of our informants mentioned the alleged tendency among police officers to seek out the 'usual suspects', that is, look for suspects primarily among people with prior convictions. Those having previously served in prison were seen as particularly predisposed for becoming the target of such a search for a culprit. Prisoners said that police very often fabricated evidence, or that criminal investigators were over-reliant on informers who may lie and give evidence against an innocent party. The problem of using informers and prison grasses to testify against defendants has been cited as a factor in more than 15 per cent of cases of wrongful convictions overturned by DNA testing promoted by the Innocence Project (Innocence Project n.d.), and various studies cite the prevalence of this phenomenon as one of the most serious problems affecting the criminal justice system (Findley 2002, Natapoff 2009). Artur, a 38-year-old drug addict and self-proclaimed career criminal sentenced to 12 years for aggravated burglary, burglary and attempted aggravated theft, recounted how he had been subjected to police violence whilst in custody – 'They left me [beaten] black and blue' – and that he had only been arrested because a 'grass' had denounced him. This prisoner admitted to aiming to perfect his burglary techniques through lessons learned in prison. He boasted that for many years he had been able to fool the police and not get caught, and held that he was convicted not because of a mistake that he himself had made, but because of a snitch:

> The police manage to do a lot of things because they have grasses. Because they don't have a crystal ball, right? … I went to prison because someone ratted me out and that's how it is, sometimes the police beat people up to get them to talk. And the police had to beat up my grass to get him to shut up. Because they found out things they didn't want to know about.

This inmate had already been in prison when he was accused of having committed crimes of assault and murder (that he insisted he had not committed). Artur spoke about confessions triggered by police violence and said that police, when they had no other evidence, would go to prison to find a culprit:

> Once I was called in … to give a saliva sample. But I wasn't obliged to give it because it was for an assault and murder back in 2002. When they called me in it was 2005. And since all those years had gone by and the police wanted to find a culprit I went there and refused [to give the saliva sample]. I won't do it, I just won't do it! … And the prison guards even said to me: 'I think you did the right thing.' They can't find the one who did it [so they think] let's go and get a guy who's already in prison. It can happen just by chance, and that time, it was my turn … The police are bigger crooks than the [people] in prison. They're real crooks! They're… the pits. [They're like this]: 'We can't find who did [the crime], there's no one we can point a finger at, look, let's go to the rubbish dump, the prison, right, OK, [let's say] it's this one.'

The practice of investigators exhorting confessions by wrongfully claiming the existence of incriminating DNA evidence or by using violence is especially problematic in light of the fact that confessions are seen as particularly strong 'evidence' of guilt, both in practical and legal terms (see also Drizin and Leo 2004, Drizin and Reich 2004, Leo 2005; for discussions of the [in]admissibility of improperly or illegally obtained DNA evidence, see Gans and Urbas 2002, Johnson and Williams 2004a). In some jurisdictions, confessions preclude the possibility of re-opening a case. A landmark decision in this regard was delivered by the Pennsylvania Supreme Court in February 2011: the court acknowledged the fact that confessions are not always 'proof' of guilt and ruled that if an individual confesses to a crime this not bar them from seeking post-conviction testing (Innocence Project 2011). In a statement that also fit the case of Peter Heidegger exactly, the court stated that: 'We need not be reminded of the countless situations where persons confess to crimes of which they are innocent, either out of a desire to cover up for the guilty person or because of a psychological urge to do so' (cf. Innocence Project 2011, see also Hall 2010).

Punitive Judges, and Lazy Lawyers?

Clearly, misconduct on the part of law enforcement officials, prosecutors, or defence lawyers can also be a reason for wrongful convictions (see also Chapter 8). The Innocence Project (n.d., see 'Government Misconduct', see also West 2010b) lists the following as 'common forms of misconduct by law enforcement officials ...: employing suggestion when conducting identification procedures; [c]oercing false confessions; [l]ying or intentionally misleading jurors about their observations; [f]ailing to turn over exculpatory evidence to prosecutors; and [p]roviding incentives to secure unreliable evidence from informants'. Forms of misconduct among prosecutors include: withholding exculpatory evidence from the defence; the mishandling, mistreating, or destruction of evidence; allowing unreliable witnesses to testify; pressuring defence witnesses not to testify; relying on unreliable or fraudulent forensic experts; and making misleading arguments overstating the probative value of testimony (Innocence Project n.d., 'Government Misconduct'). The problem of 'bad lawyering' (Innocence Project n.d., 'Bad Lawyering') which, according to the Innocence Project, ranged from failure to present defence witnesses, failure to seek DNA or serology testing, and failure to object to evidence presented by the prosecution (see West 2010a), to sleeping during trials, arguably affects defendants from poorer backgrounds more than others since the former cannot afford to pay for the best legal representatives that they could get.

The issue of being let down by defence lawyers also came up in our conversations with prisoners. Many prisoners stated that whilst the rich could afford to hire a good lawyer and prolong legal proceedings in courts for years, poor people were subjected to swift convictions, often without being given the time to properly understand what was happening.

Manuel, 27, was serving a 14-year sentence for murder and drug trafficking. He regretted that his lawyer had not told him the 'truth' and had raised false expectations about his chances of being acquitted. In his words:

> You go to court as an innocent [person], the first time you go, you're confused, right? ... I never thought I'd go to prison and then when the judge says 'you will now be taken into custody', you think 'What? I'm going where?' And the lawyer says: 'Oh, don't worry, we'll try and put an appeal in to see if we can get you out in a month or in two or three months.' I mean, he tried to give me some hope but it wasn't realistic, it was false hope.

50-year-old Karl was serving 17 years for murder; he had got into a fight with a friend when they were both on drugs, and because they both worked in the prostitution business and had firearms lying around, Karl had overreacted when he felt physically threatened by the other man and had shot him. Both his state of intoxication and lack of intention to kill the man, Karl said, should have spared him the conviction of murder, and he blamed his lawyer for failing to argue in his favour in court. Karl blamed himself for having picked that lawyer: he had chosen him, he said, because he had been one of the top defence lawyers in the area, but he had not been aware that the man had recently developed a serious alcohol problem: '[the task] was too difficult for him. He's retired now. ... The Court, of course, acted on the basis of the wrong things he had said.'

Thirty-four year old Oliver, serving an open sentence for attempted murder and attempted rape, both of which he denied having committed, claimed that a blood-stained wallet that had originally been secured as evidence at the crime scene – and had even been visible in television footage covering the crime – had 'disappeared' during the trial. His lawyer, he said, had not done anything about this, although it would very likely have been able to indicate his innocence. No evidence from the crime scene pointed to Oliver, and the only piece of evidence that did – a hair in Oliver's flat which had allegedly come from the victim – was only found after previous examinations of the flat had been unsuccessful. For Oliver, this was a clear case of contamination – i.e. the hair had accidentally, if not deliberately, been placed in his flat – yet again his lawyer did not act on this. As a result, Oliver was now 'obsessed' – as he called it – with crime scene technologies and wanted to prove his innocence. He said that during the trial he had never stopped believing that his innocence would come to light in the end: 'I always thought that it would be solved. Because it wasn't me. Up to now, I've been fighting like a wild animal [to prove my innocence…]. I pity the girl, she's a victim ... But I'm a victim too.'

Frederico, 54, had had problems with the authorities since he was a teenager. He had been given an accumulated sentence of 20 years in prison for various crimes ranging from being the leader of a criminal gang, to extortion and drug trafficking. This prisoner spoke repeatedly about errors of justice and reported how in the past he had been convicted of crimes he had not committed, simply because the judge only listened to the version of events given by the police who had allegedly found packets of drugs in his car – 'In those days I didn't even know what drugs were, I'd never seen drugs with my own eyes, only on television', Frederico said. In his opinion, 'the lawyers are incompetent, they even miss the time limits for the defence pleas' and 'the judges, because they have tried so many cases, are insensitive and don't look for 100 per cent truth, if someone has a past or has been in prison they're convinced he did the crime. And it might not be true.' It is interesting to note that the account of this interviewee reproduced the same view of a justice system unable to recognise its own errors and may not be very receptive to reviewing sentences that was cited at the beginning of this chapter:

> Interviewer: If I understood you correctly, are you saying that judges are more receptive to DNA evidence than other forms of evidence?
>
> Frederico: The problem is knowing the course these DNA analyses take. There can be a margin of error. If it's a case of murder, for example, I think they shouldn't be considered reliable, these analyses, just reliable on their own. I think other tests should be requested, from another team that does the same kind

> of work to see if their results match the others. Then [the tests] would probably be very, very reliable.

Also on the related issue of the partiality of judges or jurors, our informants' assessments and perceptions hinged on much more than whether they complied with their legal or professional duties and rules of good conduct or not. In Anton's case, who was serving a three year sentence for severe abuse of minors, the issue – according to Anton – lay with factors pertaining to the personal situation of the judges that they could not be blamed for. He told us that even if they had tried, the judge and the jurors in his case could not have been objective, as they all had children, and the judge was even pregnant at the time of his trial. Anton did not accuse them of having done him injustice in a conscious and deliberate manner but he made this remark in a very matter-of-fact way: 'The judge was pregnant, the jurors all had kids, and [child abuse] is a delicate topic in this country anyhow. They sentenced me to three years.'

We read this as a reflection of the embodied knowledge of prisoner Anton that none of us can act and think in isolation from the social relationships and circumstances we are involved in. In a way, Anton claimed that our social environment and our personal circumstances could influence sentencing behaviour in much the same way as social and demographic factors have been found by social scientists to influence voting behaviour.

Another prisoner, David, 42, was convicted of attempted murder and given a sentence of three years and ten months for accidentally running over a woman when driving under the influence of alcohol. This inmate argued that judges worried more about securing a punishment than taking into account circumstances in the personal life of the defendant that could serve to mitigate the sentence or replace it with an alternative punishment to prison. David felt disappointed with the decision of the judges since he felt that his request to use electronic tagging rather than go to prison should have been granted. He spoke of himself as someone who was capable of being reintegrated into society, also because he had a job that he could go back to upon his release. David thought that he had been treated unfairly, especially in comparison with other people who, even though they may be violent or re-offend, 'managed' to get the judges to give them alternatives to prison sentences:

> David: I had a stable life until I went to prison. And I went to prison because of a road accident.
>
> Interviewer: So it was bad luck that brought you here?
>
> David: Yes [pause]. But when a person asks the judge for something, they don't listen, they say you are a violent criminal. That's what they say. I'm still asking for a[n electronic] tag, for example, and they say I've not reintegrated, I can't go back into society.

Interviewer: You want to go home and use a tag?

David: Yes. But the judge doesn't even take the trouble to find out whether I could return to society or not, even though at the moment I know I could get work … but [the judges] aren't interested in that. All they're concerned about is keeping people [in prison] … If it's a robbery, and there are a lot of those types here who've been inside many times, if it's a robbery they give them a tag or community service. They're people who've used weapons! I don't understand why [this happens].

This prisoner's assessment of the use of DNA technology in the criminal justice system was profoundly negative; he believed that nothing would change the unjust way in which the system appears to operate. In his opinion, injustice and inequality will always prevail in trials. And he added:

David: DNA evidence in itself cannot convict anyone. I have the impression that these police officers really believe it's something that will help. Help the police to find the criminal, but it's not the truth, is it? Just because you can say that someone had this at the crime scene, it doesn't mean they are guilty. It could be planted, couldn't it?

Interviewer: Could DNA be used to try to prove someone's innocence?

David: I think so. But a lot of people are convicted without any evidence … There are people who deserve to be in here and they're sent back just so that they can carry on committing crimes, If it's someone who has been involved in a death, and it could happen to anyone, they're much more affected by this …

Interviewer: If I understand you correctly, you're saying that you think the judges always try to convict.

David: No, no that's not it [coughs]. They don't know what convicting means, they don't know what goes on in prisons. They're not reintegrating anyone into society here. Prisons are just for punishment.

The case of Emílio, 32, a Ukrainian national in Portugal, was typical of the violation of human rights that a suspect may be subjected to if they are poor, do not understand the language well and cannot make themselves properly understood. Emílio was sentenced to 15 years for murder, sexual coercion and theft, but we were left with the impression that he did not understand the reasons for his conviction very well. His remarks were partly confused and revealed a lack of familiarity with the law, his rights, and what had taken place during the trial:

> Emílio: They showed me the charge sheet for assault, robbery and rape. I went to court but the court didn't explain anything to me .... And they weren't going to believe me because I had no witnesses. They sent me to prison and I was beaten up by the other prisoners. Someone said I was a rapist and no one respects rapists here. I've been here for six months, I have work but no visitors, no clothes, nothing...
>
> Interviewer: Did they give you a DNA test?
>
> Emílio: Of course, without a lawyer or anyone else present but I let them, since they thought I was the rapist ... One of the guards grabbed my mouth and the other came and [gesture of someone being dragged by the mouth] ... it was difficult for me to speak to them [the police] in their language ...

Many other prisoners mentioned having suffered from police violence and aggression (see also Chapter 8). This was most commonly heard from recidivists and career criminals who were 'already known' by the police, so that when they were apprehended, they felt they were treated not as suspects but as convicts. This is closely related to the topic of stigma which was present, in one way or another, in every single conversation we had with the prisoners. The prisoners referred to two types of stigma – the stigma of prisoners originating in society, and the stigma – e.g. of sex offenders – among prisoners themselves (Sykes and Messinger 1960, Vaughn and Sapp 1989). Several prisoners said that DNA technologies were particularly effective in proving the truth in the case of sex crimes. Daniel, a psychology student aged 36 and sentenced to 24 years for murder, arson and grievous bodily harm, stated that stigma affected sex offenders in particular and that DNA technologies were important to prove innocence not only in the context of exoneration but also to restore the moral integrity of individuals labelled as rapists:

> Daniel: [The stigma] is very common in rape cases, which are usually very serious in moral terms, right, in social terms it's a terrible thing for a man to be convicted of rape, right...?
>
> Interviewer: Yes, yes.
>
> Daniel: And it's even worse if a man is innocent and convicted of that kind of crime. Because if a man is convicted of robbing a jeweller's store or a bank or, I don't know, something more opportunistic, [they get] labelled as an adventurer, and socially, that's not as serious [as being labelled as rapist].
>
> Interviewer: Right.
>
> Daniel: But being labelled a rapist is terrible. And DNA can at least resolve many of these cases, many of them. It already has, and that's why I say that it's an essential tool for both sides, to prove guilt or innocence...

Conclusion

What paths will the determination of guilt and innocence follow in the future? The prisoners' narratives on the potential of DNA in proving innocence, and their references to incorrect ethical and professional practices by various actors in the criminal justice system, highlight the need for further research on the root causes for wrongful convictions and on measures to minimise this risk. Should we make better use of scientific evidence, such as DNA technologies? Do we need to pay more attention to ethical procedures when biological samples are taken and more attention to the way in which information on the objectives for taking the sample is communicated to individuals subjected to these procedures (Machado and Silva 2009)? What can be done to render police interrogations more transparent, in order to minimise the risk for coercion? Do we need to reassess practices pertaining to the use of informers ('grasses', or 'snitches') in criminal investigation work? Moreover, what role will new social media, such as *Facebook* and *Twitter* and other online resources providing freely accessible information on people's networks of friends and their whereabouts at certain times, play in criminal investigations and trials at the future? Can these open source surveillance tools help decrease the risk of wrongful convictions?

Finally, will the currently increasing proliferation of initiatives dedicated to the exoneration of the wrongfully convicted also lead to the availability of solid datasets on the reasons for wrongful convictions in different jurisdictions? Although the Innocence Project was initiated in the US (Scheck, Neufeld and Dwyer 2000), similar projects now operate in Canada, New Zealand, and Australia. As Roberts and Weathered (2009: 44) note, Innocence Projects are typically associated with university law schools because of the possibility of drawing on a large pool of enthusiastic students. While Innocence Project(s) are still most active in North America, the number of organisations in Europe and other parts of the world which offer support to those claiming to have been wrongfully convicted is also on the rise (see e.g., Forejustice n.d., The Innocence Network 2008, Johnson and Williams 2004b, McCartney 2006c, Roberts and Weathered 2009, Sulzbach 2006 provides an annotated bibliography on all publications on the topic of exoneration). In addition to the important work undertaken by Innocence Projects and affiliated organisations to exonerate the wrongfully convicted, an important additional outcome of these efforts is an increase in public and stakeholder awareness of the sources of miscarriages of justice (Neufeld and Scheck 2002). In fact, the number of features and editorials in academic journals, magazines, and newspapers discussing problematic uses of forensic sciences, or calling for closer scrutiny has risen steadily in recent years (Leo 2005, see also Nature 2011).

Leo (2005: 213, see also Lofquist 2001) holds that learning about the causes of wrongful convictions cannot solve the problem of miscarriage of justice. This conclusion, he argues, is based on an unexamined assumption:

> The unexamined assumption in virtually all miscarriages writing and scholarship is that [the reasons examined for miscarriage of justice] are actual causes, and once they are identified, we will know how and why the problem of wrongful conviction occurs. This unexamined assumption is simplistic, if not misleading. This list of causes has impeded our theoretical understanding and development of the deeper psychological, sociological, and institutional causes of wrongful conviction. … Eyewitness misidentification, false confession, and police and prosecutorial misconduct are not actual *root* causes. By identifying the causes, we beg the obvious, deeper causal question: What are the causes of eyewitness misidentification? What are the causes of police-induced false confessions? What are the causes of police and prosecutorial conduct? … Scholars need to seek out *root* causes, not *legal* causes, of wrongful conviction [original emphases].

Leo also points to the work of Talia Harmon (2001a,b), who compared the cases of inmates released from death row with those who were executed, as a leading example of solid social science analysis of wrongful conviction cases, which he argues should be supplemented by analyses of rightful acquittals. Overall, scholars 'need to move beyond the legal categories and concepts handed to them by journalists and lawyers [… and] do more than descriptive case studies that recirculate the same essential ideas' (Leo 2005: 215).

Implementing technologies to strengthen protection against miscarriages of justice should be supplemented by additional measures to avoid the new risks that might be created by the expanding uses of forensic DNA technologies. One of the main risks related to the growth of more expanding uses of DNA profiling and DNA databasing is the serious implication they have in privacy and civil rights, and because 'their logic is endangering innocence, with the creation of a "suspect society"' (McCartney 2006a: 156). Some critical pronouncements that have been developed to strengthen protection against miscarriages of justice support scrutiny of the uses of scientific methods and expert evidence in courtrooms and argue for the improvement in the commitment to quality control, regulation and training related to scientific evidence (for instance, McCartney, Williams and Wilson 2010, Nuffield Council on Bioethics 2007). The prisoners' views on the exculpatory potential of DNA profiling and also their assessment of the factors that may contribute towards wrongful conviction show that it is necessary to systematically document and study cases of wrongful convictions. It is also important to create favourable contexts for the implementation of policies, practices, and legislation that will prevent wrongful convictions. Vital for this would be to invest more on educating students and practitioners in the criminal justice system (from the police, to lawyers, jurors, prosecutors and judges) about the potential for wrongful conviction and to foster the ethical responsibility that is needed in all criminal investigation procedures and trial actions.

Chapter 8
Criminal Bodies and Abusive Authorities

Introduction

This chapter discusses two core dimensions of the ways in which our interviewees spoke about their bodies: they referred to them both as useful tools and as liabilities when committing crimes, as bodies can be recognised or leave traces, and therefore lead to detection. We will argue that bodies did not start to be seen as liabilities in the era of DNA profiling, but that this situation precedes the emergence of forensic DNA technologies. Physical characteristics of offenders – usually in the form of externally visible characteristics – have always put them in danger of being recognised. Yet in the way in which DNA is seen as symbolising the 'essence' of the body, in conjunction with the fact that it is virtually impossible from protecting oneself against leaving physical traces, DNA technologies assumed a special role in the accounts of prisoners. And 'being in control' – of their lives, their 'jobs', their bodies and minds, and their surroundings – was a very central element in our conversations with prisoners. It was in this sense that the risk inherent in the offender's body has become more pronounced in era of forensic DNA technologies.

This chapter also discusses and contextualises the social processes by which the prisoners applied their knowledge of crime scene traces, and DNA traces in particular, to their own experiences of dealing with the criminal justice system. Many prisoners emphasised negative aspects of the work of police officers, for example by referring to alleged instances of police fabricating evidence or targeting ex-convicts during investigations. Other prisoners highlighted the human aspect of the work of criminal investigators in particular: police investigators deserved praise if they did their work well, contempt if they allowed their moral or professional standards to be compromised, and some prisoners told us about personal relationships with particular police officers in the sense that they 'knew them well' as a result of having encountered them frequently over a lengthy period of time.

With regard to the question of police databases in particular, prisoners did not mention the retention of fingerprints as a problem in any way, nor did they refer to fingerprint databases as potential tools to refute suspicions against the falsely accused. With regard to DNA profiles, interviewees in both countries felt that retaining these in national databases could help protect them against false accusations in the future. At the same time, the fact that their DNA profiles were stored in a centralised database was seen as deepening their stigma as convicts. This demonstrates very clearly the simultaneity of empowering and disempowering effects (Prainsack and Toom 2010) that forensic technologies, and

DNA technologies in particular, had on our informants. One of the best illustrations of the view that DNA technologies were part of a cluster of practices, attitudes, and technologies of stigmatisation was the following exchange with Jürgen, 29, convicted to five years for aggravated battery (cited in Prainsack and Kitzberger 2009: 69):

> Jürgen: I had to do that [provide a DNA sample]. They took my saliva and I had to do fingerprints. [Silence. Looks unhappy]
>
> Interviewer: Did you mind?
>
> Jürgen: Yes.
>
> Interviewer: Why?
>
> Jürgen: Because it was then that I knew: now I am a criminal. Like, now it is getting serious.
>
> Interviewer: What did you mind more, the DNA or the fingerprint part, or did you mind both the same?
>
> Jürgen: I would say: more the saliva.
>
> Interviewer: Why?
>
> Jürgen: *Because it comes from the inside*. I am of the opinion that a fingerprint one leaves everywhere in the same way, while the saliva is inside of me and this is why I mind more. [Emphasis added]

Other prisoners portrayed forensic DNA technologies as means of *reducing* the stigma attached to their status as convicted offenders. As Nelson, 35, serving a nine-year sentence for sexual abuse of a minor, burglary, theft and perjury, put it, the availability of DNA profiling forced the police to carry out a thorough investigation, rather than going for the most likely suspect and trying to 'trick' the suspect to confess to the crime (other prisoners in both countries echoed this notion). Nelson even argued in favor of the creation of a universal database as a way to prevent the police from looking suspects among previous offenders first (cited in Machado, Santos and Silva 2011: 3):

> I think it's bad that only the prison population has their genetic information there [in the database]. It should apply to everyone. In order to avoid discrimination and even more… we are the scum of society [silence] because for every crime that occurs, they [the police] will immediately go to the ones that are there [in the database]. And then the honest man might pay for the sinner's faults.

Other interviewees argued that increasing the speed and efficacy of criminal investigation through the automation of profile comparison in forensic DNA databases could help prevent certain police practices aimed at the usual suspects, such as making unfounded accusations against individuals subjected to criminal investigations in the past, and using fabricated or illegal incriminating procedures. This certainly contributed to the fact that many of our interviewees saw the existence of forensic DNA technologies overall as 'a good thing' (see Chapter 7), although this positive effect was seen as compromised by the omnipresent possibility that the technology could be abused by human actors with bad intentions.

Risky Bodies

The body is one of the main resources of the criminal. A strong, fast, and resistant body is most useful in the commission of crimes (with the exception, of course, of some white collar crimes). Also skills acquired through experience and learning from peers – like in most regular jobs – are intimately linked to physical fitness. For example, the agility and dexterity needed to steal a wallet without being noticed, and the memory and cognitive skills necessary to select targets for a burglary (Gibbs and Shelly 1982, Steffensmeier and Ulmer 2003, Sutherland 1937, Wright et al. 1995) – they require more than simply physical strength and skill – they require a certain level of physical fitness. Nevertheless, as argued above, the fact that bodies leave traces of their presence renders them a potential risk. It is perhaps also for this reason that DNA technologies were referred to by the majority of our interviewees as the principal means of identifying the perpetrator of a crime: whereas leaving fingerprints can relatively easily be avoided by wearing gloves, for example, not to leave any traces that could be analysed with the help of DNA technologies was seen as near impossible (see also Chapters 5 and 6). The particular prominence of DNA technologies in the depictions and narratives of prisoners in this respect could, however, also be influenced by the focus on DNA in public media and television series (see Chapter 4).

The prominent role of DNA evidence in the prisoners' depictions contrasts with the relatively low proportion of criminal cases where DNA evidence is actually a decisive factor. In many countries, volume crime scenes are not routinely searched for DNA traces, and even in many cases of serious crimes, DNA evidence does not play a crucial role: this is the case, for example, with alleged rapes where the question of guilt hinges on whether or not an encounter was consensual, not whether or not it took place.

DNA technologies do, however, have a special link to offenders' bodies in at least one additional respect: they enable investigators to capture, store, and automatically compare data representing material that is in every cell of our body. Thus, while DNA technologies are the potential 'allies' of those wrongfully accused, they are the enemies of people who actually commit crimes. And these technologies can also turn into enemies for those who are innocent, if the technologies are misused by authorities. What rendered the latter scenario much feared by many prisoners was that they saw it as something that could happen to anyone at any time; authorities were unpredictable, and, once a person was falsely accused, a remedy was seen as beyond his or her control; too vivid were the stories told about wrongful convictions in prison and on TV. Prisoners perceived to suffer from a lack of control over abusive authorities as well as DNA technologies: in both instances, they saw themselves as powerless, yet for different reasons. The following quote from an interview with Micael, 31, who was serving a 12-year and one month sentence for raping a woman at knifepoint, highlights the sense in which he felt he had no control over his body's leaving traces:

> Micael: It's very hard not to leave any traces. We lose hair every day – and any hair left at the crime scene contains DNA. When we speak, we release saliva … and our bodies are always shedding skin too … So we always leave some trace behind [at the crime scene].
>
> Interviewer: So this is something that's difficult to control?
>
> Micael: It is. It's not as if you can seal yourself inside a bubble and commit a crime, is it?

The impossibility of controlling the fact that the body leaves traces was also clearly illustrated in the words of Feliciano, 34, who was serving a 12-year sentence for murder:

> DNA is present in every part of the body … and because criminals are afraid they'll be identified more quickly, they are more careful about the actual crime … which might [make] people a bit sharper and a bit more balanced, [thinking] 'There are a lot more chances I'll get caught, so it's better to think twice' … or go completely in disguise [smiling], with the whole [body covered up] so you don't leave so much as an eyelash behind. Because nowadays the forensic police can get everything, maybe even a drop of sweat that might be there …

Feliciano felt that watching crime drama in order to obtain information on how to better avoid detection had the positive side-effect that one could learn lots about how the body worked in general:

> There's always a murder in the [*CSI*] series … and they talk about all the different bits of tissue and muscles and organs – on a forensic level, right, because it's, because that's their work – [and it's] very interesting. Even ordinary people watching the programme can learn something about their own bodies.

Later in the interview, Feliciano talked about the importance of understanding the body in terms of managing the crime scene, making concrete reference to the risks that can emerge both for criminals and for innocent citizens:

> The more information there is, the fewer the risks … For the actual criminal … But with this information the ordinary citizen might, I don't know … for example, if there's a murder, and someone who has had nothing to do with [the crime] turns up [at the crime scene], they're likely to touch the body, aren't they? …

Yet bodies were not only difficult to control because it was near impossible not to leave traces, but also because the use of alcohol or drugs could affect the mind and thus render the body more 'dangerous' to its owner. Bernhard, a 28-year-old burglar serving a three-year sentence, told us that because he was often high on drugs, he did not feel any pain when he cut himself and left traces at crime scenes. Bodies were thus not only liabilities if they were not fit enough to carry out the required tasks, or because it was impossible to avoid leaving traces, but also because in some instances the lack of control that the prisoner had over his own mind made him lose control over his body. According to Martim, 27, sentenced to nine years and three months in prison for rape, attempted coercion and kidnapping, alcohol was also responsible for the commission of his crime; Martim said it had made him do things that he otherwise would not have done:

> Martim: On the day I did it, when I committed the crime … I was completely drunk.
>
> Interviewer: And that's how it happened …
>
> Martim: I'm very sorry about it … nothing justifies what I did, because I've got children. If anything like this ever happened [to them], I'd go to prison for it but I'd kill the wretch who did it first. … I still ask myself why I did it. Why I went and got so drunk in the bar until the small hours of the morning and the first miserable woman who came up to me had to pay for it. And I had a wife at home! … I still feel very bad, very bad about the crime I committed and I hate people who do this. I hate myself [silence]…

The issue of control over himself (having 'lost his mind'), albeit in a different configuration, also featured in the story of Mariano, 29, sentenced to 17 years for the cruel murder of a prostitute with the help of scissors and electrical wire. Mariano explicitly stated that he had committed this crime as a result of alcohol abuse and also because, at the time, when he was only 21 years old, he believed he had been psychologically affected by having served in an army unit known for its particularly tough physical and mental training. He described how, after leaving the army, he had felt an impulse to kill:

> I was very young, I was more impulsive and I couldn't control myself [and also] I had just left the army and I had the taste of blood in my mouth, as they say … the crime I committed was very unusual [it was due to] impulses and the fact that at the time I lost my mind. After the first blow, I saw my whole life flash by me, from childhood to adulthood … after the first blow all I thought was 'my life is ruined'. I ended up taking the body into the house, I wrapped it in a sheet, called the police and stayed in the house. I felt blocked, I didn't know what to do with myself. I could have run away but I didn't. I thought about shooting myself in the head …

Mariano told us that over the years he had managed to develop a greater level of self-control to curb his impulses and that when he would be released from prison, the self-control that he had acquired would enable him to resist any impulses to violent behaviour, provided that he could control his desire to consume alcohol. Thus, very much in line with the statements of some of the Austrian prisoners who put a lot of emphasis on the psychological support that they received in prison, and on how the time they had spent in prison had helped them to change (Chapter 6 and Chapter 9), Mariano referred to his imprisonment as a vehicle to overcome his alcohol addiction.

If we keep in mind the link between control and masculinity, then this means that the time in prison had made Mariano 'more of a man' by increasing the way that he was in control of his body and his life. At the same time, however, the way in which imprisonment restricts the agency and thus the control of people over what they do, where they go, as well as their habitus, created an interesting tension in this respect. Imprisonment seemed to give some prisoners more control at one level by taking it away from them at another. This, of course, is also the way in which military organisations turn people into soldiers.

Prisoners did not, however, present their quest for more self-control as heroic success stories but usually emphasised how hard a struggle it was for them (again much in line with the psychotherapeutic imperative to 'work through' traumatic issues and destructive behaviours). Several times during the interview, Mariano referred to his inner struggle to discipline his body and his mind:

> I am impulsive and people say 'oh, he's very aggressive' but that's not true, I know I can have an argument but not become violent. I'm not a saint and sometimes I have to put my foot down, because of the situation we're in, because of where we are [in prison]. [When I hit someone] I end up punishing myself. I don't eat, I stay shut up in my cell … I go three or four days without eating … Some of the prisoners that are closer to me are amazed I'm still standing. They usually say 'You must have strong blood in you.'

Mariano's body, and his 'strong blood', was seen by him both as a guise of a much 'softer' and more sensitive inside: on the inside, he was someone who worked hard at becoming a better person. To the outside, he represented the stereotype of a murderer, the paradigmatic example of the violent, insensitive criminal who makes others suffer without any kind of compassion (Jenkins 1994, Jones and Wardle 2008, Pollak and Kubrin 2007, Seal 2010). While this 'outside' disguised a softer inside, it also guaranteed him the respect of other criminals and thus also gave him control over them:

> In prison I've already had people accusing me of beating them up and others asking me for protection … because of this so-called respect … When there are problems, I can intervene because the other inmates won't fight me. I can go and break up fights, as I have done many times. A lot of people even say that I'm fighting for justice or to keep things in order, perhaps that comes from my military training …

Thus, Mariano's strong body protected him from troubles from the outside so that he could focus on himself. But he also saw his body also as reflecting his personal identity; he discussed how the shape of his body (whether it was muscular or not) and his weight (whether he was overweight or not) reflected how secure or insecure he felt, and how well he was doing overall:

> I got very run down … I like to do a bit of body building and sometimes you need to burn off a bit of fat … But I don't feel good like that, I'd rather be a bit more … not fatter, just more muscular … [When I am thinner] I look at myself and think: 'You're going under, you're letting the system drag you down.'

Mariano thus considered the physical strength of his body as mirroring his capacity to resist 'the system'. This again reflects the multiple ways in which 'the system' and the experience of imprisonment are entangled with the issues of agency of control, which in turn are expressed partly through the physical *gestalt* and *habitus* of prisoners. While imprisonment and the situation of punishment with all its inherent restrictions and humiliations detract from the extent to which prisoners are in control, as we have seen earlier, in terms of having a clear mind and being able to be in control of one's own life, the time done in prison was portrayed by some prisoners in both countries as empowering.

Another such story of empowerment via increased self-control obtained in prison was told to us by Artur. Artur, aged 38, and sentenced to 12 years for aggravated burglary, considered he had always been a 'very successful' criminal until the day he stopped adequately weighing the risks and benefits and went on stealing sprees. For years he had managed to escape the police. He described some of his techniques for avoiding detection to the interviewer; for example, he paid attention to the movements of police patrols and changed cars when doing robberies:

> Sometimes I would steal two or three cars a night … I'd go past the police patrol, past the cops, and they aren't idiots either, they see three crooks in a car going

> backwards and forwards and they start to track the car. So we'd have to dump that car and steal another.

Eventually, it was his dependence on drugs that put him in prison, Artur said, since the need to consume cocaine and heroin 'made him' go over board; at the end, he did several burglaries every day:

> I had to rob every day, every day, because of my [drug] habit. If I hadn't gotten into drugs, I wouldn't even be here today … But because I did, and I used a lot every day, I really was forced to steal.

Artur contrasted this lack of personal control due to his abuse of drugs with the fact that he managed, on his own initiative and without medical assistance, to break his heroin and cocaine habit after being sent to prison. The following account of his relationship with drugs since entering prison was conveyed with great satisfaction:

> From the very first day in prison I thought: 'From now on I'm not taking any more drugs.' I came off drugs cold, without medication, methadone, nothing … It's known that hashish eases the 'punishment' [life in prison] because someone who is high on hashish can even forget they're in prison sometimes, they sleep better and everything. Everyone knows that hashish isn't habit forming, right? You smoke it more to forget where you are. But as I've got a child … I cut it out. I only smoke tobacco now. I don't take anything else.

Hubert, 41, who was serving a sentence of seven and a half years for sexually abusing two minors, blamed alcohol for running his life and credited the time in prison with helping him get his life back together:

> [In here] I've done lots of therapies and treatments. My behaviour has changed in many ways. I have not become a new person – that's impossible. But the behaviour has changed, the attitudes have changed a lot… Also because I stopped drinking. Or rather because I have had two and a half years to experience this, the change. Although it was hard, especially in the first year. Knowing that I would be in here for so long. And then my addiction to alcohol was still there, in the first year. And then [the awareness that there is] freedom outside, you know, that is all in the back of one's mind. [But] I did it. I made it. I realised how I started to get better. I realised what a change it was within the family and around it, with my partner, and my children. I have a daughter who is 22 years old. I realised [how much things had changed], I realised everything.

What is striking in Hubert's quote is that he referred to himself from the perspective of a psychologist or a behavioural therapist. He spoke of 'the' behaviour that had changed. Control, here, was seen as having been offered to him from the outside.

While both Hubert and Artur emphasised the ways in which they had (re-) gained control over their minds and thus over their lives while in prison, the two accounts differed in at least one crucial respect: while Hubert said he would use his newly gained control over his life to avoid making mistakes, Artur, a career criminal, aimed to use it to become a better criminal. No longer being addicted to drugs, for Artur, had two benefits: first, he no longer needed to commit burglaries indiscriminately to make money to feed the habit, and second, it enabled him to avoid leaving traces in a more efficient manner. As a good example of the behaviour of a professional, sober criminal, Artur cited the use of 'plastic bags on your feet … like they do in hospitals' to prevent leaving footprints.

Controlling Visibility

Although DNA technologies did, as discussed above, have a particularly intimate link to the prisoners' bodies and thus to their risks of being caught, DNA evidence was by no means the only way in which bodies were seen by prisoners as factors that could give them away. People's stature, their clothes, and, such as in Vincent's case, the colour of his eyes, were all factors that needed to be considered and if necessary concealed to avoid detection. Vincent, 39, was a repeat offender who was serving eight years for a number of crimes including drug trafficking, aggravated battery, and theft. For a while, Vincent's specialty had been to visit wealthy elderly women and engage them in lengthy conversations about made-up charity opportunities. While he was distracting his victims, his accomplices emptied the valuables from their flats. Vincent was good-looking in a *Men's Health* kind of way, tall, muscular, and with striking blue eyes. This is the story of how he got caught:

> [It was] an old woman who gave me away. [My accomplice] who had been with me that day told [the police] that I had done things before. [I know it was he who gave me away] because it was only he who knew that. He ratted me out. He said he knew that I had done things before, and boom, they convicted me. [Before he had told them it had been me, police] had thought [the robbers] at the jewellery store had been Russians. Nobody ever saw me [at the break-in at the jewellery store], no traces, no fingerprints, nothing. [And then], because of my blue eyes, they convicted me. I was wearing a hat, wore black clothes. Because of my body shape they recognised me [and the blue eyes]. Purely based on that, I was convicted.

Also external marks such as scars or tattoos, in the opinion of many of our interviewees, made it easier for the police to identify the perpetrator of a crime.[1] As Manuel, 27, and sentenced to 14 years for murder and drug trafficking, said:

> We are obliged to have our fingerprints taken... when we are arrested we are obliged to show tattoos or scars and have them photographed [pause] the scars I have, these [*pointing to a scar*], the police have a record of all of them, and they can even use them to look into other crimes that, that certain [other] people have committed.

Olegário, aged 31 and sentenced to three years and six months for theft and perjury, stated that great care needed to be taken to manage the most visible body features appropriately when committing a crime. He emphasised the importance of committing crimes 'in disguise', and even described a case in which a criminal had fooled the police by using a fake tattoo which he had revealed at the crime scene on purpose:

> There are people who use fake tattoos on their arms when they rob a bank. They pick up the weapon and show the tattoo and the manager, for example, sees the tattoo and it sticks [in his mind], it could be a dragon, for example, [so the witness says], look for someone with a dragon tattooed on their hand. But he doesn't really have one, it was just put on, you know? It wasn't a real tattoo. He gets rid of it and doesn't leave any traces.

The prisoners' accounts about the importance of tattoos to identify the author of a crime resembles with the work of Cesare Lombroso in the nineteenth century and his contemporaries in the field of eugenics. In a certain sense their description

---

1 Criminal identification systems have always been very concerned to include external physical features of offenders or suspects, such as tattoos, scars or birthmarks, in their records (Cole 2001). One example of contemporary practices for identifying individuals for the purposes of combating crime is the type of information recorded in the US, in the Integrated Automated Fingerprint Identification System (IAFIS). Data in the IAFIS includes fingerprints, criminal histories, mug shots, photographs of scars and tattoos, physical characteristics such as height, weight, and hair and eye colour and aliases. The system also includes civil fingerprints, mostly of individuals who have served or are serving in the U.S. military or have been or are employed by the federal government.

The IAFIS, launched in 1999, is the largest biometric database in the world, currently housing the fingerprints and criminal histories of more than 66 million subjects in the criminal master file, together with more than 25 million civil prints. It provides automated fingerprint search capabilities, instant search capability, electronic image storage, and electronic exchange of fingerprints and responses.

reproduced cultural assumptions about the 'criminal bodies' by which tattoos could be considered body marks of a professional criminal (Lombroso 2006 [1876]).[2]

The Power of Authorities

Almost all of our interviewees referred to particular practices of police officers or other actors within the criminal justice system that they found particularly problematic. Some prisoners stressed that the police were always after the 'same people', namely those who already had criminal records. Prisoners who referred to this related to themselves as individuals who had already been 'filed' in police archives.

The keeping of criminal records traditionally aims at identifying and controlling the 'habitual criminals' in particular and the 'suspect' population in general, and it should be emphasised, as many commentators have done (Caplan and Torpey 2001, Cole 2001, Williams and Johnson 2008), that since the earliest attempts by the state to solve the problems of crime by developing police identity registers the central idea has been that it is vital to include not only offenders but also those deemed likely to offend in the future (for instance, anyone who has been suspected or charged of having been involved in criminal activity).

Daniel, 36, was sentenced to 24 years imprisonment for first-degree murder as one of the perpetrators of a crime that resulted in the killing of 13 people in an arson attack. Daniel believed in the idea that people often started with small crimes and gradually got to committing more serious crimes. For this reason, he argued, investigators should collect and store as much information as possible:

> Daniel: There's a progression involved in crime … I don't like to talk like this because sometimes it looks like racism, it looks like I'm saying 'oh, that guy who stole a marble off his friend when he was six, he's going to be a criminal', no, I'm not saying that. But in life, in the real world, you know that very often there's a progression involved.

---

2 At least since the work of Lombroso and his theory that criminals are atavistic, tattoos have been considered a 'professional characteristic' of criminals and proof that can demonstrate to judges and practitioners of forensic medicine that an individual is an ex-prisoner. In Lombroso's view, criminals have a predilection for the custom of tattooing designs on their skin, either due to boredom caused by long periods of internment, or mainly because they live in a 'state of nature' quite similar to primitive men. Therefore, in the nineteenth century, tattoos were commonly seen as 'proof' that somebody was an ex-prisoner. Atavism theory saw the prevalence of tattoos among prisoners in close connection with a widespread custom amongst savages and prehistoric people. The practice of tattooing had reappeared in certain lower-class groups such as ex-convicts and sailors, so the argument went, because of 'their violent passions, blunted sensitivity, puerile vanity, and extreme laziness' (Lombroso 2006 [1876]: 62).

> Interviewer: Yes, yes.
>
> Daniel: You go from one step to the next and the kid who was stealing cars will be stealing something else tomorrow and maybe he'll end up [getting] involved in another kind of crime. So I think that a small crime, even a small crime, should go on the database. It might be useful years later.
>
> Interviewer: Why?
>
> Daniel: Because the investigator has to look at probabilities, he has to be a very practical kind of guy … he has to be cold, he has to investigate the mother, investigate the father, he has to … think 'right then, it's likely, it's likely that this could be useful to me in a few years' time'.

Many of our interviewees stated that there was a big difference between whether an individual's data were on the police files or not, explaining that usually people were only sent to prison for minor crimes (such as theft or small-scale drug dealing) if they had prior convictions. Prisoners in Portugal used the expressions 'having a dirty record' (a police record indicating that the individual has a criminal past) and 'having a clean record' (a police record indicating that the individual has served a prison sentence but that they have not committed any more offences since their release). Several of our interviewees in Portugal said that when they would get to leave prison they would want to do everything they could to keep a 'clean sheet'. What they meant with this was twofold: for some prisoners, staying clean meant not going back to committing crimes, whilst for others it meant continuing their criminal career without getting caught by the police again.

Although Austrian prisoners did not speak much about records, the accounts of prisoners in both countries focused on relationships with individual actors within the criminal justice system – very often police officers, but also judges or jurors – who were particularly bad or evil in the understanding of the prisoners. We recall, for example, Quentin, a 25 year-old serving eight years for arson, whom we encountered in Chapter 7; Quentin had said that it was the sight of a particular policeman that had upset him so much that he had confessed to everything he had been accused of doing: 'When I see him, my pocket knife opens in my pants. I tell you I start to shake when I as much as set eyes on him.' Quentin attributed a truly life-changing event, his imprisonment, to his reaction to this man. Bernhard, the burglar whom we met earlier in this chapter, said that no matter how hard he tried not look suspicious or stand out from the crowd in any way, police always had an intuition that he had been involved: 'Perhaps I've got such a "great" aura that makes them being so keen on me.' He then went on to tell us about particular instances in which certain policemen 'had it in' for him. Also other prisoners spent quite some time telling us about their relationships with certain police officers or judges who had allegedly taken an interest in them. It were usually younger men who did this, and always men who said they had been neglected in one way or another by their parents. In some instances, the relatively detailed and passionate ways in which relationships with police officers or even judges were portrayed by the prisoners could have been replacements of non-existing close relationships with other adults who were interested in them and their lives.

Virtually all prisoners agreed that their status as ex-convicts after their release would put them into the limelight of police investigations whenever a crime had been committed that 'fitted' the types of things that they had done.[3] In previous chapters we encountered stories of prisoners who felt that – especially also in high profile cases where the pressure on investigators to find the culprit was very high – the first place police looked for suspects was among (ex-)convicts. Ludwig, a 29-year-old serving 15 years for murder, even said that the fact that he had previous convictions was one of the reasons why he eventually committed a murder: he had had a female friend, Verena, with whom he had often gone out drinking. Verena's boyfriend had become increasingly annoyed with her close friendship with Ludwig. At some point, Verena and Ludwig had started sleeping together, but Verena did not want to leave her boyfriend, whom she said she loved. One day, when her boyfriend confronted Verena about her close relationship with Ludwig, so Ludwig told us, Verena said to her boyfriend that Ludwig had raped her. Verena's boyfriend became furious and 'forced' her, so Ludwig said, to report the alleged rape to the police. When he was accused, Ludwig did nothing to counter the accusation, and later on, he quietly accepted a conviction. Some months later, things escalated in the home of Verena's boyfriend, where he and Ludwig got into a fight and Ludwig stabbed him to death. Had he not had his prior convictions, Ludwig told us, all this would not have happened. Why?

> Well, in that case, after [the rape charge] I would have immediately accused her back, [reported her] for defamation. This way I would have been safe. Or at least I could have made the best out of it. They said they had evidence – but I know this was not true.

Other prisoners told stories to demonstrate their moral or intellectual superiority over the police officers of prison wards. Prison wards were usually portrayed as corrupt, heinous, and mean, and police officers were often described as a bit 'thick', aggressive, or unprofessional. Some prisoners told us that if they had not actively collaborated with police investigators to gather evidence or reconstruct their crime, they would never have found the truth. All those prisoners who looked

3 Murderers (including those who attempted it) were the only group to whom this did not apply. This can probably be explained by the fact that the murderers we interviewed mostly comprised of people who had attacked family members or lovers due to 'emotional emergencies', thus, not of typical recidivists (and they knew that police knew that). Thus for them the scenario that anyone would suspect them if a murder was committed some time in the future was rather remote. This situation may have been different for contract assassins, yet we did not have any of those among our interviewees.

down on police officers came from middle class or upper-middle class families. 37-year-old Paul, for example, who was serving 15 years for aggravated robbery and armed theft, said he had turned himself in to the police in a suicidal state. He said that even when he had confessed to everything, the police did not believe him, and he had to explain everything to them in great detail before they understood. Ingo, 43, serving a life sentence for robbery and a murder which he had committed in a faraway country, felt superior to police investigators in a twofold manner: not only because he felt he was an experienced enough criminal to outsmart police officers in general, but also because police in the country where he committed his crime were – according to Ingo – all corrupt and thoroughly disorganised. This is what Ingo told us happened when he was questioned by the police after the corpse of his victim had been found: 'I said [to them]: "Look, guys, here is my passport. Now I'll go back to my flat and if you need anything, then you call me."'

At the same time, however, prisoners had great respect for those policemen who did their job well. Crime scene investigators, for example, according to Paul deserved our respect for the great work they did – if they did it well. It seems that the same distinction between professional behaviour vs. lousy behaviour that was applied to criminal professions was, by these inmates, also applied to the work of those on the side of law enforcement.

Moral superiority on the side of the prisoners was also expressed by drawing attention to acts by police officers or other actors that were so stupid, naive, or evil that prisoners said they themselves could have never done such things. An example is the following excerpt from our conversation with Christoph, the 40-year-old kidnapper who had kept his victim locked in the boot of his car for many hours while he was waiting for ransom. It had been a particularly cold winter that year, and the woman was lucky not to have frozen to death. Christoph did not address this even once in our conversation, and neither did he tell us why he perhaps thought she would be safe in the boot of his car. Yet he got agitated when he told us about the radio transmitter attached to the bag with the (counterfeit) money that police had been left for him at a location agreed with the family of the victim. How could police do this, leave a radio transmitter in the bag? – he asked:

> What upsets me the most is that apparently a person's life does not count anything for the police. Just imagine what would have happened if they would have dealt with a loon, someone who would have found the transmitter and freaked out? I would have had sufficient time to… [silence] If they had dealt with the wrong person, the girl would not have lived that long.

Other prisoners related to the representatives of law enforcement authorities as people who, like all human beings, sometimes make mistakes. Misusing evidence, in this sense, was not something which necessarily required evil intentions but it was an inevitable side-effect of human action, which is always also influenced by emotion (see Chapter 7). This is what Karl (50, serving 17 years for murder and attempted murder) said:

> In my opinion, certainly in many things that are done [with forensic technologies], mistakes happen. See, this is just an example, I do not want to insinuate anything… [But] what happens when someone has emotions … …I know of a case of someone who got to prison, charged with mutilating the genitals of a woman, and then he [allegedly] tried to kill her. But she is still alive. He says that his flat was searched twice and nothing was found. No DNA trace. The third time [they searched the flat] they found a single hair of the girl. And now he's got [a life sentence]. I ask myself: why, when you search the flat thoroughly two times, and then [you find] a hair when you search it the third time …? I don't want to insinuate anything, but how can you protect a suspect from [investigators] tweaking a trace so that it says what they want? How do you do that? [DNA technologies] are a great tool … if they are used correctly. Which, certainly, happens 99.9 per cent of the time. But as I said, what happens if one time someone is guided by emotions, when someone says, 'we need to close the file, there needs to be a name of a perpetrator on it.' What then?

This notion was echoed by Zeno, 29, serving six years for various crimes including drug trafficking and battery. Zeno said he had a 'bad feeling' when thinking how DNA technologies in particular could be abused, although not only by police investigators but also by people in 'his circles': '[I have a] bad feeling. You give your [DNA sample] and then you can be traced everywhere. I'm afraid – I don't know how it is – I move in such circles where, when one wants to do something to another, then [false traces] could be planted… '

Deepening the Stigma

There was consensus among our informants that police investigators tended to round up the 'usual suspects' who fit a certain profile with regard to a certain crime. Several inmates referred to the stigma of being an ex-prisoner as a perpetual 'stain'; some said that efforts to reintegrate into society were futile, since they would be arrested again sooner or later anyhow, regardless of whether or not they were guilty. Mariano, whom we encountered earlier in this chapter, was very critical of the police monitoring the movements of those with prior convictions:

> Mariano: You end up committing the same crime in the same way. That's also what helps the police sometimes… the way you do things. The police get to know your movements and end up on your trail… I'll get out of prison and then, when any little thing happens, [the police will think]: 'Let's go after that one' … 'We want a conviction.' It can't be like that.
>
> Interviewer: Of course not.

> Mariano: You can't convict someone without concrete proof. Or just on suspicion, it can't be like that, because there are lots of convictions just based on suspicion.
>
> Interviewer: Right.
>
> Mariano: Someone who is wrongfully convicted will think 'now that I've been convicted and I'm not guilty I'll be a crook for the rest of my life'. No one believed me, so it'll always be the same. And it's the state that's at fault.
>
> Interviewer: Right.
>
> Mariano: There may be identical crimes because people copy [from each other] … human beings can be very adaptable and unpredictable. I committed a crime in a way that anyone who wanted to try and make me look guilty could copy.

Our interviewees knew that the police often analyse the *modus operandi* of the perpetrators of crimes. The prisoners with whom we talked about this said that police investigators will make every effort to arrange evidence, even if it had to be 'fabricated', to incriminate a suspect, and that the easiest way of arranging evidence was through witnesses making false statements or by forcing confessions or even planting DNA traces at the crime scene (see also Chapter 7). However, some prisoners depicted police officers and the practices of police investigators in more nuanced ways, reflecting a mix of acknowledgement of the good work done, admiration for the technologies they used, and worries about how they could mishandle or abuse their powers when under pressure or 'led by emotions'. Overall, however, police officers were portrayed in similar language as prisoners spoke among themselves and their fellow inmates: there were 'pros' and losers, courageous and evil people, and those who were led by emotions more than others.

Forensic DNA technologies were perceived by the inmates as instruments of 'total surveillance' of bodies and part of a continuous and insidious form of bodily surveillance (Haggerty and Ericson 2000). In other words, their perceptions of police misusing such technologies potentially meant that convicted individuals were unable to escape surveillance, thus reinforcing the stigma of delinquency. At the same time, however, DNA technologies could empower convicts insofar as they could help to prove their innocence. They were viewed as potential protective shields against dubious incriminatory police practices.[4]

---

4 Several prisoners in Portugal – not in Austria – supported the idea of creating a universal forensic database of DNA profiles and a large majority of this group argued or that DNA profiles should never be removed from the national forensic DNA database and were critical about the Portuguese law on the forensic DNA database which stipulates the mandatory removal of DNA profiles from the database at the end of judicial proceedings or at a maximum of ten years after the sentence in prison has been served (Machado, Santos

In addition to articulating the conviction that there would be a constant police intrusion in their lives following their release from prison, there was also a very evident fear of being stigmatised by 'normal' members of society after their release from prison. The word used most frequently to refer to this was 'stain'. Manuel, the 27 year-old sentenced to 14 years for murder and drug trafficking whom we quoted earlier, said that being in prison 'will brand me for the rest of my life', whilst João, aged 49 and sentenced to five years and four months for a crime considered to bear a particularly strong stigma (rape and battery), said that what he feared most was rejection by society in general:

> Of course [being in prison] stains you for life. It's something that marks you. Inside [in prison] no, [you don't feel it so much], you're still inside. When you get out, there will probably be other things that will mark you much more … Being rejected by people, because that is something that's going to happen…

There was a general lack of belief in the system's ability to provide opportunities and conditions for social reintegration by which our interviewees indicated a low level of confidence in the role played by the justice system in terms of its attempts to reintegrate ex-prisoners into society. The prisoners' expectations of social reintegration were instead associated with issues relating to employment and the kind of social networks they would find on the outside. In the opinion of our interviewees, social reintegration was 'impossible' or at least 'very difficult' due to the prevailing ex-convict stigma, which is an obstacle to finding a job and makes relationships with other people difficult.

Some prisoners argued that the removal of verbal data and information from their criminal record and police files was more important in terms of social reintegration than the actual removal of the DNA profile from the forensic database. These prisoners did not tend to associate the function and purpose of the DNA profiles with a criminal register but with an infallible tool individual identification. The logic of the stigma was based on 'classes' of people, since in the view of the interviewees the suspects were 'always the same people'. Stigma was produced by the authorities, and in this sense, was seen as independent of the biological marker (Machado, Silva and Cunha 2012).

---

and Silva 2011). The inmates' previous experiences with the criminal justice system had led to a particular redefinition of their rights and status, in which they viewed the removal of their DNA profiles from the forensic database as a lost opportunity to prove their innocence instead of a benefit, and as an opportunity for a 'clean sheet', 'cleared' of any official record that could directly identify them as the perpetrators of past crimes.

Austrian prisoners did not support a universal forensic DNA database and believed that those who had never done anything criminal should not have their DNA profiles stored in a police computer. They supported the separation line between the criminal and the non-criminal, 'normal' society exactly along the lines that politics and polities suggested it to be drawn.

Conclusion

Police databases may hold a variety of information, including criminal histories, fingerprints, DNA profiles and samples, photographs, and data on external physical characteristics such as height, weight, and hair and eye colour. Our interviewees mentioned the body as being of particular relevance, not only as a resource for successfully committing a crime but also as an important risk factor. Bodies may become incapacitated indirectly due to alcohol or drug abuse or mental instability. In addition, bodies can betray the perpetrator of a crime, since bodily substances – saliva, hair, blood, semen – can easily be shed or released and remain at the scene of the crime, leading to conviction.

What seems to be unique about DNA technologies vis-à-vis other forensic techniques and technologies is that it can be found in every cell of the body and symbolises its essence (see Chapter 5). At any given moment it could reveal the identity of its originator. In the words of one of the prisoners, 'DNA is present in all cells and is unique to each individual. [The police] can even find out *who someone is* from their sweat.' [emphasis added]

Whilst DNA serves to identify individuals, other physical characteristics have significant external visibility and remain extremely important for linking a certain body to a specific criminal act. A strong muscular body with scars, tattoos and bullet wounds corresponds to the body of the criminal that circulates in popular culture and amongst the authorities and the prisoners themselves. The prisoners we interviewed referred several times to the importance of scars and tattoos in the process of identifying the perpetrator of a crime.

The human body has always been used to classify and identify individuals – by skin colour, gender, appearance and body language. Physical features may serve not only to identify people but also to anticipate danger in the context of surveillance (Aas 2006) on the basis of cultural assumptions about how a criminal body looks like. In addition, the DNA profile allows for new methods of identification based on a positive/negative, true/false binary code that creates the illusion of certainty, the exclusion of doubt and the perception of technological infallibility, minimising any ambiguities since it distances itself from verbal communication and virtually eliminates the possibility of doubt, negotiation and uncertainty (Aas 2006: 151).

As is the case with DNA profiles, other forms of data derived from bodies exist which are largely invisible unless the equipment required to read them is available (such as iris and retina scanning, fingerprints, facial or voice recognition, etc.). Biometric identification and DNA profiling have rendered ever more parts of the body 'readable' (Van der Ploeg 1999). The fact that DNA samples can be collected from both trace materials at crime scenes and from individual suspects means that criminal investigators now have access to a powerful new form of body data and body surveillance. Increasing efforts on the part of the state to secure the identification of individuals through body data can be found in societies that are less tolerant of citizen suspects. As Lynch and McNally argued, '[a]lthough "selves" are deeply implicated, suspect identity is primarily an object and product of policing and forensic expertise, rather than a technically defined basis for the formation of individual and group identity' (2009: 284).

One challenge will be to determine how, in the near future, new and old forms of identification can be combined. The data we have obtained for this book seem to indicate that new forms of identification will not replace the old methods but rather reinforce each other in shifting the focus of surveillance towards potential offenders and re-offenders who are thus submitted to a form of 'categorical suspicion' (McCartney 2004).

Chapter 9
Conclusion

In this book we explored how prisoners described and interpreted the rules and practices by the police and other actors in the justice system to utilise bodily traces to establish a link between a specific criminal act and a specific person. We examined how these interpretations interacted with prisoners' understandings of themselves, their crimes, their futures, and with their understandings of others. Prisoners' accounts also seemed to reflect their own experiences when dealing with the criminal justice system; this is probably the reason why their narratives very often focused on the value and utility of forensic technologies, police work, and the courts. In this concluding chapter, we will contextualise the nuances in prisoners' assessments of the police and judicial use of forensic technologies. Some of these nuances may seem as contradictions at first sight: for example, while the large majority of our respondents saw DNA technologies in particular as a very effective tool for the identification of criminals, and recognised its value for exculpation and exoneration, they also raised serious doubts. These doubts mostly pertained to the possible mis- and abuse of technologies, and to the supposed deterrent effect of forensic technologies for crime prevention and deterrence. The prisoners expressed various concerns regarding the uses and effects of tracing technologies that could usefully to inform policy debates.

Chapter Overview: Putting our Findings in Context

In the Introduction, we gave an overview of our methodology, definitions and discussions of key terms and concepts, and situated our study in the larger field of research. We argued that prisoners are a population whose views and attitudes have not received a lot of attention so far in the academic literature on forensic technologies. We also showed that the cases of Austria and Portugal provide fruitful examples for comparison because of the particular similarities and differences that they represent. With regard to the use of a national DNA database, for example, Austria and Portugal are very different. Austria was one of the first countries in Europe to set up a national DNA database (in 1997), and currently holds one of Europe's most largest DNA databases if measured according to the proportion of the population who have profiles stored in it. In Portugal, in contrast, a national DNA database was set up only in 2008, preceded by a lengthy debate among policy makers about inclusion criteria and other system design properties. Such a broader discussion was largely absent in Austria; even if stake holders within the criminal justice system had tried to instigate a wider debate, it is doubtful that substantial issues regarding its use and its potential expansions would have been discussed due to the lack of any experience with centralised DNA databases in the mid-1990s.

Austria and Portugal are also very different with regard to public attitudes towards genetic technologies – with Austria having a long tradition of public 'bio-scepticism' (see Chapter 2), which is absent in Portugal – and with regard to general demographic parameters including socio-economic ones, such as unemployment rates and GDP (*Gross Domestic Product*, i.e., the market value of all final goods produced in a country in a given period).[1] Similarities between the countries are manifold as well: as pointed out in the Introduction, both countries are in continental Europe, and their criminal justice systems display the typical mixture between inquisitorial and adversarial elements typical for the European continent. In both nations, private service providers play a relatively small part in criminal justice (e.g., forensic science service provision, prison administration, etc.). In both countries, corruption – including political corruption – has been recognised as a problem and has affected public trust in governmental institutions.

Chapters 2 and 3 highlight the differences and similarities between the two countries by discussing the history of fingerprinting and forensic DNA profiling – representing two of the most prominent crime scene technologies – in both national contexts, including the current legislative and regulatory provisions and informal practices pertaining to them. Starting with the Austrian case (Chapter 2), we argued that the tension between the relatively high level of public trust in public institutions, which has recently been eroded by widely discussed scandals of alleged miscarriage of justice as well as political corruption, provides an important framework in which the data from interviews with Austrian prisoners should be interpreted. We held that the current crisis of trust in public institutions in Austria, together with the aforementioned public scepticism towards genetic technologies in particular, helps to understand the cautious and restrained way in which policy makers and representatives of governmental authorities in Austrian think and talk about forensic technologies. The forensic DNA database, for example, although having been set up as one of the first centralised forensic DNA databases world-wide, has not followed the path of rapid expansion that we saw in countries such as the UK. The Austrian DNA database is still mostly restricted to storing profiles from convicted offenders and crime scene traces.

1 According to the statistics office at the European Commission, Eurostat, unemployment (defined as the proportion of unemployed persons as a percentage of the total labour force) in autumn 2011 was at about 12 per cent in Portugal, and about 3.5 per cent in Austria (Eurostat 2011). The same source estimates the GDP per capita expressed in Purchasing Power Standards (PPS) at the level of 125 for Austria, and at 81 for Portugal (these figures indicate the relation of the GDP in PPS in both countries in relation to the average of the 17 EU member states. This means that if the index of a country exceeds 100, then the GDP per capita in this country is above the EU-27 average; if it is below 100, then the opposite is the case; Eurostat 2010).

Chapter 3 discusses the emergence of fingerprinting and DNA profiling and databasing as criminal identification techniques in Portugal, and describes the core characteristics of the Portuguese criminal justice system and procedure. It also draws attention to a growing public sentiment that corruption is on the rise. The institutions seen to be most affected by this are politics, business, police and the judiciary (Transparency International 2010). Similar to the Austrian case, this situation provides an important frame of reference for the interpretation of the Portuguese data. Unlike their Austrian counterparts, however, Portuguese media seem to be relatively unaffected by the crisis of trust, and media reports are often seen as reliable accounts of the truth. The Portuguese media coverage of the famous case of the young Madeleine McCann, who disappeared from her family's vacation residence in Portugal in 2007, included severe criticism of the conduct of Portuguese police and criminal justice authorities. In comparison with Austria, open criticism of police and criminal justice authorities seems to be more explicit and more pronounced in Portuguese media. Nevertheless, there was no apparent difference in how Austrian and Portuguese prisoners viewed the criminal justice system in their respective countries; in both cases, the way that prisoners spoke about their experiences and relations to criminal justice authorities was characterised by a combination of contempt, intimidation, suspicion, and understanding (i.e. the affirmation of the values that criminal justice authorities should represent).

Let us take a closer look at how the groups of prisoners we interviewed in Austria and Portugal compared against each other. Demographically the characteristics of prisoners interviewed in both countries were relatively similar. Our interviewees in both countries were relatively young on average (over half of our interviewees were between 25 and 35 years old), and the majority was unmarried. In this respect, the prisoners we interviewed were 'typical' of the prison population also in other countries. As Tonry (2001: 12064 – 5) summarised at the beginning of this century,

> Most prisoners in every country are young, male, unmarried, and economically and socially disadvantaged, and have extensive criminal records. Large percentages are drug dependent and committed their crimes under the influence of alcohol or other drugs. Women constitute only 3 to 8 percent of prisoners in most countries.

Also with respect to incarceration rates (the proportion of the total population currently in prison), Austria and Portugal are relatively similar: at the beginning of the 2000s, 131 out of every 100,000 people in Portugal were incarcerated, and 85 out of every 100,000 people in Austria (Christie 2001: 7248).[2]

2 According to this author, Portugal had the highest incarceration rate in Western Europe, followed by the UK with 124 in 100,000. Iceland had the lowest incarceration rate with only 29 prisoners for every 100,000 people. In Eastern Europe, the Russian Federation

As we saw in Chapters 4–8, overall, although there was considerable variation among individual prisoners on how they viewed crime scene work and tracing technologies, and in their accounts of their personal pasts, presents, and futures in connection with the story of their (alleged and actual) crimes, there were no great differences between the Portuguese and Austrian groups. The only two aspects where we found considerable group differences between Austrian and Portuguese prisoners were, first, views on the benefits and dangers of a universal DNA database: some of the Portuguese prisoners, but none of the Austrian ones, thought that such a universal DNA database would be a positive development. The second aspect concerned dominant ways of explaining criminal behaviour and deviance. This became apparent when our interviewees were asked for their opinions on the deterrent function of forensic technologies in general and DNA databases in particular. Although the majority of both Austrian and Portuguese prisoners were sceptical of a deterrent effect of forensic and DNA technologies on potential (re-)offenders, there were differences between the groups in their main underlying rationales: while some of our Portuguese interviewees thought the use of technology to deter potential offenders to be mostly futile because crime was in the 'nature' of many people, none our Austrian informants voiced such views. In contrast, many of our Austrian interviewees were 'social essentialists' when it came to explaining the aetiology of criminal behaviour: criminals were not born, but made by their environment. Our approach to explaining the differences between the two groups entailed two dimensions: with regard to the more positive attitudes towards the idea of a universal DNA databases among Portuguese prisoners, we contended that this situation could be seen as mirroring the differences in policy debates between the two countries: while the option of introducing a universal DNA database had been discussed Portugal during the period in which the Portuguese DNA database and its legal framework were designed (although this plan was abandoned because of the costs involved and concerns about the protection of human rights), this possibility has never been on the agenda in Austria, where policy makers and stake holders have been hostile towards the idea of significantly expanding the DNA database beyond the groups already included (mostly convicted offenders).

The great overlap between prisoners' views and policy debates in the two respective countries raise interesting questions about the different discursive structures that render particular solutions as possible and necessary. One of these questions related to the stigma of being an ex-convict and of having one's DNA profile and fingerprints included in forensic databases. Our data suggest that the perceptions of stigma associated with the inclusion of an individual's profile in a DNA database are also different in the two groups of Austrian and Portuguese prisoners. As argued by Prainsack and Kitzberger (2009: 70), the fact that the state held a record – in this case, a profile in the DNA database – which is based

'leads' the list with 640 prisoners per 100,000 inhabitants; yet this number is still lower than in the US (709 per 100,000, Christie 2001: 7248–9).

on something that was extracted from the body of a convict, did add and deepen the somatic dimension of their stigma. This feeling of 'being marked for life' may result from the actual experience of being included in the database, but also from the fact that the range of cases in which Austrian legislation allowed the removal of profiles from the database was more limited than in Portugal (see Chapter 2). Against this backdrop, it does not seem entirely implausible to suspect that the unanimous hostility with which Austrian prisoners met the idea of a universal database could be (at least partly) related to the notion that the surveillance and stigma that they were already subjected to was so intrusive that they did not want it to be enforced on the rest of society, namely on their families and friends.

In the Portuguese case, the experience of the stigma associated with inclusion in a DNA database had a prospective character, given that the database was not operational at the time of the interviews. Moreover, the prisoners' attitudes were most likely also be influenced by their previous experience with law enforcement authorities and their practices directed towards known criminals and ex-convicts: Portuguese prisoners in particular emphasised that individuals with prior convictions were particularly vulnerable to surveillance mechanisms and discriminatory police practices.

While some Portuguese prisoners liked the idea of a universal DNA database, the vast majority favoured a scenario in which convicted offenders and suspects should have their profiles included. The majority also thought that profiles, once uploaded to the DNA database, should be retained. This was seen as both benefitting criminal investigations and exculpating wrongly suspected individuals. There was an interesting link between the ways in which prisoners saw the exculpatory capacity of DNA profiles on the national database on the one hand, and the chances of ex-convicts for social reintegration on the other: because DNA profiles could clear somebody who was wrongfully suspected, and because ex-convicts were more likely than others to suffer from this fate, the DNA database assumed, in this respect, the role of a catalyst for reintegration: with the help of the DNA database, the ex-prisoner would be 'left alone'.

With regard to the widespread social essentialism among Austrian prisoners with regard to how they accounted for the occurrence of crime, we suggested that this could be due to the pronounced penal welfarism in Austria (Chapter 6). As Simon (2001: 12608) summarised, since the nineteenth century, punishment has been seen as serving four different functions: deterrence, prevention (or incapacitation), rehabilitation (or reform), and retribution. At different times, by different social or criminal theorists, and within different policy approaches, priorities were usually given to one of these over the others. In Austria, penal welfarism – as a variant of the rehabilitation imperative – became very pronounced during the reforms of the criminal justice system in the 1970s. This has led to a situation where prisoners have typically access to, and are encouraged to make use of, a wide range of services and programmes that aim at helping them to understand the social and psychological 'causes' of their road to deviance and crime, to 'work through' psychological traumata that are conducive to precarious lifestyles, and to change behavioural patterns accordingly. Especially long-term prisoners, like most of the prisoners in our Austrian group, are routinely offered group therapy and frequently also individual psychological counselling. The adoption of a psychological vernacular of the reflexive self is seen as a sign of rehabilitative success (Prainsack and Kreissl 2011). This context must be taken into consideration when noting that although the interviews were opened with a very general request to 'tell me something about your life, your background, your family, how you grew up, anything that you are willing to share', all prisoners immediately drew attention to factors in their lives that in a judicial context could be seen as mitigating circumstances: parents who deserted their children, or who always argued, mothers who were prostitutes, or the traffic accident which had traumatised the young boy, were highlighted in accounts of the prisoners' childhoods and youths. In addition, while narratives of the more recent past were often non-chronological and episodic, accounts of 'growing up' were typically presented in a 'neat linear' (Evans and Wallace 2008: 493) fashion, giving the impression that these stories had been well-rehearsed in the context of psychological counselling.[3]

The moral elements of prisoners' narratives took on several different forms. Very often inmates saw themselves as victims of fate: they had met or dealt with 'the wrong people', or they had been disappointed or 'seduced' by an evil-minded former partner, family member, or friend. These fateful interactions were portrayed as the key mechanisms leading to criminal behaviour. Very frequently, psychological and moral arguments and narratives came together in biographical accounts of our informants. This often created life narratives following a common plot: early deprivation led to stigmatisation and secondary deviance which then, in turn, resulted in a criminal career. We also encountered narratives revolving around the notion of sudden strikes of fate and misfortune: successful life courses and careers were seen as sabotaged by circumstances that 'forced' our informants off the tracks.

There were no substantive differences between the Austrian and the Portuguese prisoners' accounts for why crime occurred, in their own cases, and in the cases of others. However we could notice that while the explanations of Austrian prisoners were overall dominated by vocabulary derived from therapeutic language and moral frames, in the case of Portuguese prisoners they referred more to the role of prisons as 'schools of crime' by mentioning that someone who have been in a prison would probably re-offend again (in this sense, imprisonment was also considered an additional cause for crime to happen).

In Portugal the humanitarian tradition within the penal system dates back to the late eighteenth century. Portugal was the first country in the world to abolish death penalty by law, in 1867. The last time the death penalty was actually applied

3 This stands in contrast to what Evans and Wallace (2008: 493) reported from their interviews with male prisoners in a UK prison: 'One of the first patterns to emerge was that these men did not necessarily tell their life stories in a neat linear fashion.' The large role of psychotherapy in the Austrian penal system is a possible explanation for this difference.

in Portugal was in 1772. The idea of penal welfarism still plays an important role today and the Portuguese penal system is founded on a rhetoric of reintegration – that is, on the idea that the main function of a prison sentence is to re-socialise inmates (Gomes et al. 2003). The Portuguese justice system offers a range of flexibility measures intended to prepare the prisoner for his or her release, such as, for example, the issuing of temporary licenses for leaves of absence. There are also other practices designed to promote inmates' social reintegration like attending professional training courses, and benefiting from psychological counselling and support. However, like in various other countries, these social reintegration policies have shown a rather limited range in practice, which has led some authors to claim that social reintegration via imprisonment is impossible to achieve (Carlen and Tombs 2006, McMahon 1992). Factors held responsible for the relative inefficacy of social reintegration policies in Portuguese prisons (Gomes et al. 2003) are the focus on psychological explanations of crime, rather than on the complexity of the anti-social and exclusionary characteristics of their living conditions, in political and institutional discourses (Cunha and Bastos 2007, Neves 2007). Moreover, frequent complaints are heard about the scarcity of resources and the inadequacy of prison facilities for promoting the necessary psychological counselling to inmates (Gomes et al. 2003: 205–454). In their conversations with us, Portuguese prisoners also mentioned that social reintegration was difficult for them because reintegration programmes, they argued, were ill-designed: they were seen to be excessively bureaucratic, lacking sufficient human resources, or staffed with insufficiently trained people (for more details see Machado et al. 2011). In Austria, in contrast, social and psychological services were either praised by inmates, or they were not commented on. None of the Austrian prisoners criticised the way that they were set up, or their efficacy.

What both Austrian and Portuguese prisoners had in common was that the majority of individuals in each group held the social stigmatisation of convicts and ex-convicts responsible for problems with rehabilitation and re-socialisation. Their stigma as convicts and ex-convicts – represented by their criminal record – was described as an obstacle in finding a job after release, and for maintaining and building family and social relationships during imprisonment and afterwards.

There were strong similarities in Austrian and Portuguese prisoners' narratives regarding sources of information about DNA, with the media playing an important role in the construction of representations about the power and certainty of DNA, as well as in providing knowledge about the sort of biological traces that may lead to identification. In Chapter 4, we looked at the sources of information on forensic and crime scene technologies that prisoners said were most useful for them. From where did they know how to avoid leaving traces at crime scenes (if at all), and what sources did they trust? As the title of this book indicates, public media – and here, most prominently television crime drama – were mentioned by most prisoners as crucial sources of information. Rather than uncritically accepting as truth what they saw on television, however, TV portrayals of crime scene work and tracing technologies were compared with their own experiences with criminal investigation, as well as with experience of peers and friends. Thus, we argued that prisoners' representations of DNA technologies and their uses in criminal investigation cannot simply be explained by the *CSI* effect. Although the extent to which they trusted media depictions of crime scene technologies varied between individual prisoners, what all had in common was that the farther a particular technology was removed from human intervention, and the greater the extent to which it was automated, the more reliable it was thought to be by our interviewees. In other words, machines were trusted to produce reliable and objective knowledge to a much greater extent than humans were. In the prisoners' reflections on television crime drama, this notion was mirrored also in overall positive assessments of the accuracy with which forensic technologies were portrayed to work *in principle*, and with how they were used by humans in criminal investigation. For example, while most of our interviewees thought that DNA analysis in the laboratory reliably produced correct results – exactly as portrayed in series such as *CSI* – the speed at which police solved crimes on TV was unrealistic.

The often heard suspicion that science-and techno-centric crime drama has an unintended educational effect on people was supported by accounts of many of the prisoners in our study. Even if they did not agree that everything portrayed on *CSI* was realistic, they did learn about new techniques and technologies available to the police and occasionally discussed these with fellow prisoners – although not many of our interviewees referred to conversations with peers as important components of their 'forensic awareness' (Beauregard and Bouchard 2010). As we argued in the conclusion to Chapter 4, probably because details about crime scene work and forensic technologies were topics which were not discussed in isolation but instead embedded in thick narratives of the commission and detection of (alleged or actual) crimes, very few prisoners referred to conversations with fellow inmates as important sources of instrumental knowledge about crime scene work. At the same time, this was probably the most significant difference between crime scene work and technologies portrayed in television crime drama on the one hand, and 'real life crime' on the other: while on television the technological tools tend to overshadow other aspects of the story, in real life they rarely do.

As we discussed in Chapter 5, the focus on human action as a source of error and mistakes was not only restricted to accidental errors but also to deliberate abuse and misconduct. Prisoners drew attention to the practice of police investigators lying to suspects about the availability of incriminating evidence to elicit confessions, and to the risk that forensic technologies could be mis- or abused by the police. Also here, DNA technologies seemed to play a special role: because of the high extent to which they were believed to be automated and removed from the realm of human intervention and interpretation, they were believed to be more robust also with regard to the possibility of forgery and abuse. While some of our informants thought that one could forge 'anything else', including fingerprints, DNA could not be forged, neither by the offender nor by the police. Thus the only way in which police could misuse forensic DNA technologies was by planting evidence, or by lying about its existence.

We argued that the power that our informants attributed to forensic DNA technologies in particular had effects on their own self-understanding, and on how they saw their future. Because DNA evidence was seen as especially 'hard' and truthful, the story that it told took precedence over alternative stories that prisoners may have had to offer. Thus, the agency of prisoners was constrained even further; not only were they restricted in what they could do and where they could go, but also the scope of what they could truthfully say determined by external constraints. The scope of their possible claims to truth and accuracy when talking about their lives and their crimes were delineated by the accounts that the evidence told. It is in this light that *CSI*-hero Gil Grissom's famous statement that 'the evidence doesn't lie' obtains a broader meaning: it is a statement about the authority of the accounts of some over the accounts of others.

In Chapter 6 we took the 'special powers' attributed to crime scene technologies, and forensic DNA technologies in particular, as a starting point to discuss the often heard claim that their use had a deterrent effect on potential (re-)offenders. Assumptions that such a deterrent effect exists are typically used to justify or argue for the expansion of the use of forensic technologies. Our case in point are DNA databases, which in most countries have been expanding continuously since they were first set up, both in terms of inclusivity of groups of people whose profiles are stored, and in terms of the scope of purposes that they can be used for. As we saw in that chapter, the narratives of prisoners did not corroborate the deterrence argument: most prisoners believed that crime would never cease to exist, either because (some) people have crime in their 'nature', or because people are pushed into crime by difficult social and familial circumstances (we already discussed the differences between prisoners in Portugal and Austria in this respect). The common understanding was that there was no easy remedy for criminal behaviour, and it could certainly not be achieved by means of expanding of police databases. Some of our interviewees also said that while forensic technologies were helpful for catching the less skilled and sophisticated offenders – including those who committed crimes under the influence of alcohol or drugs – the real professionals among the criminals would always outsmart the police. Although the increasing use and sophistication of tracing technologies were seen to make the life of all career criminals harder, it could not really hurt the best of them. Moreover, there was wide consensus among prisoners that forensic technologies could not possibly have a deterrent effect on those offenders who committed their offences and crimes out of impulses, affect, or in a state of intoxication. This means that the deterrence argument would not be applicable to the offenders of many severe crimes – such as murderers of family members or lovers, or many sex offenders.

Most prisoners used our conversations about forensic technologies also as an opportunity to position themselves in either of these groups. For example, highlighting that they had no interest whatsoever in knowing about forensic technologies was used to corroborate some prisoners' self-presentations as principally good and law abiding citizens; their crime had been committed in a state of emergency, or it had been an accident, and they should really not 'be there' (in prison). Others were open about not intending to embrace a 'normal' lifestyle after their release but instead aiming to earn their living outside the realm of the legal. Men who said things to this effect tended to pronounce their highly professional attitude and their forensic awareness.

The scepticism towards the claimed deterrent effect of forensic technologies prevalent among the prisoners we interviewed corresponds with results from other research studies, which so far have not provided robust evidence for any sort of deterrent effect of forensic technologies. It should be kept in mind, however, that the focus on the question of whether or not there is a deterrent effect diverts our attention away from other effects that forensic technologies have. The storage of personal data – including DNA profiles – in a centralised database, for example, involves potential threats to a range of individual rights, such as the right to privacy, the right to liberty, the right to moral and physical integrity, the dignity of individuals and the presumption of innocence. It also shifts attention increasingly towards *potential* offenders (including potential re-offenders) and thus reinforces an atmosphere of prospective policing. This is not a banal detail in societies that are becoming less tolerant towards 'risky citizens'. As Hacking (2003) pointed out, discourses focusing on the *risk* of crime, rather than actual crime, symbolise fears not only about actual loss but about the stability of core values such as private property, privacy, and liberty. Thus, Hacking argues, reactions to crime extend beyond the 'real' harm done to the punishment of symbolic pollution of these values. The prisoners we interviewed associated a very particular risk with crime, namely the risk of stigma faced by those who are and were in prison.

At the end of Chapter 6 we also highlighted that some authors give different weight to the accounts of prisoners when they talk about themselves, and when they talk about others. As Cunha (2002) noted, prisoners have been found to reproduce common stereotypes about delinquency and the motivations of delinquents. While we agree that this should be kept in mind when interpreting the data from our interviews with prisoners, we hold that this is not a compelling enough argument to dismiss prisoners' accounts about others, and about the motivations and reasons for criminal behaviour more generally, as necessarily biased or informed by dubious motivations. We voiced our conviction to the idea that the production of the 'I', the 'we', and the 'other', is inevitably interlinked. Looking at our interviewees' perspectives on others, and their motivations and plans, also enables us to trace the roles that forensic technologies play in providing points of reference for notions of belonging and of difference in various contexts: 'good citizens' vs. 'criminals', convicts vs. the criminal justice system, and the stigmatised against those who stigmatise them.

In Chapter 7 we turned to another increasingly important role that crime scene technologies have assumed in the last two decades: they have become a crucial tool for the exoneration of convicted people. We started the chapter by differentiating exoneration – the reassessment of the guilt of an individual who has already been convicted – from exculpation, which involves the exclusion of an individual from a group of suspects and typically takes place during the early stages of criminal investigation, or relatively early during the trial. We drew attention to the important work of the Innocence Project, an initiative of defence lawyers in the US who work *pro bono* on appealing court decisions and applying for the re-opening of cases where it seems likely that people were convicted innocently. As analyses of first sets of data from the US have shown, many such wrongful convictions were based upon problematic or even bizarre uses of crime scene technologies, reaching from fingerprint misidentification, to 'experts' testifying on the apparent similarity of hair samples. Also non-technological evidence, such as eyewitness evidence, has been found to be a frequent cause for wrongful convictions. Fortunately, the original Innocence Project, pioneered in the US, has served as a role model for similar projects in other countries including Canada, New Zealand, and Australia. Also in some European countries we now see similar initiatives emerging. In this context it is probably not surprising that none of our interviewees mentioned the Innocence Project by name, although many prisoners did acknowledge that forensic technologies had the potential to incriminate as well as to exculpate and exonerate. In Austria, the so-called Heidegger case – the story of a young man convicted for the alleged murder and robbery of a woman in Salzburg, who was later exonerated and compensated – served as a frequent point of reference for prisoners to express their concerns about the workings of the criminal justice system. Again here, those prisoners who articulated worries about mistakes – or deliberate abuses of evidence – happening within the criminal justice system focused on the agency of humans, not on machines. None of the prisoners mentioned the possibility that wrongful convictions could result from errors or mistakes made by machines, not by humans (this applies also to our interviews with prisoners in Portugal).

We closed chapter 7 by referring to the work of the American legal scholar Richard Leo, who voiced general concerns about how discussions about miscarriages of justice and wrongful convictions are taking place. According to Leo (2005: 213), learning about the causes of wrongful convictions cannot solve the problem of miscarriage of justice. Leo highlights that there is an 'unexamined assumption in virtually all miscarriages writing and scholarship', namely that problems such as false eyewitness evidence, problematic use or interpretation of forensic technologies and techniques such as blood analysis, tool mark analysis or dactyloscopy, are actual causes of miscarriages, which Leo argues they are not: they are symptoms of underlying root causes. Thus, Leo encourages scholars to examine the underlying sociological, demographic and legal factors that contribute to the apparently – in some countries – rather frequent occurrence of wrongful convictions. We echo Leo's call for such deeper analysis. Sociologists and STS scholars have been able to make significant contributions to more critical our understandings of law, science, and society: one of the most impactful contributions has been STS has challenged the relatively unproblematic way in which scientific and technological knowledge is embedded in legal systems.

However there are other aspects of law which have not yet seen the same level of critical scrutiny from STS scholars, such as the notion of the convict: rarely any STS account treats convicts as stake holders, or challenges the supposed fixed meaning of the term; some accounts even equate convicts with actual offenders, thereby accepting several truth claims inherent in legal systems: namely that all convicted people are guilty; that the expertise of convicts pertaining to the science and technology used in legal processes is to be subordinated to, or to be ignored at the cost of, the expertise of other experts; and that such expertise on the side of convicts is not to be recognised as professional expertise. With this book we hope to have made a small start to complicate these assumptions.

Other authors, including practitioners and experts within the criminal justice system, have suggested various measures to strengthen protection against miscarriages of justice, support scrutiny of the uses of scientific methods and expert evidence in courtrooms and argue for the improvement in the commitment to quality control, regulation and training related to scientific evidence (for instance, Nuffield 2007, McCartney, Williams and Wilson 2010). We would like to draw special attention also to the work of Mnookin and colleagues (2011), who argued that the forensic sciences 'do not currently possess – and absolutely must develop – a well-established scientific foundation' (Mnookin et al. 2011: 726). They called for a shift within forensic science towards a stronger focus on science than on law: 'to shift from a quasi-adversarial perspective to a research orientation' (Mnookin et al. 2011: 731), in which peer-review should be a matter of cause, and publications should not be limited to results which are deemed desirable: '...errors should be recognized as an inevitable part of any human enterprise. Errors should be acknowledged rather than swept under the carpet' (Mnookin et al. 2011: 743). Also the Report of the US National Research Council (2009) – while highlighting the comparatively solid scientific basis of forensic DNA analysis in comparison with other forensic technologies – called for further research into cognitive bias and its effects on forensic decision making; for the standardisation of lab reports and technical terms, especially those pertaining to associations between evidence and its possible source; and for the development of a mandatory code of ethics for forensic practice (see Mnookin et al. 2011: 732–40 for a summary of the recommendations of the report). Although the NRC report was addressed to the forensic science community in the US in particular, its assessments and recommendations have been discussed far beyond the borders of the US, and they continue to be seen by many stake holders as applying to forensic sciences in many countries across the globe. We would add that in order to create a positive atmosphere for the implementation of policies which will help to reduce the frequency of wrongful convictions, it is vital to dedicate funds to carry out research into the sociological and demographic factors fostering wrongful convictions, to educating students and practitioners in avoiding these factors, and to foster awareness of ethical responsibilities.

Chapter 8 focused on the body of the criminal, or the alleged criminal, as both a tool and a risk factor in the commission of crimes, and in the quest to avoid detection and conviction. This ambivalence of the bodily dimension was articulated by some of our interviewees in both countries. While, particularly among 'career criminals', having a strong, able, masculine body was seen as an asset, our interviewees also referred to bodies – their own, and those of others – as impediments: bodies can become incapacitated indirectly due to alcohol or drug abuse or mental instability, or they can betray the perpetrator of a crime by leaving behind its marks or substances. By focusing on the corporeal dimension of criminal bodies, we did not mean to imply that either the prisoners, or we, as authors of this book, assumed a clear distinction between the realm of the body and the realm of the mind; especially in the context of issues such as intoxication or drug addiction, the link between these two dimensions was clearly apparent also in the narratives of prisoners. What we sought to do by focusing on the corporeal dimension of crime and those who (allegedly or actually) commit crimes was to provide room for the aforementioned ambivalence as both an asset and a risk factor. While we acknowledged that human body has always been used to classify and identify individuals – by skin colour, gender, appearance and body language – the advancement of tracing technologies, including technologies for automated facial recognition, and DNA analysis, has started to shift the balance in the favour of the latter. Our interviewees' descriptions of how one should commit crimes – namely by covering the body as completely as possible, conceal the true colours of one's iris, etc. – represent attempts not only to render the body invisible (as it could still leave behind substances if invisible), but to make it disappear.

In sum, our interviewees' understandings of tracing technologies were complex and nuanced: prisoners in both countries saw forensic technologies as something positive overall: not only because it helped to catch the 'truly' bad guys, but also because it helped to maintain societal order (!), and something that could 'prove' guilt or innocence. While career criminals said that the increasingly intense use of sophisticated technologies made their lives harder, some prisoners co-opted crime scene technologies as their allies: crime scene technologies could help exculpate or exonerate them, and also 'force' police to carry out a thorough investigation rather than go for the usual suspects right away. The concept of situated dis/empowerment (Prainsack and Toom 2010) applied to our interviewees' representations of crime scene technologies in respect to their own lives and selves: depending on the particular situation and context, technologies were seen as constraining the scope of their agency, or as increasing it. It is noteworthy that with the exception of the two aspects discussed at the beginning of this concluding chapter – the issue of risks and benefits of a universal DNA database, and discussions of the causes for criminal behaviour – there were no apparent group differences between prisoners in Austria and Portugal also in this respect. The large overlap of views and understandings of prisoners in both groups could partly stem from the similarities between Austria and Portugal regarding the way that criminal justice is organised, besides all the aspects that people share in common due to the similarity of practices and life worlds due to the fact of incarceration. An additional reason for the similarities between the understandings of Austrian and Portuguese prisoners could be the existence of a global imagery of criminal investigation, conveyed by blockbuster television crime series.

Opportunities and Need for Further Research

Apart from the need for more empirical research into the sociological and demographic factors that influence the prevalence of wrongful convictions, there are a number of areas where further research would be important. For example, although comparative social science work on social and regulatory aspects of forensic sciences has started to be undertaken, so far it has been mostly a comparison at macro-levels; more studies drawing on empirical fieldwork at crime scenes, policing agencies, and other places in the criminal justice system would be very welcome. Detailed studies into how particular tracing techniques and technologies are used in practice, both as single-case studies and at comparative levels, would also be highly useful to inform debates about the efficiency, and about the effects, of such use.

The uses of forensic DNA profiling and databasing necessarily bring into debate civil rights and values like privacy, dignity and equality. We hope we have added knowledge in this realm by discussing how individuals themselves might be more implicated in the construction of suspects' identities and in the redefinition of the rights and status of suspect body, by taking into account how knowledge about collection and databasing of DNA profiles has effects on the self-management of those whose action and identities are captured in this specific method of surveillance.

Our data also suggest that new forms of identification are unlikely to entirely replace older methods, but instead that they will reinforce each other in shifting the focus of surveillance towards potential offenders and re-offenders who are thus submitted to a form of 'categorical suspicion' (McCartney 2004). In addition, the alleged capacity of DNA technologies to provide identification in an objective and secure manner appears to be a factor that may be used to strengthen public trust in the justice system and the criminal investigation agencies. However, the study of modes of public confidence in DNA databases has been limited to the representations and expectations of 'law abiding citizens' so far. Therefore, the need remains for more comparative studies in order to achieve a better understanding of how convicted offenders, or 'risky citizens' (i.e. those seen as likely to offend, or re-offend), react to the growing use of DNA technologies in criminal investigation. Similarly, the kind of impacts these databases may have on crime prevention and deterrence has yet to be fully understood.

Finally, the experiences and views of the prisoners in our study illustrate how forensic technologies can widen the power gap between authorities and elites. We would like to end with a call for the greater inclusion of perspectives not only of prisoners and offenders, but of marginalised groups more widely, in the academic debate in this field, as well as in policy making.

Afterword:
Forensic DNA and the Human Sciences

Robin Williams

Introduction

This book, the previous chapters of which you should have read before turning to this afterword, is an important addition to the human science literature on a cluster of recent and closely related technological innovations in criminal justice – forensic DNA profiling and databasing. In the pages that follow, I situate this study within the wider field to which it contributes and also comment on what is distinctive about Helena Machado's and Barbara Prainsack's analysis. I begin by making some remarks about the recent history of DNA profiling and databasing before going on to consider how several human science scholars have advanced our understanding of the ambitions of forensic science stakeholders in general and forensic genetics stakeholders in particular. Following these sections I discuss the authors' novel empirical study of prisoners' perceptions of police and judicial uses of forensic genetics, before concluding with some observations on several ongoing social and technical issues concerning forensic DNA profiling and databasing.

Forensic Genetics and Criminal Investigations

From the first announcement in *Nature* of the discovery of 'hypervariable minisatellites' within the human genome by Alec Jeffreys and his colleagues (Jeffreys, Wilson and Thein 1985), through to the most recent controversy surrounding the reliability of so-called 'Low Copy Number' DNA analysis of biological material recovered from crime scenes (see, for example, Budowle, Eisenberg and van Daal 2009 and Buckleton and Gill 2010), there has been constant scientific, political and cultural attentiveness to the development of forensic genetic technologies and their uses for the investigation of crime and the prosecution of offenders in an increasing number of jurisdictions.

Numerous state actors – especially policing authorities – have responded enthusiastically to the promise of each of the many new developments in forensic DNA profiling and databasing that have occurred over almost three decades of scientific and investigative work. There have been ongoing advances in the chemistry and uses of the various workhorse STR multiplexes used in most jurisdictions, but also in the more specialised uses of Y-STRs and of mitochondrial sequencing.[1] In addition, innovatory investigative applications of these technologies continue to appear, including 'familial searching', 'mass screening', 'phenotypical inferencing' and 'bio-geographic ancestry' analysis. It seems to have become generally accepted that the majority of these applications are more effective in supporting investigations and prosecutions wherever legislation permits criminal investigators to take, use and retain biological samples from a large number of crime scenes and from many categories of individual subjects. For this reason, there is a strong – global – expansionary tendency in which relevant authorities in more jurisdictions collect and retain samples and profiles from an increasing number of people in searchable forensic DNA databases, or databanks.[2]

However, various academic, legal, and civil society groups, especially those that have applied to the forensic field bioethical resources relevant to deliberating the collection and use of human genetic material, have reacted more critically to these expanding applications. Central to such negative responses has been a concern with the potential effects of the increased surveillance of citizens made possible by the expansion of forensic DNA profiling and databasing, as well as questions about what agencies will have access to DNA samples and profiles and for what purposes. Problems have also been raised about the governance of this new domain, especially in light of the typically restricted participation of non-police actors in key policy and decision-making fora.[3] There has been particular criticism of instances of unthinking enthusiasm for increasing the size and scope of forensic DNA databases, and also of the use of unsupported assumptions about the relationship between genetic and phenotypical characteristics.[4]

---

1 For a recent review of current issues in the scientific basis of forensic genetics, see Gill and Clayton (2009).

2 A survey of the number of criminal jurisdictions in which DNA samples were taken from various individuals, profiled and retained for subsequent forensic purposes was disseminated by INTERPOL (2009), and the European Network of Forensic Science Institutes (ENFSI) also regularly reviews relevant legislation and policy across Europe (see http://www.enfsi.eu/). Despite this overall growth trajectory, there remain significant differences between the willingness and the capacity of different nation states to invest in the relevant scientific and ICT infrastructures necessary for the establishment of wide-scale forensic DNA databasing. Observations on these comparative – political and economic issues – can be found in Wilson (2009), Jasanoff (2010) and in a number of the substantive chapters in Hindmarsh and Prainsack (2010).

3 Of course there are large differences in the way in which governance regimes have been established and modified in different jurisdictions over the last decade. Comparisons can usefully be made – for example – between the slow acceptance in England and Wales of the necessity of external involvement in, and ethical scrutiny of, the UK National DNA Database on the one hand and the foresight of the Irish Government's plans for independent oversight of its planned national forensic DNA database on the other.

4 I include in this latter group, critical studies of the way in which individuals and agencies who have promoted the use of DNA profiling for inferring possible 'visible characteristics' of criminal suspects, have deployed problematic concepts of 'race' and/

Despite these kinds of objections, claims for the operational utility and the scientific standing of forensic DNA profiling and profile comparison are increasingly accepted by investigators, advocates and judges in most criminal jurisdictions. Equally, the value of forensic DNA databasing is recognised widely by criminal justice policymakers and legislators in a very large number of nation states. Perhaps surprisingly, the rising confidence in these forensic applications has also contributed to an increasing scepticism of claims for the reliability and validity of other, more traditional forms of forensic science knowledge and expertise. This unanticipated consequence of the success of one particular forensic discipline for the fate of others has most recently surfaced in the critical report of the United States National Research Council (2009) on the scientifically problematic condition of a large number of forensic disciplines especially, but not exclusively, fingerprinting, ballistics, bitemark, toolmark and fibre comparison.[5]

Human Science Perspectives and Policy Interventions

This rich agonistic field, in which issues of scientific credibility, social policy, and criminal justice practice constantly jostle one another, has received the attention of a number of human science scholars who have brought to its cultivation a range of more general interests and resources. Unsurprisingly, many of the most penetrating of these contributions have been made by those affiliated to the interdisciplinary domain of science and technology studies, and especially those with an interest in exploring the complex and often problematic relationship between the knowledge systems and local practices of science and the (civil and criminal) law. Central to the development of this area of scholarship was work that appeared more than a decade ago in a special issue of Social Studies of Science *Contested Identities: Science, Law and Forensic Practice* edited by Michael Lynch and Sheila Jasanoff

or 'ethnicity'. Troy Duster's work has been a major inspiration to these studies, and other aspects of the relationship between DNA databasing and social inequality. His Foreword to this book explains his outlook, and his and other papers in Krimsky and Sloan (2011) represent the most recent attempt to explore this topic in detail.

5 The NRC's representation of forensic genetics as the exemplary forensic science discipline, and the implications of this for other disciplines has been the subject of considerable commentary in the literature. See, for example, Cole (2010), Murphy (2010) and Thompson (2009). This history of earlier NRC efforts to deal with the arrival of forensic genetics is discussed by several writers, especially Aronson (2007) and Kaye (2010). For Cole and Lynch (2010), the specific comparisons made in the NRC report between DNA profile matching and fingerprint comparison instantiates what they earlier described as an 'inversion of credibility'. In their account, early DNA profiling advocacy made rhetorical use of the previously established forensic discipline of fingerprinting (most obviously by the use of the term 'DNA Fingerprinting'). However current portrays of the relationship between the two forensic technologies now usually claim the existence of well-grounded scientific support for the former in contrast to the weaker rational foundations for the latter.

(1998).[6] Since that time (and drawing on their previous bodies of work), both Jasanoff and Lynch have continued to provide powerful general theoretical inspiration as well as specific conceptual tools for critical analysis in this field. Their common concern to develop work informed by the trope of 'co-production', which stresses the interdependence of social and natural orderings, has had a strong influence on many recent studies of many scientific and technological developments.[7] In addition, an especially relevant variant of this underlying theme (which pays particular attention to forensic DNA profiling and databasing) is Lynch and McNally's notion of 'biolegality' which foregrounds the constant and mutual adjustment of judicial, policing and scientific imperatives and considerations in the instutionalisation of these technological affordances.[8] Finally, the analysis of what happens in the variety of deliberative fora in which actors and agencies claim and contest evidence for the effectiveness of forensic DNA profiling and databasing for crime control, has been aided by understanding the dependency of these arguments on particular 'civic epistemologies' – a neologism coined by Jasanoff whose potential she has explored as part of her comparative analysis of the way that key actors and agencies in different societies have dealt with a variety of scientific and technological innovations (see, for example, Jasanoff 2005). These, and other related, conceptual innovations, have informed the work of a number of other scholars who have contributed to a growing body of literature on the claims and uses of forensic science in general and forensic genetics in particular.[9]

These theoretical and empirical contributions have been supplemented by the work of legal academics who have published diagnostic accounts of the relationship between scientific reasoning (in forensic genetics and other forensic fields) and legal discourse. For example, David Kaye's (2010) recent account of the history of forensic DNA profiling covers many of the topics that have been of interest for this scholarly group, especially those who work in the US. However there are

---

6 Many, but not all of the papers on forensic DNA profiling in this collection, centred on its contested application in the trial of OJ Simpson for the murder of his ex-wife and her male companion. A focus on this important case lent coherence to the collection but also meant that issues of the logic and propriety of forensic DNA databasing (which had already begun to emerge in the UK), as well as consideration of the developing uses of DNA profiling outside of the United States, were less thoroughly covered. Nevertheless, Lynch (and McNally) had already begun – in 1995 – a groundbreaking UK based ESRC funded study Science in a Legal Context: DNA Profiling, Forensic Practice, and the Court. Much of this research was later published in Lynch, M., Cole, S., McNally, R., and Jordan, K. (2008).

7 The clearest account of this perspective, along with several examples of its application is Jasanoff (2004b).

8 See Lynch, M. and McNally, R. (2009)

9 This is not the place for a full list of these scholars but, in addition to those mentioned elsewhere in this chapter, many of them contributed to Hindmarsh and Prainsack (2010). Others deserving of particular mention include Gerlach (2004), Lawless (2010) and McCartney (2006a).

many other commentators whose writing has advanced our understanding of some of the more intractable differences that emerge when the perspectives of genetic scientists and population-genetic statisticians are confronted by the reasoning preferences of judges and advocates. The issues raised by the introduction of DNA evidence into criminal prosecutions in England and Wales, as well as in other jurisdictions based on English jurisprudence, have been especially vigorously pursued by several scholars, especially Roberts (e.g., 2002, 2009 and Roberts, Willmore and Davis 1993), Redmayne (e.g., 1995, 2001), Steventon (1993, 1998), Edmond (2000, 2004) and Gans (e.g., 2007 and Gans and Urbas 2002).

A number of other studies of DNA profiling and databasing have been less concerned to chart the course of scientific or juridical disputes about the working of these technologies, and more concerned to test claims of their operational value to criminal investigators. Here, criminological interests tend to displace those of legal scholarship or science and technology studies, and academic ambitions may more easily complement the demands for evidence arising from criminal justice policymakers and state agencies involved in allocating relevant police and/or forensic science provider budgets.

Whilst earlier efforts to accumulate evidence capable of determining the value of DNA profiling and databasing to criminal investigations largely originated from the UK, and was almost all funded by the Home Office (see, for example, Burrows et al. 2005, Prime and Hennelly 2003, Williams 2004), many of the more recent studies have been carried out in the US, mostly funded by the National Institute of Justice. Two of these have been especially ambitious. Roman and his colleagues (Roman et al. 2008) carried out the first randomised control trial of the use of forensic DNA profiling across several US police districts in which the results of burglary investigations in which DNA evidence was collected but not analysed, were compared with those in which such evidence was made available to investigators. A second major study, of the role of forensic science in general in securing prosecutions, but also providing separate data on DNA profiling, has recently been completed by Peterson and others (Peterson, Sommers, Baskin and Johnson 2010). This work followed the course of the investigations of a number of different kinds of crime (including homicide, rape, aggravated assault, robbery, and burglary), through the criminal justice system in order to assess the contribution of forensic science to the outcome of investigations and prosecutions. Whilst a range of forensic evidence types was considered, particular attention was given to DNA analysis because of its ability to provide individualising evidence capable of associating particular suspects to crime scenes.[10]

10 The findings of this study are too complex to summarise here, but it is worth noting that the two crime types in which DNA evidence most strongly figured were homicide and rape. This may seem unsurprising, although it does not in fact accord with research findings from the UK where there has a strong drive to include DNA evidence collection in the routine examination of burglary and car crime scenes.

The wider social and political implications of the expanding uses of this technology have also been explored in several academic and policy studies. In the United Kingdom, two major agencies – the Nuffield Council on Bioethics, and the Human Genetics Commission – have both published substantial critical reports on the distinctively forceful legislative and operational developments in DNA databasing that occurred in England and Wales between the establishment of the National DNA Database in 1995 and the decision of the Council of Europe's European Court of Human Rights (ECrHR) in the case of S and Marper v. the UK Government.[11] It is difficult to assess the effective influence of these two bodies, even though the latter, at least until recently, was the major and authoritative source of advice to Government on all issues related to human genetics. However, it is worth noting that the ECrHR ruling referred to above made specific use of some of the arguments about DNA sample and profile retention made by the Nuffield Council on Bioethics in their 2007 report. In addition, the monitoring group Genewatch UK have also been actively interrogating official statements and statistics on the National DNA Database for a number of years as well as appearing before the several House of Commons Committees that have inquired into aspects of forensic DNA profiling and databasing in England and Wales.[12] In the US, the American Civil Liberties Union has frequently criticised the state and federal expansion of DNA collection and retention (see Krimsky and Simoncelli 2011), and the American Society of Law, Medicine and Ethics sponsored a series of national workshops and conferences on US developments in DNA profiling, attended by many of the major academic, scientific and operational experts in the field between 2003 and 2006.[13]

Finally, human science scholars have contributed to our awareness of the sources, distribution, and quality of knowledge about DNA profiling and databasing amongst individuals from a range of social categories. Police officers' knowledge of forensic genetics has always been seen to be limited and problematic since the beginning of its appearance within investigations in the 1990's. Whilst there have been no studies that have focussed solely on forensic genetics, studies of the general forensic awareness of police officers have usually shown large variation and serious shortcomings (see, for example, Saulsbury et al. 1994). Forensic providers (often in association with key policing policy actors) in the UK and elsewhere have sought to raise police awareness of the possibilities and limitations of DNA profiling, but the results of these efforts have never been systematically evaluated.

11 See Nuffield Council on Bioethics (2007) and Human Genetics Commission (2001, 2002 and 2009).

12 Genewatch UK publications on forensic DNA databasing are available at http://www.genewatch.org/

13 Papers presented at, or influenced by, these meetings were published in Lazer (2004) and in Noble and Moulton (2006).

It is also widely asserted, especially by forensic scientists themselves, that knowledge amongst advocates and judges of many of the details of DNA profiling and profile comparison is often unsatisfactory (especially but not exclusively their understanding of key statistical issues in the application of these technologies to investigations and prosecutions). One very interesting recent study by several New Zealand scholars (Grace et al. 2011) has explored this in detail and shown the difficulties encountered by judicial actors in efforts to grasp the typically Bayesian reasoning preferences of forensic DNA scientists. This same publication has also produced evidence on lay understandings of DNA profiling, a topic which has been of considerable interest elsewhere, but rarely the subject of rigorous empirical research. Much of the work on the so-called '*CSI* effect' (to which forensic DNA is often asserted to be a major contributor) has recently been critically summarised by Cole and Dioso-Villa (2009), but it continues to be a controversial topic that is treated with a variable level of seriousness by different scholars.[14]

Tracing Technologies

Common to almost all of the studies and reports listed above has been a critically interrogative stance to the history of claims-making over the contested place of forensic genetics in contemporary social formations, in particular with claims-making about the contribution of this science and its associated technologies to the goals of personal safety and collective security. This has been so, whether the focus of such studies has been on the scientific underpinning, and practical accomplishment, of forensic DNA profile generation and comparison, the trajectories of mutual adjustment between the everyday work of forensic genetics and the preoccupations of judicial actors, the formation and implementation of legislation on the collection, retention and use of DNA samples and profiles, the evaluation of the value of DNA profiling and databasing for effective criminal investigations and reliable prosecutions, or the way in which the arrival of this technology has renewed traditional debates about the balance between imperatives of personal safety and collective security on the one hand, and fundamental commitments to human dignity and individual privacy on the other.

---

14 In the mid-1800s, a representation of criminal investigation fully informed by forensic science emerged in which Locard's (in)famous 'law' or 'principle' (usually simplified and rendered as 'every contact leaves a trace'), was combined with a version of the 'method' advocated by the fictional Sherlock Holmes ('the observance of trifles'). This representation has continued to hold sway over professional and public imaginations of the power of these practices ever since. Indeed, whilst much has been made of the recent discovery of the hypermodern '*CSI* effect', it is clear that public interest in the seemingly spectacular accomplishments of forensic practitioners predates this phenomena by at least a century (see Thomas' (2000) analysis of the factual and fictional portrayal of emerging forensic technologies of the late nineteenth century).

The work of Helena Machado and Barbara Prainsack, in this publication and in their other independently written papers on this general topic, is informed by and contributes to several of these interrogative preoccupations. Both have arrived at them via a longer history of work on other aspects of genetic science and its deployment within medical contexts. However, since turning their attention of forensic issues, and before completing this book, Machado has already written about the Portuguese deliberations on the establishment of a national DNA database and on an especially well-known recent criminal investigation in the Algarve. Prainsack's interest in forensic genetics was developed in the course of a larger study of the governance of DNA research databanking, and has already led to a number of publications on the development of forensic DNA databasing, the emergence of regimes for the exchange of forensic DNA profile information between criminal jurisdictions, and the logic of phenotypical inference-making.

The early chapters of this book make use of these previous – and ongoing – studies in order to explain why and how this technology has been embraced by many criminal jurisdictions. The authors explore the history of modern state ambitions for security, and describe the growth of forensic DNA databases as one of the manifestations of that ambition (albeit accompanied by an interest in the uses of other forms of bio-information), in particular in an attempt to anchor knowledge of the history and actions of individual (especially criminal) actors in immutable facts of their bodies. This general exploration is given more detailed texture by considering the differing trajectories of these developments in two European Nation States – Austria and Portugal. In the former we see a developing forensic DNA profiling and databasing regime that somewhat resembles that of the world's first forensic DNA databasing jurisdiction (England and Wales) except that fewer categories of individuals are at risk of having their DNA samples taken, and also that the power to retain DNA profiles and samples is also much more limited. Nevertheless, it is clear that forensic DNA profiling is well embedded in Austrian criminal investigation, and that there is also enthusiasm amongst relevant state agencies to participate in the new arrangements for the international exchange of forensic bioinformation between Austria and other EU States under the Prüm Treaty (as well as with other non EU States through Interpol).

In contrast to this more-or-less standard Northern European and North American trajectory, however, Portugal provides us with a more unusual (and problematic) forensic DNA databasing history. Whilst recent police uses of DNA profiling have been very limited (at least when compared with those jurisdictions where its uses are increasingly common in the investigation of property crime as well as sexual and violent crime), there has been sufficient political support to announce a plan to establish a universal DNA database of the whole population in support of criminal investigations. However, this plan was subsequently abandoned because of the costs involved and concerns about the protection of human rights. Instead the Portuguese law has made it possible for citizens to volunteer their samples for inclusion on such a DNA database. The DNA profiles of volunteers are kept indefinitely or until permission is revoked, while the profiles of convicts are retained up to a maximum of ten years after the end of their sentence. Unsurprisingly, the number of individuals who have come forward to donate voluntarily is vanishingly small.

In later chapters the authors complement their contribution to existing research and scholarship on the nature and scope of forensic genetics by providing the first systematic account of the views of DNA profiling and databasing held by prisoners convicted of criminal offences (and held in Austrian and Portuguese prisons). In the UK, several consultations (by the Nuffield Council on Bioethics, the Human Genetics Commission and the Home Office) invited the views of members of the public on the use of forensic DNA profiling and on the inclusion and retention regimes appropriate to the National DNA Database of England and Wales. A small number of respondents to these invitations identified themselves as having direct experience of their DNA being taken and retained in relation to specific criminal investigations. However, until the two parallel studies reported in this book, no researchers have tried systematically to explore the experiences and views of convicted offenders. Their own words nicely express their exploration as the effort to consider:

> ... how prisoners views on forensic technologies, the work of police and courts, the body and instances of surveillance, processes of exclusion and social categorisation, are interrelated with media representations of criminality, crime investigation, prisons and prisoners, and also with the inmates own experiences when dealing with the criminal justice system.

Many aspects of prisoners' experiences and views are analysed in the course of this book, but I will confine my remarks to just two of them. First, the authors have written about the 'forensic awareness' of the prisoners that they interviewed – especially their awareness of what biological material forensic scientists are able to collect from crime scenes, the kind of analysis they can carry out, and the inferences that can be drawn from those analyses. This is an interesting topic to consider, if only because police officers and forensic scientists themselves are rarely consistent in what kinds of knowledge of these matters they most want to disseminate to the general public (and to criminal actors as members of that public). On the one hand, it is commonly argued that knowledge of the potential of forensic DNA to assist investigations will deter individuals from committing crime for fear of an increased chance of their detection. On the other hand, however, there is a claim that revealing too many details of the routines of DNA recovery and profiling will either cause criminals to take additional forensic precautions, change their preferences for the kind of crime they undertake, or encourage them in more extreme efforts to eliminate any traces that they fear leaving at crime scenes (for example by setting fire to properties).

Some, but not all, of the prisoners interviewed in the course of this study had made efforts to discover what they could about the collection of biological materials at crime scenes and the uses of DNA profiles obtained from these materials. Many had only begun this following their conviction and, though some may plan to bank the knowledge for future use, not all of the prisoners who participated, saw themselves as career criminals. Others saw the exculpatory advantages of DNA evidence, especially in situations where they distrusted the police to honestly collect and present other forms of non-forensic science evidence. This plurality of narratives – of awareness, guilt, innocence and accident – that recur throughout these accounts cannot easily be summarised except perhaps to say that they reflect many more general views of forensic DNA profiling, albeit filtered through the pragmatic relevancies of those who once engaged in just the kind of actions that the technology was designed to capture (and even deter).

Mention of deterrence brings me to the second theme in prisoners' talk that I wanted to mention: views of the utility of forensic DNA databases. The majority view expressed by prisoners was that the establishment and expansion of such databases would not help to deter crime, although there were some differences in the views expressed in the two jurisdictions, with some of the Portuguese prisoners being more optimistic about this aspect of socio-legal engineering. There seemed to be little support for the extension of criminal databases into universal databases, since again prisoners expressed distrust of relevant authorities to govern their uses fairly. Yet prisoners are not experts in deliberating these issues, and they suffer from the same lack of relevant evidence concerning database effectiveness in detecting and/or deterring offenders from which all other – professional and lay – commentators also suffer. They do, of course know something of the risks to their own criminal conduct posed by the growing collection and storage of this kind of forensic bioinformation. However, Machado and Prainsack are keen not to over-privilege DNA technologies in this respect, reminding us that they are only one '... of a cluster of practices, attitudes, and technologies of stigmatisation' which these offenders confronted in and as a result of their criminalised actions.

Conclusion

Throughout their detailed analysis of various – ruling and subject, operational and policy, police and judicial, scientific and legislative – perspectives on contemporary forensic genetics, Machado and Prainsack encourage us to reflect on many aspects of this technology, and what we imagine to be both its contribution and its challenge to a number of contemporary social values. Informed debate on the uses of forensic DNA profiling an databasing necessarily brings into play consideration of a large number of values, most obviously, but not exclusively, those of justice, equality, security, privacy, dignity, freedom, autonomy and solidarity. The growth of forensic DNA databases continues apace despite the necessary caution over inclusiveness and retention regimes that European States have now to observe following the judgement of the ECrHR in the aforementioned case of S and Marper v. The United Kingdom. Profiling methods keep on improving, with new STR multiplexes making it possible to retrieve usable biological material from sources previously too contaminated by environmental and other local factors to permit successful profiling. Controversy continues, especially in the US, but also in some part of Europe about the use of 'familial searching', and phenotypical analysis remains an ambition for some and a hazard for others. Not all jurisdictions are comfortable with the analysis of the very small amounts of DNA typically amplified in 'Low Template Analysis', and the role of human judgement in disambiguating two, three, or even four person mixtures remains contentious. The old DNA Wars are long gone, but this does not mean the end of DNA controversies. Ongoing human science analysis of the sources, nature and resolutions of these scientific and operational promises, problems, and controversies will continue to be needed to challenge the credibility of unthinking assertions, and to provide a more secure evidence base on which to support rational decision making in this domain. This book contributes powerfully to such analysis.

Glossary

AFIS: Automated Fingerprint Identification System. It is a biometric identification system using digital imaging technology to obtain, archive and search dactyloscopic data. In the process of establishing someone's identity in the context of an arrest, or for the purpose of criminal investigation in many jurisdictions, fingerprints and palm prints are routinely taken and AFIS is searched to see whether the person's prints match latent prints from crime scenes, or whether the person's prints are already stored in the database under a different name.

Arguido: In Portugal, the legal term for an official suspect, i.e., a person against whom a formal accusation has been made or inquiry procedures have been instigated.

Bertillonage (also Bertillon-system): A system of criminal identification developed by the French criminologist and anthropologist Alphonse Bertillon at the end of the nineteenth century. The Bertillon-system comprised the detailed description of suspects and convicts on the basis of a large set of standardised measurements of the body, a narrative description (*portrait parlé*), photographs, and, if applicable, the registration of unusual characteristics such as moles or scars. It rendered possible the first systematic archiving of data obtained for criminal identification. It was superseded by dactyloscopy (fingerprinting) as the primary method of archiving and searching data pertaining to criminal identification in the first decades of the twentieth century.

Bioinformation: There is no authoritative definition of the term. Drawing upon the way the term is employed in the Nuffield Council on Bioethics' Report on *The Forensic use of Bioinformation: Ethical Issues* (2007), we use it to signify data derived from the analysis of a range of physical or biological characteristics of a person (most prominently, DNA data and fingerprints).

CNPD: *Comissão Nacional de Protecção de Dados*, the Portuguese Data Protection Authority.

Código de Processo Penal: The Portuguese Code of Criminal Procedure.

***CSI* effect**: A concept employed by scholars, and increasingly also practitioners and public media, to capture the notion that the wide popularity of techno-centric crime drama on TV (such as the US crime series *Crime Scene Investigation: CSI*) has influenced what people expect from forensic technologies, and in particular from DNA analysis.

***CSI* effect effect**: This term was coined by Simon Cole and Rachel Dioso-Villa (2009), signifying the phenomenon that *assumptions* about how people's expectations and behaviours have changed on the basis of public media representations of forensic technologies have started to change the expectations and behaviour of actors within the criminal justice system. This, these authors argue, often works in favour of prosecutors: because prosecutors are seen as confronted with increasingly overblown expectations regarding the presentation of scientific evidence, publics and stake holders tend to sympathise with them and view their stances and arguments more favourably.

Dactyloscopy: The method of ridge analysis in human skin (typically fingers and palms).

DNA Expansion Programme: A programme launched in the UK in 2000, with the aim of increasing the growth of the NDNAD until DNA profiles of all known offenders would be centrally stored.

'DNA Wars': In the aftermath of the first uses of DNA evidence in criminal investigations and at court in the 1980s, a heated discussion among experts and practitioners ensued about whether or not DNA evidence was robust enough for this purpose. The outcome of this 'war' is well known; not only has DNA evidence found entrance in criminal justice systems all over the world, but it is widely seen as the new 'gold standard' in forensic science – a process which Lynch (2004; see also Lynch et al. 2008) aptly referred to as 'inversion of credibility'.

EU: European Union.

Eurodac: The Eurodac system is based on EU Council Regulation 2725/2000. It is run by a central unit within the European Commission and consists of a central database containing fingerprints as well as particular types of personal information about the originator of the print (EU country of origin; sex; place and date of asylum application, or place and date of the apprehension of the person; reference number; date of taking of the fingerprints; date of transmission of the print to the central Eurodac unit).

Eurojust: Eurojust is a judicial cooperation body within the EU. Its function is to aid and help coordinate measures against serious crime which affect the territory of more than one EU member country.

Europol: Europol is a law enforcement agency supporting law enforcement in EU countries. In particular, its mission is to tackle problems of transnational and European relevance, such as counter-terrorism, organised crime, etc.

Exculpation: Involves the exclusion of an individual from a group of suspects. It typically takes place during the early stages of criminal investigation or the trial.

Exoneration: Entails a reassessment of the guilt of an individual who has already been convicted. Exoneration thus involves the re-opening of a case and can free wrongfully convicted people from prison (see also 'Innocence Project').

Familial searching: If DNA profiles in a database do not result in a 'full match', that is, if two profiles are not identical at all but most tested loci, it is likely that the genetic proximity between the two profiles is relatively close. Depending on how many markers match, the 'almost matching' profile could come from a parent, sibling, child, cousin, uncle, etc. of the person in the database. Only few countries allow the results of so-called 'familial searching' to be used in investigations.

Forensic awareness: Beauregard and Bouchard (2010) use this notion to describe experience and knowledge pertaining to the avoidance of leaving traces at crime scenes on the side of offenders.

Function creep: The concept refers to the observation that technological infrastructures that were set up for a particular purpose often start to be used for wider purposes (Dahl and Sætnan 2009). Once infrastructures are set up, it becomes difficult to prevent them from being used more widely.

(Forensic) Graphology: Handwriting analysis that gives indications as to the person's state of mind at the time of producing a particular document, or to examine what may be suspicious or fraudulent documents.

Heidegger case: The case of the Austrian Peter Heidegger, who – in 1993 – was wrongfully convicted of robbing and murdering 28-year-old taxi driver Claudia Deubler, mostly on the basis of false eye witness evidence. He was exonerated in 2003.

IAFIS: Integrated Automated Fingerprint Identification System in the U.S. Data in the IAFIS include fingerprints, criminal histories, mug shots, photographs of scars and tattoos, physical characteristics such as height, weight, and hair and eye colour and aliases. The system also includes civil fingerprints, mostly of individuals who have served or are serving in the U.S. military or have been or are employed by the federal government. It is currently thought to be the largest biometrical database in the world.

Innocence Project: A US-based litigation and public policy organisation founded in 1992, which has taken a pioneering role in exonerating wrongfully convicted individuals (mainly) through DNA testing. The Innocence Project has become a leading example in how forensic technologies can be used to tackle and sometimes rectify miscarriages of justice, and it has spurred many similar initiatives in other countries.

Joana case: Joana Cipriano Guerreiro was an 8-year-old Portuguese girl who disappeared from her home in the village of Figueira (region of Algarve), in 2004, seven miles from where Madeleine McCann was last seen in 2007. The detective in charge of the investigation in Joana's case, Gonçalo Amaral, would later be the same to lead the searches for Madeleine McCann.

Johann 'Jack' Unterweger (1950 –1994) case: Unterweger was an Austrian serial killer whose victims were mostly sex workers. First convicted of a 1974 murder, he was released in 1990 after a public campaign by intellectuals and personal friends of Unterweger who regarded him as a textbook example of rehabilitation. Upon his release from prison, Unterweger became a journalist and a minor celebrity, but within months of his release started killing again. He committed suicide following a conviction for several counts of murder in 1994.

Madeleine McCann case: The case pertains to the unresolved disappearance of a three-year-old English girl, Madeleine McCann, during a family holiday in a beach resort in Portugal in May 2007. In terms of media coverage and public attention all over the world, the criminal investigation following her disappearance has been one of the most high-profile cases in this century.

Mechanical objectivity: Theodore Porter (1996) famously used this term to refer to the greater authority bestowed upon 'impersonal numbers' in many spheres of our political, economic, and social realities than on human experience and judgment.

Modus operandi: The particular pattern of crime commission; the mode in which a crime is committed. The analysis of the *modus operandi* (or 'MO'), can give investigative clues linking a crime scene to a particular suspect, or different crime scenes to one another.

Natascha Kampusch case: Natascha Kampusch, an Austrian female, was abducted at the age of 10 on 2 March 1998. Kampusch was held captive in a secret cellar by her kidnapper Wolfgang Priklopil for more than eight years, until she escaped on 23 August 2006. Her captor, Wolfgang Priklopil, could not be charged as he committed suicide when he found out that Ms Kampusch had escaped.

NDNAD: The National DNA Database in the UK. It is the oldest and largest centralised forensic DNA database in Europe, and one of the largest worldwide.

Night Stalker case: Also known as the "Minstead Rapist", regards a man who brutally assaulted and raped a number of elderly women in the South East London area of England between 1992 and 2009. DNA samples were taken and found to match the DNA profiles obtained from semen found on the victims. Delroy Grant denied his involvement with the crimes and instead blamed his ex-wife of having planted the evidence against him. Grant was convicted of 29 counts of rape, robbery and assault on 24 March 2010.

Penal welfarism: The idea that the punishment that criminals receive should also help them to become better citizens and people, and that the punishment should help them acquire skills to do so.

Persons of happenstance (*Gelegenheitspersonen*): In Austria, this definition applies to individuals under no suspicion who might have left their DNA at the crime scene for legitimate reasons and may be asked to provide a DNA sample for elimination purposes. Typically, these are partners, family members, flat-mates, and neighbours, cleaning personnel, but sometimes also victims.

Phantom of Heilbronn case: The case of the 'phantom of Heilbronn' comprised a large-scale multinational police search for an unknown female offender, until it turned out that the DNA found at the crime scenes had come from a factory worker packaging the cotton swabs that were used for the securing of crime scene traces.

Phenotypic profiling: The use of DNA analysis in order to obtain information about externally visible traits, and/or the likely ethnic background, of a person. This information cannot be obtained from traditional (STR-based) DNA profiles, but necessitates a special kind of analysis that is not routinely carried out when DNA is secured at crime scenes, or samples are taken from people. Phenotypic profiling can give investigative clues with respect to perpetrators, suspects, and victims (if the latter cannot be identified by other means – e.g. severely mutilated or decomposed corpses).

Prüm Decision (and Prüm Convention): On 27 May 2005, the so-called Prüm Convention – named after the German town where the meeting took place – was signed by representatives of seven European countries, Belgium, Germany, Spain, France, Luxembourg, The Netherlands, and Austria. It was driven by the conviction that the measures of the Schengen Convention (abolishing border controls and enhancing police cooperation) and the provisions of the former so-called Third EU Pillar (Police and Judicial Cooperation in Criminal Matters) were not sufficient to address growing levels of cross-border crime. In June 2007, the core parts of the Convention were transposed into EU Law (2008/615/JHA, 2008/616/JHA); the so-called Prüm Decision became effective in August 2008. By August 2011, all EU countries were obliged to have rendered their central databases on vehicles, fingerprint, and DNA data searchable (on a hit/no hit basis) to authorities of other EU countries. Not all countries met this deadline.

S and Marper v. United Kingdom case: On 4 December 2008, the European Court of Human Rights (ECrHR) delivered its Grand Chamber Judgment in the case of *S and Marper v. the United Kingdom*. The case was brought to the Court by Michael Marper and another young man known only as 'S', whose fingerprints and DNA profiles were stored in the English police database following their arrest in 2001. Charges had been dropped in both the case of Marper (arrested on harassment charges) and of S (at age 11 arrested for attempted robbery). In the absence of convictions, both men demanded their fingerprints and DNA data be removed from the database. In both cases, the Court of Appeal ruled against this. Having exhausted all legal remedies in the UK, the two men turned to the ECrHR, arguing that retention of their fingerprints, DNA profiles, and DNA samples represented infringements of their rights to private life as provided in Article 8 of the European Convention on Human Rights (1950). In its judgment, the Court acknowledged a violation of Article 8. The Court also expressed a particular concern for possible risks of stigmatisation, arguing that the presumption of innocence of the applicants had been infringed by the retention of their samples and data in the absence of conviction. This concern was deemed particularly relevant with regard to minors. Discussions are still ongoing on how exactly practices should and will change following the judgment.

Schengen *acquis* (also Schengen Treaty): In 1995, five EU member countries – Belgium, France, Germany, Luxembourg, and the Netherlands – signed the so-called Schengen agreement (named after the town in Luxembourg where it was signed). The aim of this international treaty was to facilitate the free movement of persons across borders within the area, which practically meant the abolishment of border controls. Portugal, Spain, Italy, and Austria joined the Treaty in 1997. Two years later, the Treaty of Amsterdam adopted the Schengen agreement into EU law and rendered it part of the so-called *acquis communautaire* (the body of laws, regulations, and rules in the EU that new accession countries take over when they join the EU). However the countries which now implement the Schengen agreement are not entirely congruent with EU member countries: While EU countries Ireland and the UK opted out of Schengen, several non-EU members, Iceland, Norway, and Switzerland, voluntarily opted into Schengen. This means that any non-EU resident holding a Schengen visa can also travel to these three non-EU states without passing any border controls. In addition, three micro-countries that are neither EU members nor Schengen signatories are de-facto part of the Schengen area due to their bilateral agreements with their surrounding countries: Monaco, San Marino, and Vatican City.

Situated dis/empowerment: Barbara Prainsack and Victor Toom coined this term to highlight the simultaneity of both empowering and oppressive effects of surveillance. The notion of situated dis/empowerment, they argue, 'helps us to see the ways in which empowering and disempowering effects of surveillance are always intertwined and often mutually constitutive' (Prainsack and Toom 2010: 1118).

SPG: Austrian Security Police Act (*Sicherheitspolizeigesetz*).

StPO: The Austrian Code of Criminal Procedure (*Strafprozessordnung*).

STR Multiplex: The term refers to the most common kits for DNA analysis in forensics. STR stands for Short Tandem Repeats, which are repeats of chains of nucleotides on the genome. Different people have different numbers of repeats at the same location of their genome; if several different loci are looked at, the chance that two different people coincidentally have the same number of repeats in all loci is very small. This is the underlying principle of DNA profiling.

Universal DNA database: A centralised DNA database for police and forensic uses that comprises profiles of all residents of a country.

VIS AFIS: Visa Information System used in the EU. VIS AFIS is based on Regulation (EC) 767/2008. Data recorded on VIS are: information on the applicant and on the visas requested, issued, refused, annulled, revoked, or extended; photographs; fingerprint data; links to previous visa applications and to the application files of individuals travelling together.

References

Aas, K.F. 2006. 'The body does not lie': identity, risk and trust in technoculture. *Crime, Media, Culture*, 2(2), 143–58.

Agnew, R. 1990. The origins of delinquent events: an examination of offender accounts. *Journal of Research in Crime and Delinquency*, 27(3), 267–94.

Agnew, R. 1992. Foundation for a general strain theory. *Criminology*, 30(1), 47–87.

Águas, C. et al. 2009. DNA databases and biobanks: the Portuguese legal and ethical framework, in *New Challenges for Biobanks: Ethics, Law and Governance*, edited by K. Dierickx and P. Borry. Antwerp & Oxford: Intersentia, 209–23.

Alschuler, A.W. 1979. Plea bargaining and its history. *Columbia Law Review*, 79(1), 1–43.

Altheide, D. and Coyle, M.J. 2006. Smart on crime: the new language for prisoner release. *Crime, Media, Culture*, 2(3), 286–303.

Altheide, D. and Devriese, D. 2007. Perps in the news: a research note on stigma. *Crime, Media, Culture*, 3(3), 382–9.

Aronson, J.D. 2007. *Genetic Witness: Science, Law, and Controversy in the Making of DNA Profiling*. New Brunswick, NJ: Rutgers University Press.

Asplen, C. 2004. *The Application of DNA Technology in England and Wales*. [Online]. Available at: http://www.ncjrs.gov/pdffiles1/nij/grants/203971.pdf [accessed: 21 June 2011].

Austin, J. et al. 2007. *Unlocking America: Where and How to Reduce America's Prison Population*. Washington, DC: The JFA Institute.

Barondess, J.A. 1996. Medicine against society. Lessons from the Third Reich. *Journal of the American Medical Association*, 276(20), 1657–61.

Baskin, D.R. and Sommers, I.B. 2010. Crime-show-viewing habits and public attitudes towards forensic evidence: the 'CSI effect' revisited. *The Justice System Journal*, 31(1), 97–113.

BBC News. 2009. 'DNA bungle' haunts German police. *BBC News* [Online, 28 March] Available at: http://news.bbc.co.uk/2/hi/europe/7966641.stm [accessed: 21 January 2011].

BBC. 2011. How they caught… the Night Stalker. *Crime Watch*. [Online, 31 March] Available at: http://www.bbc.co.uk/crimewatch/solved/howtheycaught/htc_night_stalker.shtml [accessed: 9 April 2011].

Beauregard, E. and Bouchard, M. 2010. Cleaning up your act: forensic awareness as a detection avoidance strategy. *Journal of Criminal Justice*, 38(6), 1160–6.

Beck, U. 1992. *Risk Society: Towards a New Modernity*. London: Sage.

Bhati, A. 2010. *Quantifying the Specific Deterrent Effects of DNA Databases* [Online: Justice Policy Center, The Urban Institute]. Available at: http://www.urban.org/uploadedpdf/412058_dna_databases.pdf [accessed: 24 June 2011].

Bieber, F.R. 2006. Turning base hits into earned runs: improving the effectiveness of forensic DNA data bank programs. *The Journal of Law, Medicine & Ethics*, 34(2), 222–33.

Boavida, M.J. 2005. *Portugal Plans a Forensic Genetic Database of its Entire Population.* [Online: NewropMag]. Available at: http://www.newropeans-magazine.org/index.php?option=com_content&task=view&id=2059&Itemid=121 [accessed: 31 January 2011].

Bradbury, S. and Feist, A. 2005. *The Use of Forensic Science in Volume Crime Investigations: A Review of the Research Literature* [Online: Home Office Online Report 43/05]. Available at: http://www.homeoffice.gov.uk/publications/science-research-statistics/research-statistics/police-research/hoor4305?view=Binary [accessed: 24 June 2011].

Brewer, P. and Ley, B. 2010. Media use and public perceptions of DNA evidence. *Science Communication* 32(1), 93–117.

Brezina, T. and Piquero, A. 2003. Exploring the relationship between social and non-social reinforcement in the context of social learning theory, in *Social Learning Theory and the Explanation of Crime: A Guide for the New Century*, edited by R. Akers and G. Jensen. New Brunswick, NJ: Transaction, 265–88.

Briody, M. 2004a. DNA databases and effects on volume crime, in *The Effects of DNA Evidence on the Criminal Justice Process*. Ph.D. thesis by Michael Briody. School of Criminology and Criminal Justice, Faculty of Arts, Griffiths University, 176–358.

Briody, M. 2004b. The effects of DNA evidence on homicide cases in court. *Australian and New Zealand Journal of Criminology*, 37(2), 231–52.

Briody, M. and Prenzler, T. 2005. D.N.A. Databases and property crime: a false promise? *Australian Journal of Forensic Sciences*, 37(2), 73–86.

Brown, D. 2007. Madeleine officer charged over another missing girl. *The Times*. [Online, 11 June] Available at: http://www.timesonline.co.uk/tol/news/world/europe/article1913175.ece [accessed: 26 February 2011].

Buckleton, J. and Gill, P. 2010. A universal strategy to interpret DNA profiles that does not require a definition of low-copy-number. *Forensic Science International: Genetics*, 4(4), 221–7.

Budowle, B., Eisenberg, A.J. and van Daal, A. 2009. Low copy number typing has yet to achieve 'general acceptance'. *Forensic Science International: Genetics Supplement Series 2*, 551–2.

Burrows, J. et al. 2005. *Forensic Science Pathfinder Project: Evaluating Increased Forensic Activity in Two English Police Forces*. London: Home Office.

Bynum, T., Cordner, G. and Greene, J. 1982. Victim and offense characteristics: impact of police investigative decision-making. *Criminology*, 20, 301–18.

Cabral, M. et al. 2003. *Desigualdades Sociais e Percepções da Justiça* [*Social Inequalities and Perceptions of Justice*]. Lisboa: Instituto de Ciências Sociais [in Portuguese].

Cafepress. 2011. T-shirt: 'People lie. The evidence doesn't'. [Online]. Available at: http://www.cafepress.co.uk/+people_lie_evidence_doesnt_womens_dark_tee,85706521[accessed: 3 February 2011].

Caplan, J. and Torpey, J. 2001. *Documenting Individual Identity: The Development of State Practices in the Modern World*. Princeton: Princeton University Press.

Carlen, P. and Tombs, J. 2006. Reconfigurations of penalty. The ongoing case of the women's imprisonment and reintegration industries. *Theoretical Criminology*, 10(3), 337–60.

Cauchi, J.A. and Knepper, P. 2009. The empire, the police, and the introduction of fingerprint technology in Malta. *Criminology & Criminal Justice*, 9(1), 73–92.

Cavender, G. and Deutsch, S.K. 2007. CSI and moral authority: the police and science. *Crime, Media, Culture*, 3(1), 67–81.

Center on Wrongful Convictions 2005. *The Snitch System* [Online: Northwestern University School of Law]. Available at: http://www.innocenceproject.org/docs/SnitchSystemBooklet.pdf [accessed: 27 February 2011].

Charmaz, K. 1990. 'Discovering' chronic illness: using grounded theory. *Social Science and Medicine*, 30: 1161–72.

Charmaz, K. 2000. Grounded theory: objectivist & constructivist methods, in *Handbook of Qualitative Research*, 2nd edition, edited by N. Denzin and Y. Lincoln. Thousand Oaks, CA: Sage, 509–35.

Cheliotis, L.K. 2010. The ambivalent consequences of visibility: crime and prisons in the mass media. *Crime, Media, Culture*, 6(2), 169–84.

Christie, N. 2001. Imprisonment: sociological aspects, in *International Encyclopedia of the Social & Behavioral Sciences*, edited by N.J. Smelser and P.B. Baltes. Oxford, UK: Elsevier Sciences, 7248–51.

Clemmer, D. 1940. *The Prison Community*. New York: Rinehart and Co.

Cloward, R., and Ohlin, L. 1960. *Delinquency and Opportunity*. New York: Free Press.

Code of Criminal Procedure. 2007. Enacted by Decree-Law 78/87, 17 February, republished by Law 48/2007, 29 August. [Online: Procuradoria-Geral Distrital de Lisboa]. Available at: http://www.pgdlisboa.pt/pgdl/leis/lei_mostra_articulado.php?nid=929&tabela=leis&ficha=1&pagina=1 [accessed: 31 January 2011].

Cole, S.A. 2001. *Suspect Identities: A History of Fingerprinting and Criminal Identification*. Harvard: Harvard University Press.

Cole, S.A. 2010. Acculturating forensic science: what is 'scientific culture' and how can forensic science adopt it? *Fordham Urban Law Journal*, 38, 435–72.

Cole, S.A. and Dioso-Villa, R. 2007. CSI and its effects: media, juries, and the burden of proof. *New England Law Review*, 41, 435–70.

Cole, S.A., and Dioso-Villa, R. 2009. Investigating the 'CSI effect': media and litigation crisis in criminal law. *Stanford Law Review*, 61(6), 1335–73.

Cole, S.A. and Lynch, M. 2010. DNA profiling versus fingerprint evidence: more of the same?, in *Genetic Suspects: Global Governance of DNA Profiling and Databasing*, edited by R. Hindmarsh and B. Prainsack. Cambridge, UK: Cambridge University Press. 105–27.

Connor, S. 2003. Take everyone's fingerprint, says pioneer. *The Independent* [Online, 3 February] Available at: www.independent.co.uk/news/science/take-everyones-dnafingerprint-says-pioneer-596474.html [accessed: 18 March 2010].

Conti, R. 1999. Psychology of false confessions. *The Journal of Credibility Assessment and Witness Psychology*, 2(1), 14–36.

Costa, S. 2003. *A Justiça em Laboratório. A Identificação por Perfis Genéticos de ADN – Entre a Harmonização Transnacional e a Apropriação Local* [*Justice in the Laboratory. Identification by DNA profiles – Between Transnational Harmonization and Local Appropriation*]. Coimbra: Almedina [in Portuguese].

Cunha, M.I. 2002. *Entre o Bairro e a Prisão: Tráfico e Trajectos* [*Between the Housing Project and the Prison: Trafficking and Trajectories*]. Lisboa: Fim do Século [in Portuguese].

Cunha, M.I. 2008. Closed circuits: kinship, neighborhood and imprisonment in urban Portugal. *Ethnography*, 9(3), 325–50.

Cunha, M.I. 2010. Race, crime and criminal justice in Portugal, in *Race, Crime and Criminal Justice: International Perspectives*, edited by A. Kalunta-Crumpton. New York: Palgrave Macmillan, 144–61.

Cunha, M.I. and Bastos, C. 2007. Introdução [Introduction]. *Análise Social*, XLII(185), 977–83 [in Portuguese].

Cutter, A.M. 2006. To clear or to convict ? The role of genomics in criminal justice. *Genomics, Society and Policy*, 2(1), 1–15.

Dahl, J.Y. and Sætnan, A.R. 2009. 'It all happened so slowly': on controlling function creep in forensic DNA databases. *International Journal of Law, Crime and Justice*, 37(3), 83–103.

Dâmaso, E. 2007. Críticas inglesas [English criticism]. *Correio da Manhã* [Online, 11 May] Available at: http://www.cmjornal.xl.pt/detalhe/noticias/opiniao/eduardo-damaso/criticas-inglesas?nPagina=3 [accessed: 15 March 2011] [in Portuguese].

Decree 175/2011. *Tabela de Preços das Perícias Forenses* [*Price Table of Forensic Exams*]. [Online: Diário da República Electrónico]. Available at: http://www.dre.pt/pdf1s/2011/04/08200/0246802474.pdf [accessed: 30 April 2011] [in Portuguese].

Deliberation 3191/2008, 3 December. *Regulamento de Funcionamento da Base de Dados de Perfis de ADN* [*Regulation of the Functioning of the DNA Profiles Database*]. [Online: Diário da República Electrónico]. Available at: http://www.dre.pt/pdf2sdip/2008/12/234000000/4888148886.pdf [accessed: 31 January 2011] [in Portuguese].

Deutsch, S.K. and Cavender, G. 2008. CSI and forensic realism. *Journal of Criminal Justice and Popular Culture*, 15(1), 34–53.

DGSP. 2009. *Reclusos Existentes em 31 de Dezembro, Segundo a Instrução, Sexo e Nacionalidade* [*Existing Inmates on 31 December, According to Education, Sex and Nationality*]. [Online] Available at: http://www.dgsp.mj.pt/backoffice/uploads/anuais/20100302020332RecExist_Inst-Sex-Nac.pdf [accessed: 15 July 2011] [in Portuguese].

Dobash, R.E. and Dobash, R.P. 2011. What were they thinking? Men who murder an intimate partner. *Violence Against Women*, 17(1), 111–34.

Doyle, J. 2005. *True Witness: Cops, Courts, Science, and the Battle Against Misidentification*. New York: Palgrave Macmillan.

Drizin, S. and Leo, R. 2004. The problem of false confessions in the post-DNA world. *North Carolina Law Review*, 82, 891–1007.

Drizin, S. and Reich, M. 2004. Heeding the lessons of history: the need for mandatory recording of police interrogations to accurately assess the reliability and voluntariness of confessions. *Duke Law Review*, 52, 619–46.

Dror, I.E. and Hampikian, G. 2011. Subjectivity and bias in forensic DNA mixture interpretation. *Science and Justice*, 51 (4), 204-208.

Dror, I.E. and Mnookin, J. L. 2010. The use of technology in human expert domains: challenges and risks arising from the use of automated fingerprint identification systems in forensic science. *Law, Probability and Risk*, 9(1), 47–67.

Dundes, L. 2001. Is the American public ready to embrace DNA as a crime-fighting tool? A survey assessing support for DNA databases. *Bulletin of Science, Technology & Society*, 21(5), 369–75.

Durão, S. 2008. *Patrulha e Proximidade – Uma Etnografia da Polícia em Lisboa* [*Patrol and Proximity – A Police Ethnography in Lisbon*]. Coimbra: Almedina [in Portuguese].

Durnal, E. 2010. Crime scene investigation (as seen on TV). *Forensic Science International*, 199(1–3), 1–5.

Duster, T. 2004. Selective arrests, an ever-expanding DNA forensic database, and the specter of an early-twenty-first-century equivalent of phrenology, in *The Technology of Justice: DNA and the Criminal Justice System*, edited by D. Lazer. Cambridge, MA: MIT Press, 315–34.

Duster, T. 2006a. Explaining differential trust of DNA forensic technology: grounded assessment or inexplicable paranoia? *Journal of Law, Medicine & Ethics*, 34(2), 293–300.

Duster, T. 2006b. The molecular reinscription of race: Unanticipated issues in biotechnology and forensic science. *Patterns of Prejudice*, 40(4–5), 427–41.

Duster, T. 2008. DNA dragnets and race: larger social context, history and future. *GeneWatch*, 21(3–4), 3–5.

[The] *Economist*. 2010. The 'CSI effect'. [Online, 22 April]. Available at: http://www.economist.com/node/15949089 [accessed: 3 February 2011].

Edmond, G. 2000. Judicial representations of scientific evidence. *Modern Law Review*, 63: 216–51.

Edmond, G. (ed.). 2004. *Expertise in Regulation and Law*. Aldershot, UK: Ashgate.

ENFSI 2010. *ENFSI Survey on DNA-databases in Europe December 2010* [Online]. Available at: http://www.enfsi.eu/get_doc.php?uid=346 [accessed: 24 June 2011].

Ericson, R.V. and Haggerty, K. 1997. *Policing the Risk Society*. Oxford: Oxford University Press.

Ericson, R.V. and Shearing, C.D. 1986. The scientification of police work, in *The Knowledge Society: The Growing Impact of Scientific Knowledge on Social Relations*, edited by G. Bohme and N. Stehr. Dordrecht: D. Reidel Publishing Company, 129–59.

EU. 2010a. *'Eurodac' system* [Online: European Union: Europa: Summaries of EU legislation]. Available at: http://europa.eu/legislation_summaries/justice_freedom_security/free_movement_of_persons_asylum_immigration/l33081_en.htm [accessed: 7 January 2011].

EU. 2010b. *Schengen Information System II* [Online: European Union: Europa: Summaries of EU legislation]. Available at: http://europa.eu/legislation_summaries/other/l33183_en.htm [accessed: 7 January 2011].

EU. 2010c. *VIS Regulation* [Online: European Union: Europa: Summaries of EU legislation]. Available at: http://europa.eu/legislation_summaries/justice_freedom_security/free_movement_of_persons_asylum_immigration/l14517_en.htm#KeyTerms [accessed: 7 January 2011].

EU. 2010d. *The Schengen area and cooperation* [Online: European Union: Europa: Summaries of EU legislation]. Available at: http://europa.eu/legislation_summaries/justice_freedom_security/free_movement_of_persons_asylum_immigration/l33020_en.htm [accessed: 7 January 2011].

EU Council. 2008. *Council Framework Decision 2008/977/JHA of 27 November 2008 on the protection of personal data processed in the framework of police and judicial cooperation in criminal matters*. [Online]. Available at: http://eur-lex.europa.eu/LexUriServ/LexUriServ.do?uri=OJ:L:2008:350:0060:01:EN:HTML [accessed: 6 January 2011].

European Commission. 2006. Europeans and biotechnology in 2005: patterns and trends. *Eurobarometer 64.3* [Online, July]. Available at: http://ec.europa.eu/public_opinion/archives/ebs/ebs_244b_en.pdf [accessed: 21 January 2011].

European Commission. 2010. Europeans and biotechnology in 2010: winds of change? *Eurobarometer 73.1* [Online, October]. Available at: http://ec.europa.eu/public_opinion/archives/ebs/ebs_341_winds_en.pdf [accessed: 21 January 2011].

Eurostat. 2010. *GDP Per Capita in Purchasing Power Standards (PPS) (EU-27=100)*. [Online]. Available at: http://epp.eurostat.ec.europa.eu/tgm/table.do?tab=table&init=1&plugin=1&language=en&pcode=tsieb010 [accessed: 31 August 2011].

Eurostat. 2011. *Harmonised Unemployment Rate by Gender – Total*. [Online]. Available at: http://epp.eurostat.ec.europa.eu/tgm/graph.do?tab=graph&plugin=1&language=en&pcode=teilm020&toolbox=type [accessed: 31 August 2011].

Eusébio, J.C. et al. 2007. Judiciária na pista do raptor [Police on the kidnapper's trail]. *Correio da Manhã* [Online, 6 May] Available at: http://www.cmjornal.xl.pt/detalhe/noticias/exclusivo-cm/judiciaria-na-pista-do-raptor [accessed: 15 March 2011] [in Portuguese].

Evans, T. and Wallace, P. 2008. A prison within a prison? The masculinity narratives of male prisoners. *Male and Masculinities*, 10(4), 485–507.

Findley, K. 2002. Learning from our mistakes: criminal justice commission to study wrongful convictions. *California Western Law Review*, 38(2), 333–53.

Finn, J. 2005. Photographing fingerprints: data collection and state surveillance. *Surveillance & Society*, 3(1), 21–44.

Fontes, L. 2011. Lei ameaça dois mil registos de ADN que a PJ recolheu [Law threatens two thousand DNA records that the PJ collected]. *Diário de Notícias* [Online, 6 May] Available at: http://www.dn.pt/inicio/portugal/interior.aspx?content_id=1749615 [accessed: 31 January 2011] [in Portuguese].

Forejustice. n.d. *Websites or Web Pages Around the World That are Devoted Wholly or in Part to Exposing Various Aspects of Wrongful Convictions* [Online]. Available at: http://forejustice.org/wc/wrongful_conviction_websites.htm [accessed: 27 February 2011].

Fosdick, R.B. 1915. The passing of the Bertillon System of Identification. *Journal of the American Institute of Criminal Law and Criminology*, 6(3), 363–9.

Foucault, M. 1975. *Discipline and Punish: The Birth of the Prison*. New York: Random House.

Freckelton, I. and Selby, H. 2002. *Expert Evidence: Law, Practice, Procedure and Advocacy*. Pyrmont, N.S.W.: Lawbook Co.

Fróis, C. 2008. Bases de dados pessoais e vigilância em Portugal: análise de um processo em transição [Personal databases and surveillance in Portugal: Analysis of a process in transition], in *A Sociedade Vigilante. Ensaios Sobre Identificação, Vigilância e Privacidade* [*The Surveillant Society. Essays about Identification, Surveillance and Privacy*], edited by C. Fróis. Lisboa: Imprensa de Ciências Sociais, 111–34 [in Portuguese].

Gamero, J.J. et al. 2007. Spanish public awareness regarding DNA profile databases in forensic genetics: what type of DNA profiles should be included? *Journal of Medical Ethics*, 33(10), 598–604.

Gans, J. 2007. Catching Bradley Murdoch: tweezers, pitchforks and the limits of DNA sampling. *Current Issues in Criminal Justice*, 19, 34–48.

Gans, J. and Urbas, G. 2002. DNA identification in the criminal justice system. *Australian Institute of Criminology*, 226, 1–6.

Garrett, B. 2010. The substance of false confessions. *Stanford Law Review*, 62(4), 1051–119.

Garrett, B. and Neufeld, P. 2009. Invalid forensic science testimony and wrongful convictions. *Virginia Law Review*, 95, 1–96.

Gepp, J. 2007. Der geliebte Psychopath [The beloved psychopath]. *Falter* [Online, 28 November], 48. Available at: www.falter.at/web/print/detail.php?id=598 [accessed: 5 January 2011] [in German].

Gerlach, N. 2004. *The Genetic Imaginary: DNA in the Canadian Criminal Justice System*. Toronto: University of Toronto Press.
Ghoshray, S. 2007. Symposium – The 'CSI-effect': the true effect of crime scene television on the justice system: CSI and its effects: circumstantial evidence, reasonable doubt, and jury manipulation. *New England Law Review*, 41, 533–60.
Gibbs, J.J. and Shelly, P.L. 1982. NCCD research review: Life in the fast lane: a retrospective view by commercial thieves. *Journal of Research in Crime and Delinquency*, 19(2), 299–330.
Gill, P. and Clayton, T. 2009. The current status of DNA profiling in the UK, in *Handbook of Forensic Science*, edited by J. Fraser and R. Williams. Cullompton, Devon: Willan Publishing, 29–56.
Glaser, B.G. and Strauss, A.L. 1967. *The Discovery of Grounded Theory: Strategies for Qualitative Research*. New York: Aldine de Gruyter.
Glover S. and Lait, M. 2003. Lack of funds stalls rampart probe: the LAPD seeks private donations so that an independent panel can begin investigating the department's handling of the scandal. *Los Angeles Times*, 6 November, B1.
Goffman, Erving. 1959. *The Presentation of Self in Everyday Life*. London: Penguin.
Goffman, Erving. 1986 [1963]. *Stigma: Notes on the Management of Spoiled Identity*. New York: Simon & Schuster.
Gold, S. 2003. 35 are pardoned in Texas drug case. *Los Angeles Times*, 23 August, A11.
Gomes, C. et al. 2003. *A Reinserção Social dos Reclusos. Um Contributo para o Debate sobre a Reforma do Sistema Prisional* [*The Social Reintegration of Inmates. A Contribution Towards the Reform of the Prison System*]. OPJP, CES: Coimbra [in Portuguese].
Gottfredson, M. and Gottfredson, D. 1988. *Decision Making in Criminal Justice: Toward the Rational Exercise of Discretion*. New York: Plenum Press.
Grabher, R. 2007. *2865 Tage. Der Fall Peter Heidegger*. [*2,865 days. The Peter Heidegger case*]. Vienna: Czernin [in German].
Grace, V. et al. 2011. *Forensic DNA on Trial: Science and Uncertainty in the Courtroom*. Litchfield Park, AZ: Emergent Publications.
Graham, E. 2008. DNA reviews: predicting phenotype. *Forensic Science, Medicine, and Pathology*, 4, 196–9.
Griffin, T. and Miller, M. 2008. Child abduction, AMBER alert, and crime control theater. *Criminal Justice Review*, 33(2), 159–76.
Gross, H. 1908. *Kriminalistische Tätigkeit und Stellung des Arztes* [*Criminalistic practice and the position of the physician*]. Vienna: Braumüller [in German].
Gudjonsson, G. 2003. *The Psychology of Interrogations and Confessions: A Handbook*. Chichister: John Wiley & Sons.
Hacking, I. 2003. Risk and dirt, in *Risk and Morality*, edited by R.V. Ericson and A. Doyle. Toronto: University of Toronto Press, 22–47.

Haddow, I. 2008. *Debating Ethics of DNA Database* [Online: BBC News online]. Available at: http://news.bbc.co.uk/1/hi/uk/7177152.stm [accessed: 18 March 2010].

Haggerty, K. and Ericson, R.V. 2000. The surveillant assemblage. *British Journal of Sociology*, 51(4), 605–22.

Hall, A. and Leidig, M. 2006. *Girl in the Cellar: The Natascha Kampusch Story*. London: Hodder & Stoughton.

Hall, M. 2010. Weird science. *Texas Monthly* [Online, May 2010] Available at: http://www.texasmonthly.com/cms/printthis.php?file=feature2.php&issue=2010-05-01 [accessed: 10 April 2011].

Hamel, J., Dufour, S. and Fortin, D. 1993. *Case Study Methods*. London: Sage Publications.

Hamlin, J.E. 1988. The misplaced role of rational choice in neutralization theory. *Criminology*, 26, 3, 425–38.

Harmon, T. 2001a. Guilty until proven innocent: an analysis of post-Furman capital errors. *Criminal Justice Policy Review*, 12(2), 113–39.

Harmon, T. 2001b. Predictors of miscarriages of justice in capital cases. *Justice Quarterly*, 18, 949–68.

Harrison, M. 2002. Dallas police frame and deport Hispanics. *The Razor Wire*, 6(1). [Online: The November Coalition]. Available at: http://www.november.org/razorwire/rzold/27/page03.html [accessed: 29 September 2011].

Heindl, R. 1922. *System und Praxis der Daktyloskopie. Und der sonstigen technischen Methoden der Krimalpolizei* [*System and Practice of Dactyloscopy, and Other Technical Methods of Criminal Policing*]. Berlin: De Gruyter [in German].

Heinemann, T., Lemke, T. and Prainsack, B. (eds.) 2012 (forthcoming). Risky profiles: societal dimensions of forensic uses of DNA technologies. *New Genetics & Society*, Special issue.

Heumann, M. 1978. *Plea Bargaining: The Experiences of Judges, Jurors, and Defense Attorneys*. Chicago: University of Chicago Press.

Hicks, T. et al. 2010. Use of DNA profiles for investigation using a simulated national DNA database: Part I. partial SGM plus® profiles. *Forensic Science International: Genetics*, 4(4), 232–8.

Hindmarsh, R. 2008. Australian biocivic concerns and governance of forensic DNA technologies: confronting technocracy. *New Genetics and Society*, 27(3), 267–84.

Hindmarsh, R. 2010. Biosurveillance and biocivic concerns, from 'truth' to 'trust': the Australian forensic DNA terrain, in *Genetic Suspects: Global Governance of DNA Profiling and Databasing*, edited by R. Hindmarsh and B. Prainsack. Cambridge, UK: Cambridge University Press, 262–87.

Hindmarsh, R. and Prainsack, B. (eds.) 2010. *Genetic Suspects: Global Governance of DNA Profiling and Databasing*. Cambridge, UK: Cambridge University Press.

Hochstetler, A., Copes, H. and Williams, J.P. 2010. 'That's not who I am:' how offenders commit violent acts and reject authentically violent selves. *Justice Quarterly*, 27(4), 492–516.

Holmgren, J.A. and Fordham, J. 2011. The CSI effect and the Canadian and the Australian jury. *Journal of Forensic Sciences*, 56(S1), S63–S71.

Home Office. 2003. *The National Policing Plan 2004–2007*. [Online]. Available at: http://webarchive.nationalarchives.gov.uk/20100413151441/http://police.homeoffice.gov.uk/publications/national-policing-plan/natpolplan2004_7.html [accessed: 24 June 2011].

Home Office. 2005. *DNA Expansion Programme 2000-2005: Reporting Achievement*. Forensic Science and Pathology Unit. London: Home Office.

Home Office. 2009. *Keeping the Right People on the DNA Database: Science and Public Protection*. [Online]. Available at: http://www.nio.gov.uk/consultation_paper_-_keeping_the_right_people_on_the_dna_database.pdf [accessed: 23 June 2011].

Howitt, D. 2002. *Introduction to Forensic and Criminal Psychology*. Essex, UK: Pearson Education Limited.

Huey, L. 2010. 'I've seen this on CSI': criminal investigators' perceptions about the management of public expectations in the field. *Crime, Media, Culture*, 6(1), 49–68.

Hughes, T. and Magers, M. 2007. The perceived impact of crime scene investigation shows on the administration of justice. *Journal of Criminal Justice and Popular Culture*, 14(3), 259–76.

Human Genetics Commission. 2001. *Whose Hands on Your Genes? A Discussion Document on the Storage Protection and Use of Genetic Information*. [Online]. Available at: http://www.hgc.gov.uk/UploadDocs/DocPub/Document/business_consultations2maintext.pdf [accessed: 28 September 2011].

Human Genetics Commission. 2002. *Inside Information: Balancing Interests in the Use of Personal Genetic Data*. [Online]. Available at: http://www.hgc.gov.uk/UploadDocs/Contents/Documents/iiintroduction.pdf [accessed: 28 September 2011].

Human Genetics Commission. 2009. *Nothing to Hide, Nothing to Fear? Balancing Individual Rights and the Public Interest in the Governance and Use of the National DNA Database*. [Online]. Available at: http://www.hgc.gov.uk/UploadDocs/DocPub/Document/Nothing%20to%20hide,%20nothing%20to%20fear%20-%20online%20version.pdf [accessed: 28 September 2011].

Humes, E. 2009. *Guilt by the Numbers: How Fuzzy is the Math That Makes DNA Evidence Look So Compelling to Jurors*. [Online: California Lawyer: a Daily Journal Publication]. Available at: http://www.callawyer.com/clstory.cfm?eid=900572&ref=updates [accessed: 2 September 2009].

Innes, M. 2001. 'Crimewatching': homicide investigations in the age of information. *Criminal Justice Matters*, 43(1), 42–3.

Innes, M. and Clarke, A. 2009. Policing the past: cold case studies, forensic evidence and retroactive social control. *The British Journal of Sociology*, 60(3), 543–63.

[The] Innocence Network 2008. *Innocence Network Member Organizations* [Online, The Innocence Network]. Available at: http://www.innocencenetwork.org/members.html [accessed: 27 February 2011].

Innocence Project. n.d. [Online]. Available at: http://www.innocenceproject.org/ [accessed: 27 February 2011].

Innocence Project 2009a. *National Academy of Sciences Urges Comprehensive Reform of U.S. Forensic Sciences* [Online: Innocence Project]. http://www.innocenceproject.org/Content/National_Academy_of_Sciences_Urges_Comprehensive_Reform_of_US_Forensic_Sciences.php# [accessed: 27 February 2011].

Innocence Project 2009b. *Wrongful Convictions Involving Unvalidated or Improper Forensic Science that Were Later Overturned through DNA Testing* [Online: Innocence Project]. http://www.innocenceproject.org/docs/DNA_Exonerations_Forensic_Science.pdf [accessed: 27 February 2011].

Innocence Project 2011. *Pennsylvania Supreme Court Rules That a Confession Does Not Bar Access to Post Conviction DNA Testing* [Online: Innocence Project]. Available at: http://www.innocenceproject.org/Content/Pennsylvania_Supreme_Court_Rules_That_a_Confession_Does_Not_Bar_Access_to_Post_Conviction_DNA_Testing.php [accessed: 27 February 2011].

INTERPOL. 2009. *INTERPOL Handbook on DNA Data Exchange and Practice*. INTERPOL: Lyon.

Irwin, J. and Cressey, D. 1962. Thieves, convicts and the inmate culture. *Social Problems*, 10, 142–55.

Jackson, J. and Bradford, B. 2009. Crime, policing and social order: on the expressive nature of public confidence in policing. *The British Journal of Sociology*, 60(3), 493–521.

Jacobs, B.A. 2010. Serendipity in robbery target selection. *British Journal of Criminology*, 50(3), 514–29.

Jacobs, B.A. and Wright, R. 1999. Stick-up, street culture, and offender motivation. *Criminology*, 37(1), 149–72.

Jasanoff, S. 1998. The eye of everyman: witnessing DNA in the Simpson trial. *Social Studies of Science*, 28(5–6), 713–40.

Jasanoff, S. 2004a. DNA's identity crisis, in *DNA and the Criminal Justice System: The Technology of Justice*, edited by D. Lazer. Cambridge, MA: MIT Press, 337–55.

Jasanoff, S. (ed.). 2004b. *States of Knowledge: The Co-Production of Science and Social Order*. London: Routledge and Kegan Paul.

Jasanoff, S. 2005. *Designs on Nature: Science and Democracy in Europe and the United States*. Princeton, NJ: Princeton University Press.

Jasanoff, S. 2006. Just evidence: the limits of science in the legal process. *Journal of Law, Medicine & Ethics*, 34(2), 328–41.

Jasanoff, S. 2010. Foreword, in *Genetic Suspects: Global Governance of Forensic DNA Profiling and Databasing*, edited by R. Hindmarsh and B. Prainsack. Cambridge, UK: Cambridge University Press, xix–xxiv.

Jefferson, J. 2008. Cold hits meet cold facts: are DNA matches infallible. *Transcript*, University of California, Berkeley – School of Law, Spring, 40(1), 29–33.

Jeffreys, A., Wilson, V. and Thein, S.L. 1985. Hypervariable 'minisatellite' regions in human DNA. *Nature*, 314, 67–73.

Jenkins, P. 1994. *Using Murder: The Social Construction of Serial Homicide*. New York: Aldine de Gruyter.

Jewkes, Y. 2002. *Captive Audience: Media, Masculinity and Power in Prisons*. Cullompton, Devon: Willan Publishing.

Jewkes, Y. 2004. *Media and Crime*. London: Sage.

Jewkes, Y. 2007. Prisons and the media: the shaping of public opinion and penal policy in a mediated society, in *Handbook on Prisons*, edited by Y. Jewkes. Cullompton, Devon: Willan Publishing, 447–66.

Johnson, P. and Williams, R. 2004a. DNA and crime investigation: Scotland and the 'UK National DNA Database'. *The Scottish Journal of Criminal Justice Studies*, 10, 1–9.

Johnson, P. and Williams, R. 2004b. Post-conviction DNA testing: the UK's first 'exoneration' case? *Science and Justice*, 44(2), 77–82.

Jones, P.J. and Wardle, C. 2008. 'No emotion, no sympathy': the visual construction of Maxine Carr. *Crime, Media, Culture*, 4(1), 53–71.

Kahn, J. 2009. Race, genes and justice: a call to reform the presentation of forensic DNA evidence in criminal trials. *Brooklyn Law Review*, 74(2), 325–75.

Kampusch, N. 2010. *3,096 Days*. London: Penguin.

Kassin, S.M. 2008. The psychology of confessions. *Annual Review of Law and Social Science*, 4(1), 193–217.

Kaye, D.H. 2010. *The Double Helix and the Law of Evidence*. Cambridge, MA: Harvard University Press.

Kaye, D.H. and Smith, M.E. 2004. DNA databases for law enforcement: the coverage question and the case for a population-wide database, in *DNA and the Criminal Justice System: The Technology of Justice*, edited by D. Lazer. Cambridge, MA: MIT Press, 247–84.

Kayser, M. and Schneider, P.M. 2009. DNA-based prediction of human externally visible characteristics in forensics: motivations, scientific challenges, and ethical considerations. *Forensic Science International: Genetics*, 3(3), 154–61.

Kim, Y.S., Barak, G. and Shelton, D.E. 2009. Examining the 'CSI-effect' in the cases of circumstantial evidence and eyewitness testimony: multivariate and path analyses. *Journal of Criminal Justice*, 37, 452–60.

Kobilinsky, L., Liotti, T.F. and Oeser-Sweat, J. 2004. *DNA: Forensic and Legal Applications*. Hoboken, NJ: John Wiley & Sons.

Kraske, M. 2008. Polit-Skandal in Österreich – Fall Kampusch droht die Große Koalition zu sprengen [Political Scandal in Austria – The Kampusch case threatens to rock the coalition government]. *Der Spiegel* [Online, 18 February]. Available at: http://www.spiegel.de/politik/ausland/0,1518,535894,00.html [accessed: 21 January 2011] [in German].

Kreisky, E. 1992. Der Staat als "Männerbund". Der Versuch einer feministischen Staatssicht [The state as a 'male syndicate'. Attempting a feminist view of the state], in *Staat aus feministischer Sicht* [*The State from a Feminist Viewpoint*], edited by Elke Biester et al. Berlin: Verlag für Sozialwissenschaften, 53–62 [in German].

Krimsky, S. and Simoncelli, T. 2011. *Genetic Justice: DNA Data Banks, Criminal Investigations, and Civil Liberties*. New York: Columbia University Press.

Krimsky, S. and Sloan, K. (eds). 2011. *Race and the Genetic Revolution: Science Myth and Culture*. New York: Columbia University Press.

Kruse, C. 2010a. Producing absolute truth: CSI science as wishful thinking. *American Anthropologist*, 112(1), 79–91.

Kruse, C. 2010b. Forensic evidence: materializing bodies, materializing crimes. *The European Journal of Women's Studies*, 17(4), 363–77.

Kruse, C. 2012 (forthcoming). The importance of context: widening the perspective on forensic evidence. *New Genetics & Society. Special Issue.*

Law 57/98, 18 August. *Estabelece os Princípios Gerais que Regem a Organização e o Funcionamento da Identificação Criminal* [*Establishes the General Principles that Rule the Organisation and Functioning of Criminal Identification*]. [Online: Diário da República Electrónico]. Available at: http://dre.pt/pdf1sdip/1998/08/189A00/40434047.pdf [accessed: 31 January 2011] [in Portuguese].

Law 45/2004, 19 August. *Estabelece o Regime Jurídico das Perícias Médico-legais e Forenses* [*Establishes the Legal Regulation of Forensic and Legal-medical Examinations*]. [Online: Diário da República Electrónico]. Available at: http://dre.pt/pdf1sdip/2004/08/195A00/53625368.pdf [accessed: 31 January 2011] [in Portuguese].

Law 5/2008, 12 February. *Aprova a Criação de uma Base de Dados de Perfis de ADN para Fins de Identificação Civil e Criminal* [*Aproves the Creation of a DNA Profiles Database for Civil and Criminal Investigation Purposes*]. [Online: Diário da República Electrónico]. Available at: http://dre.pt/pdf1sdip/2008/02/03000/0096200968.pdf [accessed: 31 January 2011] [in Portuguese].

Law 49/2008, 27 August. *Aprova a Lei de Organização da Investigação Criminal* [*Aproves the Law for the Organisation of Criminal Investigation*]. [Online: Diário da República Electrónico]. Available at: http://dre.pt/pdf1sdip/2008/08/16500/0603806042.pdf [accessed: 31 January 2011] [in Portuguese].

Lawless, C. 2010. Managing epistemic risk in forensic science: sociological aspects and issues. *Sociology Compass*, 6, 381–92.

Lazer, D. (ed.). 2004. *The Technology of Justice: DNA and the Criminal Justice System*. Cambridge, MA: MIT Press.

Leake, J. 2007. *The Vienna Woods Killer: A Writer's Double Life*. London, UK: Granta Books.

Lee, H. and Tirnady, F. 2004. *Blood Evidence: How DNA is Revolutionizing the Way We Solve Crimes*. Cambridge, MA: Perseus Publishing.

Leo, R. 2005. Rethinking the study of miscarriages of justice: developing a criminology of wrongful conviction. *Journal of Contemporary Criminal Justice*, 21, 201–23.

Levine, H.G. and Small, D.P. 2008. *Marijuana Arrest Crusade: Racial Bias and Police Policy in New York City – 1997-2007* [Online: New York Civil Liberties Union]. Available at: http://www.nyclu.org/files/MARIJUANA-ARREST-CRUSADE_Final.pdf [accessed: 2 October 2011].

Ley, B., Jankowski, N. and Brewer, P.R. 2012. Investigating CSI: portrayals of DNA testing on a forensic crime show and their potential effects. *Public Understanding of Science*, 21(1), 51–67.

Lofquist, W. 2001. Whodunit? An examination of the production of wrongful convictions, in *Wrongly Convicted: Perspectives on Failed Justice*, edited by S. Westervelt and J. Humphrey. Newark, NJ: Rutgers University Press, 174–98.

Lombroso, C. 2006 [1876]. *Criminal Man*. Translated and with a new introduction by M. Gibson and N.H. Rafter. Durham, NC: Duke University Press.

Lynch, M. 2003. God's signature: DNA profiling, the new gold standard in forensic science. *Endeavour*, 27(2), 93–7.

Lynch, M. 2004. 'Science above all else': the inversion of credibility between forensic DNA profiling and fingerprint evidence, in *Expertise in Regulation and Law*, edited by G. Edmond. Aldershot, UK: Ashgate, 121–35.

Lynch, M. et al. 2008. *Truth Machine: The Contentious History of DNA Fingerprinting*. Chicago: University of Chicago Press.

Lynch, M. and McNally, R. 2009 Forensic DNA databases and biolegality: the co-production of law, surveillance technology and suspect bodies, in *Handbook of Genetics and Society: Mapping the New Genomics Era*, edited by P. Atkinson, P. Glasner and M. Lock, Routledge: London, 283–301.

McCartney, C. 2004. Forensic DNA sampling and the England and Wales National DNA Database: a sceptical approach. *Critical Criminology*, 12(2), 157–78.

McCartney, C. 2006a. *Forensic Identification and Criminal Justice: Forensic Science, Justice and Risk*. Cullompton, Devon: Willan Publishing.

McCartney, C. 2006b. The DNA expansion programme and criminal investigation. *British Journal of Criminology*, 46(2), 175–92.

McCartney, C. 2006c. Liberating legal education? Innocence projects in the US and Australia. *Web Journal of Current Legal Issues* [Online], 3. Available at: http://webjcli.ncl.ac.uk/2006/issue3/mccartney3.html [accessed: 10 April 2011].

McCartney, C., Williams, R. and Wilson, T. 2010. *The Future of Forensic Bioinformation*. [Online]. Available at: http://www.law.leeds.ac.uk/assets/files/research/ccjs/forensic-bioinformation-report.pdf [accessed: 20 June 2011].

Machado, H. 2011. Arguido or no: the Portuguese DNA database. *GeneWatch*. [Online]. Available at: http://www.councilforresponsiblegenetics.org/GeneWatch/GeneWatchPage.aspx?pageId=374[accessed: 20 December 2011].

Machado, H. and Santos, F. 2009. The disappearance of Madeleine McCann: public drama and trial by media in the Portuguese press. *Crime, Media, Culture*, 5(2), 146–67.

Machado, H. and Santos, F. 2011. Popular press and forensic genetics in Portugal: expectations and disappointments regarding two cases of missing children. *Public Understanding of Science*, 20(3), 303–18.

Machado, H. and Silva, S. 2009. Informed consent in forensic DNA databases: volunteering, constructions of risk and identity categorization. *BioSocieties*, 4, 335–48.

Machado, H. and Silva, S. 2010. Portuguese forensic DNA database: political enthusiasm, public trust and probable issues in future practice, in *Genetic Suspects: Global Governance of Forensic DNA Profiling and Databasing*, edited by R. Hindmarsh and B. Prainsack. Cambridge: Cambridge University Press, 218–39.

Machado, H. et al. 2011. *Stained Bodies: Prisoners' Perceptions of the DNA Database for Criminal Investigation Purposes and their Perspectives of Social Reintegration*. [Online: Centro de Estudos Sociais]. Available at: http://dnadatabase.ces.uc.pt/list_documents.php [accessed: 15 July 2011].

Machado, H., Santos, F. and Silva, S. 2011. Prisoners' expectations of the national forensic DNA database: surveillance and reconfiguration of individual rights. *Forensic Science International*, 210(1–3), 139–43.

Machado, H., Silva, S. and Amorim, A. 2010. Políticas de identidade: perfil de DNA e a identidade genético-criminal [Politics of identity: DNA profiles and the genetic-criminal identity]. *Análise Social*, XLV(196), 537–53 [in Portuguese].

Machado, H., Silva, S. and Cunha, M. 2012 (forthcoming). Multiple views of DNA surveillance: the surveilled, the surveillants and the academics, in *Crime, Security and Surveillance*, edited by N. Zurawski et al. The Hague, The Netherlands: Boon Eleven Publishers.

M'Charek, A. 2008. Contrasts and comparisons: three practices of forensic investigation. *Comparative Sociology*, 7, 387–412.

M'Charek, A., Toom, V., and Prainsack, B. 2011. Bracketing off populations does not advance ethical reflection on EVCs: a reply to Kayser and Schneider. *Forensic Science International: Genetics*, DOI: 10.1016/j.fsigen.2010.12.012.

McMahon, M. 1992. *The Persistent Prison: Rethinking Decarceration and Penal Reform*. Toronto: University of Toronto Press.

Madureira, N. 2003. A estatística do corpo: antropologia física e antropometria na alvorada do século XX [The statistics of the body: physical anthropology and anthropometry in the dawn of the XXth century]. *Etnográfica* 7(2), 283–303 [in Portuguese].

Marcelino, V. 2011. Base de dados da PSP está ilegal [PSP's database is illegal]. *Diário de Notícias* [Online, 06 February] Available at: http://www.dn.pt/inicio/portugal/interior.aspx?content_id=1776871&page=-1 [accessed: 31 January 2011] [in Portuguese].

Marques, T.P. 2005. *Crime e Castigo no Liberalismo em Portugal*. Lisboa: Livros Horizonte [in Portuguese].

Marshall, L. 2004. The innocence revolution and the death penalty. *Ohio State Journal of Criminal Law*, 1(573), 573–84.

Maruna, S. and Copes, H. 2005. What have we learned from five decades of neutralization research? *Crime and Justice*, 32, 221–320.

Mason, P. 2006. Lies, distortion and what doesn't work: monitoring prison stories in the British media. *Crime, Media, Culture*, 2(3), 251–67.

Mayr, W. 2010. Jörg Haider's legacy: corruption scandals shake faith in Austrian democracy. *Der Spiegel* [Online, 7 November]. Available at: http://www.spiegel.de/international/europe/0,1518,721596-2,00.html [accessed: 17 January 2011].

Mays, G.L., Fields, C.B. and Thompson, J.A. 1991. Preincarceration patterns of drug and alcohol use by jail inmates. *Criminal Justice Policy Review*, 5(1), 30–52.

Meβner, D. 2010a. Erkennungsdienstliche Behandlung verdächtiger Personen. Über technisierte Identifizierung durch Fotografie, Anthropometrie und Daktyloskopie [Criminal identification of suspects. On identification technologies: photography, anthrometry, and dactyloscopy], in *Ermitteln, Fahnden und Strafen. Kriminalitätshistorische Studien vom 16. bis zum 19. Jahrhundert* [*Investigate, search, and punish. Studies in criminal history from the sixteenth to the nineteenth century*], edited by A. Griesebner and G. Tschannett. Vienna: Löcker, 225–49 [in German].

Meßner, D. 2010b. Volksdaktyloskopie: Das Fingerabdruckverfahren als Überwachungsphantasie zwischen Ausweitung und Widerstand [General Dactyloscopy: fingerprinting as surveillance phantasy between extension and resistance]. *Journal for Intelligence, Propaganda and Security Studies (JIPSS)*, 4(1), 23–35 [in German].

Minor, W.W. 1980. The neutralization of criminal offense. *Criminology*, 18(1), 103–20.

Mnookin, J.L. 2008. Of black boxes, instruments, and experts: testing the validity of forensic science. *Episteme*, 5(3), 343–58.

Mnookin, J.L. et al. 2011. The need for a research culture in the forensic sciences. *UCLA Law Review*, 58, 725–79.

Moniz, H. 2009. A base de dados de perfis de ADN para fins de identificação civil e criminal e a cooperação transfronteiras em matéria de transferência de perfis de ADN [DNA profiles database for civil and criminal identification purposes and transborder cooperation in matters of transferring DNA profiles]. *Revista do Ministério Público*, 120(Oct/Dez), 145–56 [in Portuguese].

Mopas, M. 2007. Examining the 'CSI effect' through an ANT lens. *Crime, Media, Culture*, 3(1), 110–17.

Moreira, A. 1960. O problema da identificação [The problem of identification]. *Estudos Jurídicos. Estudos de Ciências Políticas e Sociais*, 40, 222–35. Lisboa: Junta de Investigações do Ultramar. Centro de Estudos Políticos e Sociais [in Portuguese].

Murphy, E. 2007. The new forensics: criminal justice, false certainty, and the second generation of scientific evidence. *California Law Review*, 95(3), 721–97.

Murphy, E. 2008. The art in the science of DNA: a layperson's guide to the subjectivity inherent in forensic DNA typing. *Emory Law Journal*, 58(2), 489–512.

Murphy, E. 2010. What 'strengthening forensic science' today means for tomorrow: DNA exceptionalism and the 2009 NAS report. *Journal of Law, Probability & Risk*, 9, 7–24.

Nance, D.A. and Morris, S.B. 2005. Juror understandings of DNA evidence: an empirical assessment of presentation formats for trace evidence with a relatively small random-match probability. *Journal of Legal Studies*, 34(2), 395–444.

Natapoff, A. 2009. *Snitching: Criminal Informants and the Erosion of American Justice*. New York: New York University Press.

National Research Council. 2009. *Strengthening Forensic Science in the United States: A Path Forward* [Online: National Research Council, Committee on Identifying the Needs of the Forensic Sciences Community]. Available at: http://www.ncjrs.gov/pdffiles1/nij/grants/228091.pdf [accessed: 24 June 2011].

Nature. 2011. Courtroom drama. *Nature*, 471, 548.

NECN. 2011. Alabama jails get DNA testing kits. *NECN* [Online, 20 April]. Available at: http://www.necn.com/04/20/11/Alabama-jails-get-DNA-testing-kits/landing_nation.html?&blockID=3&apID=659dd6726cda49448b5b5a49c01918a2 [accessed: 24 April 2011].

Nelkin, D. and Lindee, S. 1995. *The DNA Mystique: The Gene as a Cultural Icon*. New York: W.H. Freeman.

Neufeld, P. and Scheck, B. 2002. Toward the formation of 'Innocence Commissions' in America. *Judicature*, 86, 98–105.

Neuschatz, J. et al. 2007. The mitigating effects of suspicion on post-identification feedback and on retrospective eyewitness memory. *Law and Human Behavior*, 31(3), 231–47.

Neves, T. 2007. A defesa institucional numa instituição total: o caso de um centro de internamento de menores delinquentes [Institutional defence in a total institution: the case of a juvenile delinquents' internment centre]. *Análise Social*, XLII (185), 1021–39 [in Portuguese].

Neyround, P. and Disley, E. The management, supervision and oversight of criminal investigation, in *Handbook of Criminal Investigation*, edited by T. Newburn et al. Cullompton, Devon: Willan Publishing, 549–71.
Noble, A.A. and Moulton, B.W. 2006. Symposium – DNA fingerprinting and civil liberties. Special issue of *The Journal of Law, Medicine and Ethics*, 34(2), 141-475.
Nuffield Council on Bioethics 2007. *The Forensic Use of Bioinformation: Ethical Issues* [Online: Nuffield Council On Bioethics]. Available at: http://www.nuffieldbioethics.org/sites/default/files/The%20forensic%20use%20of%20 bioinformation%20-%20ethical%20issues.pdf [accessed: 31 January 2011].
Oppel, R.A. 2011. Sentencing shift gives new leverage to prosecutors. *The New York Times* [Online, 25 September]. Available at: http://www.nytimes.com/2011/09/26/us/tough-sentences-help-prosecutors-push-for-plea-bargains.html [accessed: 3 October 2011].
ORF news. 2010. Jagd auf Phantomtäter [Hunting for phantom perpetrators]. *ORF news* [Online, 12 August]. Available at: http://news.orf.at/stories/2008494/2008492/ [accessed: 21 January 2011] [in German].
ORF noe. 2010. Kritik an DNA-Massentests für Ermittler [Critics to DNA mass-testing of investigators]. *ORF noe* [Online, 11 August]. Available at: http://noe.orf.at/stories/461977/ [accessed: 21 January 2011] [in German].
ORF Science. 2004. EU: Hohe Ablehnung von Genfood in Österreich [EU: Strong Rejection of Gene-food in Austria] *ORF Science* [Online]. Available at: http://science.orf.at/science/news/131467 [accessed: 21 January 2011] [in German].
Parenti, C. 1996. Police crime. *ZMag* [Online, March]. Available at: http://zmag.org/ZMag/articles/mar96parenti.htm [accessed: 16 February 2006].
Peelo, M. 2006. Framing homicide narratives in newspapers: mediated witness and the construction of virtual victimhood. *Crime, Media, Culture*, 2(2), 159–75.
Peterson, J. et al. 2010. *The Role and Impact of Forensic Evidence in the Criminal Justice Process* [Online: National Institute of Justice]. Available at: http://www.ncjrs.gov/pdffiles1/nij/grants/231977.pdf [accessed: 25 June 2011].
Piquero, A., Farrington, D. and Blumstein, A. 2007. *Key Issues in Criminal Career Research: New Analyses of the Cambridge Study in Delinquent Development*. Cambridge: Cambridge University Press.
Podlas, K. 2006. The 'CSI effect': exposing the media myth. *Fordham Intellectual Property, Media and Entertainment Law Journal*, 16, 429–65.
Polanyi, M. 1966. *The Tacit Dimension*. New York: Doubleday.
Pollak, J.M. and Kubrin, C.E. 2007. Crime in the news: how crimes, offenders and victims are portrayed in the media. *Journal of Criminal Justice and Popular Culture*, 14(1), 59–83.
Porter, T. 1996. *Trust in Numbers: The Pursuit of Objectivity in Science and Public Life*. Princeton: Princeton University Press.
Portuguese Government 2005. *Programa do XVII Governo Constitucional* [*Programme of the XVII Constitutional Government*]. [Online: Presidência do Conselho de Ministros] Available at: http://www.portugal.gov.pt/pt/

Documentos/Governos_Documentos/Programa%20Governo%20XVII.pdf [accessed: 31 January 2011] [in Portuguese].

Prainsack, B. 2008. Forum on the Nuffield report *The Forensic Use of Bioinformation: Ethical Issues*: An Austrian perspective. *BioSocieties*, 3, 92–7.

Prainsack, B. 2009. Book review: Truth machine: The contentious history of DNA fingerprinting by M. Lynch, S.A. Cole, R. McNally and K. Jordan, Chicago, University of Chicago Press, 2009. *Critical Policy Studies*, 3(1), 143–5.

Prainsack, B. 2010a. Key issues in DNA profiling and databasing: implications for governance, in *Genetic Suspects: Global Governance of DNA Profiling and Databasing, edited by R. Hindmarsh and B. Prainsack.* Cambridge, UK: Cambridge University Press, 15–39.

Prainsack, B. 2010b. Partners in crime: The use of forensic DNA technologies in Austria, in *Genetic Suspects: Global Governance of DNA Profiling and Databasing*, edited by R. Hindmarsh and B. Prainsack. Cambridge, UK: Cambridge University Press, 153–74.

Prainsack, B. and Gmeiner, R. 2008. Clean soil and common ground: the biopolitics of human embryonic stem cell research in Austria. *Science as Culture*, 17(4), 377–95.

Prainsack, B. and Kitzberger, M. 2009. DNA behind bars: other ways of knowing forensic DNA technologies. *Social Studies of Science*, 39(1), 51–79.

Prainsack, B. and Kreissl, R. 2011. The Molecular Leviathan? Forensic DNA technologies in life-stories of male prisoners in Austria. Work in progress, London and Vienna.

Prainsack, B. and Toom, V. 2010. The Prüm regime. Situated dis/empowerment in transnational DNA profile exchange. *British Journal of Criminology*, 50, 1117–35.

Prainsack, B. and Toom, V. 2012 (forthcoming). Performing the Union: the Prüm Decision and the European dream. *Studies in the History and Philosophy of Science.*

Pratt, T.C. et al. 2006. This isn't CSI: estimating the national backlog of forensic DNA cases and the barriers associated with case processing. *Criminal Justice Policy Review*, 17(1), 32–47.

Prime, R. and Hennelly, L. 2003. *Effects of the Processing of DNA Evidence.* London: Home Office.

Prüm Convention. 2005. *Convention between the Kingdom of Belgium, the Federal Republic of Germany, the Kingdom of Spain, the French Republic, the Grand Duchy of Luxembourg, the Kingdom of the Netherlands and the Republic of Austria on the stepping up of cross-border cooperation, particularly in combating terrorism, cross-border crime and illegal migration* [Online, 27 May]. Available at: http://www.libertysecurity.org/IMG/pdf/Prum-ConventionEn.pdf [accessed: 6 January 2010].

Putniņš, A.L. 2010. An exploratory study of young offenders' self-reported reasons for offending. *Journal of Forensic Psychiatry and Psychology*, 21(6), 950–65.

Redmayne, M. 1995. Doubts and burdens: DNA evidence, probability and the courts. *Criminal Law Review*, June, 464–82.
Redmayne, M. 2001. *Expert Evidence and Criminal Justice*. Oxford: Oxford University Press.
Reiner, R. 2002. Media made criminality: the representation of crime in the mass media, in *The Oxford Handbook of Criminology*, edited by R. Reiner, M. Maguire, and R. Morgan. Oxford: Oxford University Press, 376–416.
Robbers, M. 2008. Blinded by science: the social construction of reality in forensic television shows and its effect on criminal jury trials. *Criminal Justice Policy Review*, 19(1), 84–102.
Roberts, P. 2002. Science, experts and criminal justice, in *The Handbook of the Criminal Justice Process*, edited by M. McConville and G. Wilson. Oxford: Oxford University Press, 253–84.
Roberts, P. 2009. The science of proof: forensic science evidence in English criminal trials, in *Handbook of Forensic Science*, edited by J. Fraser and R. Williams. Cullompton, Devon: Willan Publishing, 446–84.
Roberts, S. and Weathered, L. 2009. Assisting the factually innocent: the contradictions and compatibility of Innocence Projects and the Criminal Cases Review Commission. *Oxford Journal of Legal Studies*, 29(1), 43–70.
Roberts, P., Willmore, C. and Davis, G. 1993. *The Role of Forensic Science Evidence in Criminal Proceedings*. Royal Commission on Criminal Justice Study 11. London: HMSO.
Roman, J.K. et al. 2008. *The DNA Field Experiment: Cost-Effectiveness Analysis of the Use of DNA in the Investigation of High-Volume Crimes*. Washington, D.C, Urban Institute – Justice Policy Center.
Saks, M. and Koehler, J.J. 2005. The coming paradigm shift in forensic identification science. *Science*, 309(5736), 892–5.
Sampson, R. and Laub, J. 1993. *Crime in the Making: Pathways and Turning Points Through Life*. Harvard: Harvard University Press.
Santos, B.S. et al. 1996. *Os Tribunais nas Sociedades Contemporâneas: O Caso Português* [*The Courts in Contemporary Societies: The Portuguese Case*]. Porto: Afrontamento [in Portuguese].
Saulsbury, W., Hibberd, M. and Irving, B. 1994. *Using Physical Evidence: An Examination of Police Decision Making*. London: The Police Foundation.
Scheck, B. 2001. Preventing the execution of the innocent: testimony before the senate judiciary committee. *Hofstra Law Review*, 29(1165), 1165–71.
Scheck, B., Neufeld, P. and Dwyer, J. 2000. *Actual Innocence: Five Days to Execution and Other Dispatches from the Wrongly Convicted*. New York: Signet Publishing.
Schlosser, J. 2008. Issues in interviewing inmates. Navigating the methodological landmines of prison research. *Qualitative Inquiry*, 14, 1500–25.
Schmid, R. 2010. International biometric data exchange; European perspective [Online]. Available at: http://www.riseproject.eu/_fileupload/RISE%20

Conference/Presentations/Reinhard%20Schmid.pdf [accessed: 6 January 2011].
Schmid, R. and Scheithauer, R. 2010. Die Österreichische Nationale DNA-Datenbank [The Austrian National DNA-Database], *SIAK Journal – Zeitschrift für Polizeiwissenschaft und Polizeiliche Praxis* [*Journal for the Science and Practice of Policing*], 4, 21–31 [in German].
Schroeder, D.A. and White, M.D. 2009. Exploring the use of DNA evidence in homicide investigations: implications for detective work and case clearance. *Police Quarterly*, 12(3), 319–42.
Schweitzer, N.J. and Saks, M.J. 2007. The CSI effect: popular fiction about forensic science affects the public's expectations about real forensic science. *Jurimetrics*, 47, 357–64.
Seal, L. 2010. *Women, Murder and Femininity: Gender Representations of Women Who Kill*. Basingstoke: Palgrave Macmillan.
Seeh, M. 2010. Fall Natascha Kampusch: Entführung mit (zu) vielen Geheimnissen [The Natascha Kampusch case: Kidnapping with (too) many secrets] *Die Presse* [Online, 23 October]. Available at: http://diepresse.com/home/panorama/oesterreich/604661/Fall-Kampusch_Entfuehrung-mit-zu-vielen-Geheimnissen [accessed: 21 January 2011] [in German].
Semikhodskii, A. 2007. *Dealing with DNA Evidence: A Legal Guide*. London and New York: Routledge-Cavendish.
Shelton, D.E. et al. 2006. A study of juror expectations and demands concerning scientific evidence: does the "CSI Effect" exist? *Vanderbilt Journal of Entertainment & Technology Law*, 9(2), 331–68.
Silver, E., Felson, R.B. and Vaneseltine, M. 2008. The relationship between mental health problems and violence among criminal offenders. *Criminal Justice and Behavior*, 35(4), 405–26.
Simon, J. 2001. Punishment: social and legal aspects, in *International Encyclopedia of the Social & Behavioral Sciences*, edited by N.J. Smelser and P.B. Baltes. Oxford, UK: Elsevier Sciences, 12606–12.
Simonian, H. 2007. Karl-Heinz Grasser – life after politics. *Financial Times* [Online, 12 May]. Available at: http://www.ft.com/intl/cms/s/0/db9dc68a-0025-11dc-8c98-000b5df10621.html#axzz1WQr8XWpM [accessed: 17 January 2011].
Sky News. 2007. Footballers plead for return of Madeleine. *Sky News* [Online, 9 May] Available at: http://news.sky.com/skynews/Home/Sky-News-Archive/Article/20080641264705 [accessed: 31 January 2011].
Spencer, C. 2003. *Genetic Testimony: A Guide to Forensic DNA Profiling*. San Francisco, CA: Benjamin Cummings Publishing Company.
Steffensmeier, D. and Ulmer, J.T. 2003. Confessions of a dying thief: a tutorial on differential association, in *Social Learning Theory and the Explanation of Crime: A Guide for the New Century*, edited by R.L. Akers and G.F. Jensen. New Brunswick, NJ: Transaction, 227–64.

Steventon, B. 1993. *The Ability to Challenge DNA Evidence*. Royal Commission on Criminal Justice Research Study 9. London: HMSO.

Steventon, B. 1998. Statistical evidence and the courts – recent developments. *Journal of Criminal Law*, 62(2), 176–84.

Sulzbach, D. 2006. DNA shall prevail – postconviction DNA evidence: an annotated bibliography. *Legal Reference Servicing Quarterly*, 25(1), 39–58.

Surette, R. 1998. *Media, Crime and Criminal Justice. Images and Realities*. Belmont, CA: Thomson/Wadsworth.

Sutherland, E. 1937. *The Professional Thief: By a Professional Thief*. Chicago: University of Chicago Press.

Sykes, G.M. 2007 [1958]. *The Society of Captives: A Study of a Maximum Security Prison*, Princeton: Princeton University Press.

Sykes, G.M. and Matza, D. 1957. Techniques of neutralization: a theory of delinquency. *American Sociological Review*, 22(6), 664–70.

Sykes, G.M. and Messinger, S. 1960. The inmate social system, in *Theoretical Studies in Social Organization of the Prison*, edited by R.A. Cloward et al. New York: Social Science Research Council, 5–19.

Taylor, M. and Hirst, J. 1995. *Initial Scene Visits to House Burglaries* [Online: Home Office, Police Research Series No. 14]. Available at: http://library.npia.police.uk/docs/hopolicersold/fprs14.pdf [accessed: 23 June 2011].

Thomas, R.R. 2000. *Detective Fiction and the Rise of Forensic Science*. Cambridge: Cambridge University Press.

Thompson, W.C. 2003. Review of DNA Evidence in State of Texas v. Josiah Sutton (District Court of Harris County, Cause No. 800450). [Online]. Available at: http://www.scientific.org/archive/Thompson%20Report.PDF [accessed: 27 February 2011].

Thompson, W.C. 2009. The National Research Council's plan to strengthen forensic science: does the path run through the courts? *Jurimetrics*, 50, 35–51.

Toby, J. 1962. Criminal motivation: a sociocultural analysis. *British Journal of Criminology*, 12, 317–36.

Tonry, M. 2001. Prisons and imprisonment, in *International Encyclopedia of the Social & Behavioral Sciences*, edited by N.J. Smelser and P.B. Baltes. Oxford, UK: Elsevier Sciences, 12062–7.

Toom, V. 2010. Inquisitorial forensic DNA profiling in the Netherlands and the expansion of the forensic genetic body, in *Genetic Suspects: Global Governance of DNA Profiling and Databasing*, edited by R. Hindmarsh and B. Prainsack. Cambridge, UK: Cambridge University Press, 175–96.

Topalli, V. 2006. The seductive nature of autotelic crime: how neutralization theory serves as a boundary condition for understanding hardcore street offending. *Sociological Inquiry*, 76(4), 475–501.

Tracy, P. and Morgan, V. 2000. Big Brother and his science kit: DNA databases for 21st century crime control. *The Journal of Criminal Law and Criminology*, 90(2), 635–90.

Transparency International. n.d. [Online]. Available at: http://www.transparency.org/ [accessed: 21 January 2011].

Transparency International 2010. *Global Corruption Barometer 2010* [Online: Transparency International]. Available at: http://www.transparency.org/policy_research/surveys_indices/gcb/2010 [accessed: 31 January 2011].

Tyler, T.R. 2006. Viewing CSI and the threshold of guilt: managing truth and justice in reality and fiction. *The Yale Law Journal*, 115(5), 1050–85.

Unterweger, J. 1983. *Fegefeuer oder Die Reise ins Zuchthaus* [*Purgatory, or The Journey to Jail*]. Augsburg, DE: Maro Verlag (2nd ed.) [in German].

Van Camp, N. and Dierickx, K. 2007. *National Forensic Databases: Social-ethical Challenges & Current Practices in the EU* [Online: European Ethical-legal Papers n°9]. Available at: https://www.kuleuven.be/cbmer/viewpic.php?LAN=N&TABLE=DOCS&ID=552&PAGE=1 [accessed: 20 June 2011].

Van Camp, N. and Dierickx, K. 2008. The retention of forensic DNA samples: a socio-ethical evaluation of current practices in the EU. *Journal of Medical Ethics*, 34(8), 606–10.

Van der Ploeg, I. 1999. The illegal body: 'Eurodac' and the politics of biometric identification. *Ethics and Information Technology*, 1(4), 295–302.

Vaughn, M. and Sapp, A. 1989. Less than utopian: sex offender treatment in a milieu of power struggles, status positioning, and inmate manipulation in state correctional institutions. *The Prison Journal*, 69(2), 73–89.

Wagner, W. et al. 1998. Austria, in *Biotechnology in the Public Sphere: A European Sourcebook*, edited by J. Durant, M.W. Bauer and G. Gaskell. London: Science Museum, 15–28.

Waldram, J.B. 2009. Challenges of prison ethnography. *Anthropology News*, 50(1), 4–5.

Washington, H. 2010. Base assumptions? Racial aspects of US DNA forensics, in *Genetic Suspects: Global Governance of DNA Profiling and Databasing*, edited by R. Hindmarsh and B. Prainsack. Cambridge, UK: Cambridge University Press, 63–84.

Weir, B.S. 2004. Matching and partially-matching DNA profiles. *Journal of Forensic Science*, 49, 1009–14.

Weir, B.S. 2007. The rarity of DNA profiles. *Annals of Applied Statistics*, 1, 358–70.

Weiss, M.J. 2004. Beware! Uncle Sam has your DNA: legal fallout from its use and misuse in the US. *Ethics and Information Technology*, 6(1), 55–63.

Wells, G. and Olson, E. 2003. Eyewitness testimony. *Annual Review of Psychology*, 54, 277–95.

Wells, G. and Quinlivan, D. 2009. Suggestive eyewitness identification procedures and the Supreme Court's reliability test in light of eyewitness science: 30 years later. *Law and Human Behavior*, 33(1), 1–24.

West, E.M. 2010a. *Court Findings of Ineffective Assistance of Counsel Claims in Post-Conviction Appeals Among the First 255 DNA Exoneration Cases* [Online: Innocence Project]. Available at: http://www.innocenceproject.org/docs/Innocence_Project_IAC_Report.pdf [accessed: 10 April 2011].

West, E.M. 2010b. *Court Findings of Prosecutorial Misconduct Claims in Post-Conviction Appeals and Civil Suits Among the First 255 DNA Exoneration Cases* [Online: Innocence Project]. Available at: http://www.innocenceproject.org/docs/Innocence_Project_Pros_Misconduct.pdf [accessed: 10 April 2011].

Williams, R. 2004. *The Management of Crime Scene Examination in Relation to the Investigation of Burglary and Vehicle Crime* [Online: Home Office RDS Online Report 24/04]. Available at: http://library.npia.police.uk/docs/hordsolr/rdsolr2404.pdf [accessed: 15 July 2011].

Williams, R. 2010a. Shaping forensic science innovation. *Science & Justice*, 50(1), 4–7.

Williams, R. 2010b. DNA databases and the forensic imaginary, in *Genetic Suspects: Global Governance of DNA Profiling and Databasing*, edited by R. Hindmarsh and B. Prainsack. Cambridge, UK: Cambridge University Press, 131–52.

Williams, R. and Johnson, P. 2005. *Forensic DNA Databasing: A European Perspective. Project Interim Report (June)* [Online: University of Durham, UK]. Available at: http://www.dur.ac.uk/robin.williams/EU_Interim_Report_2005.pdf [accessed: 27 February 2011].

Williams, R. and Johnson, P. 2008. *Genetic Policing: The Use of DNA in Criminal Investigations*. Cullompton, Devon: Willan Publishing.

Williams, R., Johnson, P. and Martin, P. 2004. *Genetic Information and Crime Investigation: Social, Ethical and Public Policy Aspects of the Establishment, Expansion and Police Use of the National DNA Database* [Online: Durham University, UK]. Available at: http://www.dur.ac.uk/resources/sass/Williams_Johnson_Martin_NDNAD_report_2004.pdf [accessed: 7 July 2011].

Willing, R. 2004. 'CSI effect' has juries wanting more evidence. *USA Today* [Online, 5 August]. Available at: http://www.usatoday.com/news/nation/2004-08-05-csi-effect_x.htm [accessed: 3 October 2011].

Wilson, D.B., McClure, D. and Weisburd, D. 2010. Does forensic DNA help to solve crime? The benefit of sophisticated answers to naive questions. *Journal of Contemporary Criminal Justice*, 26(4), 458–69.

Wilson, T. 2009. Forensic science and the internationalisation of policing, in *Handbook of Forensic Science*, edited by J. Fraser and R. Williams. Cullompton, Devon: Willan Publishing, 491–522.

Wright R. and Decker, S.H. 1994. *Burglars on the Job: Streetlife and Residential Break-ins*. Northeastern University Press.

Wright, R., Logie, R.H. and Decker, S.H. 1995. Criminal expertise and offender decision making: an experimental study of the target selection process in residential burglary. *Journal of Research in Crime and Delinquency*, 32(1), 39–53.

Zamir, A. et al. 2012. The Israel DNA database – The establishment of a rapid, semi-automated analysis system. *Forensic Science International: Genetics*, 6(2), 286-9.

Index

www.ingramcontent.com/pod-product-compliance
Ingram Content Group UK Ltd.
Pitfield, Milton Keynes, MK11 3LW, UK
UKHW022131190926
475702UK00013B/1741
* 9 7 8 1 1 3 8 1 0 7 5 0 2 *